Studies in Jewish Myth and Jewish Messianism

SUNY Series in Judaica:
Hermeneutics, Mysticism, and Religion

Michael Fishbane, Robert Goldenberg, and Arthur Green, Editors

Studies in Jewish Myth
and
Jewish Messianism

Yehuda Liebes

Translated from the Hebrew
by
Batya Stein

STATE UNIVERSITY OF NEW YORK PRESS

Production by Ruth Fisher
Marketing by Theresa A. Swierzowski

Published by
State University of New York Press, Albany

For information, address the State University of New York Press,
State University Plaza, Albany, NY 12246

Library of Congress Cataloging-in-Publication Data

Liebes, Yehuda.
    Studies in Jewish myth and Jewish messianism / Yehuda Liebes :
translated from the Hebrew by Batya Stein.
        p.   cm. — (SUNY series in Judaica)
    "This volume is a selection from my articles": Introd.
    Includes bibliographical references and index.
    ISBN 0-7914-1193-1 (acid-free). — ISBN 0-7914-1194-X (pbk. : acid
-free)
    1. Mythology, Jewish.   2. Messiah—Judaism.   3. Sabbathaians.
4. Nahman, of Bratzlav, 1772–1811.   Tikun ha-kelali.   I. Title.
II. Series
BM530.L457   1993
296.1'6—dc20   91-36470
                                                                    CIP

10 9 8 7 6 5 4 3 2 1

Contents

Introduction

Historical research of Jewish religion began in the circles of the Wissenschaft des Judentums in Germany, which sought to minimize religion's national, particular elements and bring it closer to universalist and rationalist notions of religion. From its inception, this research has blurred the mythical, messianic fundations of religion that, in my view, are critical to its vitality. These views of Wissenschaft des Judentums have never ceased to influence the general public as well as scholars, but they are not the only voice. In the last century, and particularly following the national Zionist renaissance, these rejected elements began to resurface. The work of Gershom Scholem, who raised the study of Jewish mysticism, myth, and messianism to the level of an independent scientific discipline, has played a decisive role in this process. I am a disciple of Scholem, but I have attempted to break further ground. Scholem did carve out a space for myth within Judaism, but restricted it to a specific, defined realm, opposed to "ordinary" Judaism whereas, in this book, I try to show that Jewish myth spans far beyond the "ghetto" to which it has been confined. The chief uniqueness of Kabbala is not in its *mythologoumena*, in and by themselves, but in the form and in the patterns of thought in which they were expressed.

I also learned from Gershom Scholem to trace links between the domain of Jewish mysticism and the messianic idea, mainly Sabbateanism, the most important Jewish messianic movement (unless we include Christianity under this rubric) as well as the most mystical one. In this realm as well, I chose to go further than Scholem. Scholem claimed that, despite its mystical character, the main concern of Sabbateanism was historical and political redemption, which he indeed viewed as the foremost concerns of Jewish messianism in general. He thereby embraced an approach to Judaism prevalent among Christian scholars; Christians had also tended to stress the legalistic, antimystical dimension of Jewish religion. As I shall show, my view is that Sabbateanism was chiefly concerned with spiritual redemption: the redemption of religion, the redemption of God, and personal, mystical redemption.

These ideas crystallized through the development of an alternative approach to the study of Kabbala. Rather than placing the main emphasis on its abstract, ideological aspects, as if Kabbala were a philosophy, this method connects it to the personal experiences of those who created it and wonders about their true religious concerns (I discuss this method extensively elsewhere).[1] I am not alone in adopting this method and these ideas; it seems to me that other scholars have recently arrived at much the same conclusions when faced with similar problems in their use of the previous method. First among them I note my friend Moshe Idel, with whom I have been discussing these questions for the last twenty years.

This volume is a selection from my articles in these fields. "De Natura Dei" and "The Kabbalistic Myth as Told by Orpheus" represent my discussions on the problems of myth in Judaism, as well as its antiquity. I have written on these questions in a long series of articles—not included in this book—stretching over a long period, from a book on talmudic mysticism[2] to a comparison between the kabbalistic myth and the "Canaanite" myth as they appear in the modern poetry of Jonathan Ratosh.[3] I would like to single out my article on "Myth vs. Symbol," where I attempt to show that the Zohar and Lurianic Kabbala do not differ, as is commonly held, in the content of their myths but rather in their patterns of thought, in their use of language, and in the type of link they assume with the Supreme Entity.[4]

The articles on messianism and Sabbateanism have been chosen from among more than a dozen dealing not with the concrete details of the movement's history but rather with Sabbatean Kabbala or its messianic, theoretical foundations. The articles on Sabbateanism, in their original Hebrew version, are due to appear in book form (published by Mossad Bialik, Jerusalem). Furthermore, I have recently edited a large collection of Hebrew articles on Sabbateanism written by Gershom Scholem, published by Am-Oved. I also direct the reader to the English version of my lengthy article "The Messiah of the Zohar," due to appear in my forthcoming book, *Studies in the Zohar*, published by the SUNY Press.

The present book includes articles originally published in Hebrew, the language in which I produce all my work. I do this not only because Hebrew is my tongue but also because it is the language of the texts under consideration. In Kabbala, language is not only instrumental, it is vital to its essence. Readers who do not know Hebrew will therefore be limited in their ability to gain full understanding of these questions. Nevertheless, Arthur Green and others convinced me that an important layer in the study of these issues could be made available without access to language. I have therefore selected articles in which this layer seemed particularly prominent and have omitted discussions focusing on linguistic points. I would still suggest to those fluent in Hebrew that they read the original version of these articles. Batya Stein assumed the arduous task of the translation, which I have thoroughly reviewed. I hope the results show that justice was on the side of those who encouraged me to relinquish my past reservations and see this English anthology published.

1

De Natura Dei: On the Development
of the Jewish Myth

I. General Characteristics

When encountering Kabbala for the first time, many face it in dismayed trepidation: Can this be Judaism? Where is the pure monotheism we have learned to expect from studies of the Bible, Talmud, Midrash, and Jewish philosophy? The research literature does not solve this riddle and, needless to say, these questions are not discussed in the writings of those scholars who view Kabbala as an alien growth and have a vested interest in stressing them. But even Gershom Scholem, the leading scholar of Kabbala who turned it into a decisive factor in the history of the Jewish spirit, saw it as a new eruption of the myth beginning in the twelfth century. Scholem stressed the vast difference between Kabbala and "the tendency of classical Jewish tradition to liquidate myth as a central spiritual power"[1] and therefore, when searching for the mystery of Jewish "vitality," could find it only in the Kabbala.[2] This approach also reflects disbelief in the kabbalists' pretension to be *baalei kabbala*, namely, guardians of the mythical tradition, and raises the question: How did such a striking innovation find acceptance by an ancient, wise people, at the close of the Middle Ages?

In this essay, I will try to trace the outlines of an alternative answer. Essentially, Kabbala is not a new creation but a reformulation, in different form, of the same myth that has been the very heart of the Torah since time immemorial. The mythical element did not erupt in the Kabbala; rather, that is where it was given systematic formulation and set within rigid frameworks, which may have in fact restrained and weakened its personal, spontaneous vitality. Adapting an ancient myth in accord with the spirit of the times is not particular to Kabbala. This flexibility is in the very nature of myth, which unfolds in line with changing sensibilities and develops complex interactions with the surrounding culture, while preserving its continuity. To the extent that it is flexible, a myth is also conservative,

1

traditionally transmitted, and evolves through textual interpretation. I have discussed the "external" links of the kabbalistic myth elsewhere,[3] and this essay will deal with its internal development. In other words, I will try to show that the characteristic features of the biblical and the rabbinical God have been attired in the guise of the kabbalistic *sefirot*.

But there is a preliminary question: Why are we unaware today of a continuum extending from the biblical to the kabbalistic conception of divinity? We have probably been influenced by the ideas of the Enlightenment, which held the biblical and talmudic God above all myth, construing myth and Judaism as essentially contradictory. This is not just a popular truism, but an assumption adopted by most of Judaism's spokesmen, from philosophers like Hermann Cohen to distinguished scholars and philologists such as Yehezkel Kaufmann and Julius Guttman. Even Moshe David Cassuto, most of whose research was devoted to emphasizing the parallels between the Bible and Ugaritic literature, consistently attempted to show that the Bible preserved idolatry only in form, while pouring new, nonmythical content into the old vessels. If *myth* be defined as a groundless prejudice, then the assumption of an a-mythical Judaism is a total myth. Indeed, a host of scholars, most of them Gentiles, followed the opposite course and highlighted the Hebrew myth as part of the general one. However, these scholars lacked influence—especially in the field of kabbalistic research, which they did not pursue—because their work reflected an unacceptable blurring of Judaism's uniqueness, as well as a rift between biblical and later Jewish literature. Nuances of an anti-Jewish ideology can occasionally be discerned in these writings, either reflecting the Christian attempt to deny rabbinical Judaism its pretence to be the legitimate heir of biblical religion or, in the case of Jewish scholars, expressing the influence of radical Zionist historiosophy or even of "Canaanite" denials of the Exile.

The uniqueness of Judaism may be preserved without severing it from myth—the well-spring of the religious impulse. Myths are shared by all religions but are also the source of each religion's uniqueness, as they are concerned with the particular and concrete rather than with generalizations and abstractions. This emerges from the most general definition of myth, one essentially accepted by most scholars: A myth is a sacred story about the gods expressing that which the abstract word, or Logos, cannot express.[4] It is because of this sacredness that myths affect life. Those who see the Logos as the central essence have turned *myth* into a derogatory term, denoting trivial and vain inventions whereas those, like myself, who do not believe that reality can be completely reduced to logical terms, recognize myth as its culmination. Each religion has its own myth into which it absorbs and incorporates influences from other religions, and this is also true for the Jewish religion. Even Judaism's monotheistic essence is not contradictory to myth, and monotheism itself has its own, far-reaching myth. The very declaration of the unity of God is mythical in origin and, Maimonides notwithstanding, does not turn God into an abstract inapprehensible concept. Judaism's mythical elements are not a result of polytheistic influences. On the contrary, philosophical abstraction emerged in fact within Greek polytheism, and thinkers such as Maimonides laboriously attempted to graft it on to the monotheistic texts; this attempt, as we shall see later, often led to the strengthening of myths rather than to their disappearance. There was good reason for the Platonic academy to remain as the last bastion of "pagan" religion during the expansion of Christianity.

Scholars of religion such as Rudolf Otto and Mircea Eliade have already pointed out the mythical element in monotheistic religion. Martin Buber went even further and grounded his conception of Judaism in the monotheistic myth.[5] However, although Buber stressed the human attitude toward the divine as a mythical entity with whom dialogue is possible, the kabbalists were concerned with the mythical features of God Himself. Therefore, while affirming myth, Buber denied the kabbalistic gnosis (the knowledge of God's mysteries). In this essay, I am concerned with the mythical features of the one God that, through their analogy to those of the human being created in His image, enable the dialogue to take place. In my view, this is no affront to the glory of God, the *Adam Ila'a* [Man Supreme] of the Zohar, who transcends even the most sublime idea; I will also show how these features are the source of the kabbalistic gnosis odious to Buber.

True, the Jewish myth in its kabbalistic guise may be disturbing. The personal descriptions of God in the Bible and in rabbinical literature may be approached lightly, merely as legends attempting to shape individual attitudes toward God. However, the Kabbala ascribes a more defined ontological meaning to God's attributes and confines them within a conceptual range that, though not rationally apprehensible, weakens the closeness of the "I–Thou" relationship. The biblical myth may be embraced without requiring us to believe in it, but Kabbala makes more stringent demands that reach into the rational realm too; it may be for this reason that wide circles, which enjoy this complacent distinction between myth and mind, feel threatened by it. Moreover, as I shall show later, the somewhat dry and arbitrary systematization pervasive in the Kabbala may evoke a sense of alienation.

These features of the kabbalistic myth are grounded in the exegetical approach to rabbinical *midrashim* that characterize most of the early Kabbala and actually created it. Unlike the philosophical exegesis of Midrash, kabbalistic exegesis did not expound one system according to an already available one; the kabbalistic system was actually created through exegesis of the Midrash. Kabbalists fostered one Jewish myth, that of the "ten *sefirot*," which after a long development, crystallized into the ten attributes or divine hypostases[6] and became the organizing framework for the Jewish myth in its entirety. Kabbalists ascribed to a specific *sefira* all mythical references to God's attributes found in the Bible and in rabbinical literature, in line with the conceptual rigor favored by the medieaval approach and under the influence of philosophy, despite the latter's attempt to eradicate all mythical traces from Judaism. Philosophy failed in this attempt, but it did have a share in changing the shape of the myth. Philosophy affected kabbalists directly, through ideas such as the *unio mystica* and the neo-Platonic emanation, which in Kabbala fused in the mythical descriptions of attachment (*devekut*) and emanation (*atsilut*). It also affected them indirectly, by evoking their need for self-defense; to protect myth from attacks mounted from the philosophical flank, kabbalists adopted the ways of their adversaries and arrived at more conceptualized formulations of God's attributes. This conceptualization never reached the point of completely reducing mythical entities: myth always remained the heart of Kabbala and this process only strengthened it, made it more structured, and even raised its ontological status. However, a heavy price was occasionally paid, in the form of a considerable devaluation of the personal and vital nature of the Jewish myth, as we shall see further on.

This was not an inevitable consequence. Organizing the myth in the model of the ten *sefirot* can be potentially fruitful and enriching, providing the individual *mythologoumenon* with a wider range of interesting associations. This was indeed the case with the Zohar and the circles that crystallized around it.[7] The Zohar was written in a setting of wealth and security; as against the philosophical option, it built a marvelous structure from the ancestral mythical elements, which was only strengthened by the addition of kabbalistic and philosophical components. The Zohar blurs the boundaries between genres, and not in vain was it written in the mold of an ancient *midrash*. Its authors often continued creating living myths in the ancient manner and included the kabbalistic *sefirot* only when necessary and in an appropriate dosage. The *sefirot* are not included for the sake of systematization, but to deepen the old myth through new reflection, because the Zohar recognizes the freedom of mythical creativity. This freedom is granted only to the kabbalist who is "faithful" to the spirit of religion, not to transgressors "weaving heavens of chaos," as some of the disciples and imitators of the Zohar indeed did.[8] The writers of the Zohar were wary of this, and it exists in a fruitful tension between the need to spread its message and to conceal it.[9] The multifaceted character of the Zohar explains the fascination it has exerted over its readers from the time it was written until our own days; a great deal of subsequent kabbalistic creativity is no more than attempts to systematize the zoharic myths. These attempts are not inevitably unimaginative and dull; at times, they reflect a great individual soul, as attested by the wondrous system Isaac Luria developed from the Zohar in Safad.

One need not be perplexed by the assumption that myths can be graded according to their ontological validity. A wide range of possibilities stretches between legends and parables, on the one hand, and an objective, inevitable reality, on the other. Myths do not always lay claim to absolute ontological validity, which may vary widely in line with the literary genres. In my view, it can be assumed that the mythical validity of religions based on canonized Scriptures will be particularly high. Hence, the mythical status of Judaism, Christianity, and Islam is even higher than that of the Greek myth, which gave birth to the term. Undoubtedly, in Greece as well, myth was the foundation of ritual and considered a religious truth but, since Greek religion lacked "Scriptures" in the full sense of the term, its ontological validity was lower. The changing course of myth may be traced through several literary genres in Greek religion, both from the perspective of its authors and from that prevailing in later periods. There are great differences between the status of myths in Homer's writings, which was very close to that of "Scriptures," the description of the gods in Hesiod and Orpheus, and the status of myths in the classical tragedies, where they were transformed according to the needs and inclinations of the playwrights. Furthermore, these all differ from the myths that Plato integrated in his philosophical writings.[10]

The same phenomenon is found in Jewish literature: the mythical status of the biblical stories of Creation or the Exodus differs in descriptive style and in the authority of its source from that of its midrashic amplifications. The Bible tells a flowing, detailed story in the name of God or Moses, and this authority is accepted and confirmed by the later Halakha; on the other hand, rabbinical *midrashim* are the statements of different rabbis, who are often in mutual disagreement. (Indeed, rabbinical myths themselves appear in various forms. Some were formulated in clearly mythical terms, because of literary considerations and in order to deliver a nonmythical message, as I have shown elsewhere,[11] whereas others have a prominently mythical character and will be discussed later.) However, the biblical myth is itself not the apex of the ontological scale, and this myth too can be removed from its literal context and expounded, whether in allegorical or other terms. Praxis, rather than belief in the details of the biblical myth, is the core of Jewish religion though, as we shall see later, praxis is not divorced from myth. In this regard, the credit for being the most mythical religion belongs to Christianity, which meticulously formulated the details of its myth through a series of disputes, schisms, and even wars and established them as articles of faith to be committed to memory. These features of the Christian myth reflect its contest with philosophy and its adoption of the latter's concepts,[12] in a process similar to the one described earlier regarding Kabbala. However, in Christianity this process culminated in a dangerous fusion—philosophical elements merged with the Paulinian principle of faith, which superseded the commandments and became the key to salvation. Indeed, in his epistle to the Galileans, the emperor Julian the Apostate preferred paganism to Christianity on the grounds that the Christian myth, as opposed to the pagan one, does not allow for allegorical interpretation.

The kabbalists themselves were aware of the high status of their myth. This awareness increased in the course of history and reached its peak in the kabbalistic, messianic awakening of the Sabbatean period. For the Sabbateans, identifying the true God (the "God of truth" in their terms) was a crucial aspect of their activity. Sabbetai Zevi himself had difficulty formulating exactly the nature of his God, given its elusive personal character.[13] This task became the main concern of Nathan of Gaza, Sabbatai Zevi's prophet; in his profound, extensive, and largely unpublished work, Nathan created an innovative kabbalistic system where the images of God and the Messiah are connected and shaped through their mutual influence. However, the core of Nathan's work is not theoretical definition but rather the emotional bond of faith and love joining the believers, God, and the Messiah. It was the Sabbatean theologian Abraham Miguel Cardozo who raised theoretical definition to the rank of a messianic end, devoting his numerous writings to this purpose,[14] as did his followers. In Cardozo's writings, for the first time in kabbalistic literature, there is a formulation resembling a Christian credo: "I believe with my whole heart and soul that He is the Cause of all Causes, that He is One, the only One, the singular One. . .that He shines through the ten *sefirot* of emanation. . ."[15]

The credal style, which started with Sabbateanism, occasionally appears in later Kabbala in even stronger terms and accompanied by a ritual instruction to recite it daily. It is interesting that precisely at a time when its influence was on the wane, Kabbala demanded such authority for its myth. The following excerpt appears in the *Sefer Od Yosef Hai*, by the nineteenth century Babylonian kabbalist Rav Yosef Hayyim ben Elyiahu Elhakham:[16]

> Every man should carefully recite these words every day, including the Sabbath and the Holidays, before the portion on the *akeda* [the sacrifice of Isaac]. This declaration is greatly needed for the ways of mystery, and these are its words: "I believe with my whole heart and soul that God Our Lord is the Cause of all Causes, that He created the ten *sefirot* which are *keter, hokhma* and *bina, hesed, gevura* and *tiferet, netzah, hod, yesod* and *malkhut* and His Light is revealed and hidden in the Supreme *Keter,* and from there it shines upon the letter *Yod,* which is *hokhma"*. . .

After the kabbalistic description, it goes on to state: "It is my belief and my wish before the Holy One, blessed be He, with my whole heart and with a willing soul, to completely eliminate all strange, unfit, harmful and forbidden thoughts as well as all thoughts which are, God forbid, heretical, and all bad reflections and all bad, unfit, harmful and forbidden images."[17]

This text is followed by detailed halakhic instructions concerning the ways of "eliminating" heretic thoughts, borrowed from the laws about the disposal of leavened bread during Passover. As far as I have been able to ascertain, this text was not printed in the prayerbooks and was circulated in a special booklet, undated, printed in Jerusalem several times. We may perhaps infer from this as well that, despite the Kabbala's high ontological status in the kabbalists' eyes, belief in it did not become normative for the general public or for the leadership. The normative status of the kabbalistic myth is lower than that of Maimonides's thirteen articles of faith, which lack a prominently mythical character and were accepted into the liturgy.

Further evidence of the high status of the kabbalistic myth may be found in its liturgical uses; from the sixteen century onward, kabbalistic excerpts were extensively included in prayerbooks. These excerpts range from short allusions, such as the formula *leshem yihud* [for unity], stated before performing the commandments, all the way to long passages meticulously describing kabbalistic beliefs. Many of these excerpts appear in the first anthology of kabbalistic liturgy, *Sha'arei Zion* [The Gates of Zion], which Nathan Neta Hanover compiled shortly before the advent of Sabbateanism. In this anthology we find, for instance, the passage *Petah Eliyyahu* from the introduction to the *Tikkunei Zohar*, which preceeds the prayers in Sephardi communities; this passage, though not worded as a credo, is a general summary of the kabbalistic myth. We should also include under this rubric the well-known book *Hemdat Yamim* [The Beloved of Days]— unquestionably Sabbatean—which suggests that kabbalistic *kavvanot* [devotional intentions] be turned into a text to be recited aloud. Indeed, this process began even earlier, as attested by the many kabbalistic *piyutim* [ritual songs] for various occasions; although of lesser liturgical validity, some of these *piyutim* were occasionally printed in prayerbooks.

The first kabbalists were already aware of the ontological importance of myth, even if they did not establish it as a dogma or integrate it into normative liturgy. By liturgy I refer to words and deeds, not to intentions—which are obviously the core of Kabbala since its inception—or to practices adopted by closed circles at its early stages of development.[18] This awareness of the importance of myth is expressed in the very claim that Kabbala constitutes a distinct phase in the understanding of religion that is different from textual or midrashic interpretation, as well as in the names ascribed to it, such as *Derekh Emeth* [The Path of Truth] in Nahmanides' Commentary on the Bible; *Orah Keshot* [The Path of Truth], *Raza de-Hokhmeta* [The Mystery of Wisdom], or *Raza de-Meheimanuta* [The Mystery of Faith] in the Zohar. It is also reflected in the precautions and secrecy in which the first kabbalists shrouded their knowledge,[19] as well as in their consistent abstention from introducing any innovations in the body of knowledge handed down to them. The latter approach was prevalent among Gerondian kabbalists and their leader Nachmanides,[20] as against the creativity displayed by circles associated with the Zohar, to which we referred earlier.

In this essay, my concern is with myth itself, as it is revealed in the texts. I am not concerned with the sociological or psychological role of myth, or with the circumstances of its creation. Therefore, I will not be relating to the whole field of research on these aspects of myth, from Jung extending to Levi-Strauss and their disciples as well as their opponents, which has recently elicited a tremendous volume of work. I am interested in precisely those facets of myth that cannot be reduced to general concepts. Furthermore, I do not use the term *myth* in the amplified meaning adopted by the social sciences, where it includes additional concepts, ideologies, and spiritual approaches, which would obscure my intention. I adhere to the original meaning of the word, which denotes a story about the gods and their nature, adapted to the one God of Jewish religion. God's unity determines His nature; it also has a mythical aspect that, in my eyes, is the source of life of the Jewish religion.

II. Talmud and Kabbala:
God's Actions as Reflected in His Attributes

We shall first examine several passages of rabbinical literature exposing the character and attributes of the talmudic God, in order to illustrate the continuities and contrasts between the Talmud and the Kabbala noted in the previous section. Obviously, we can no more than touch on this diverse and monumental body of literature, created by widely different circles over many centuries. I use the conventional term *rabbinical* as a matter of convenience although, in every respect, delimiting this literature is an impossible task due to the difficulties of defining the time span, social strata, scope of relevant literature and literary genre, as well as the rabbis' concepts and beliefs.

Examples were chosen mainly from the Babylonian Talmud and its tannaitic *beraitot*, given the Talmud's central place in Jewish literature and its quality as a clear, early document, less influenced by outside currents of thought and marked by stronger mythical leanings. I will show how these examples blend into a myth with uniform features, albeit not one formulated as a fixed and articulated credo. These features assume various guises, in accordance with the needs of the exegete and the "mythological validity" of his claims. The recurrence of these features and their close integration into the halakhic and religious ethos, as well as the continuity between the Bible and the Kabbala that we shall discuss later, will point to a myth in the full sense of the term. It will then become clear that these are not vain assertions, as alleged by those intent on "purifying" and blurring the essence of religion.

Still, it is not my claim that this myth is "the rabbinical view," as there is no "rabbinical view." Broadly different and even mutually contradictory statements appear in this literature, including the Talmud, and I intend only to indicate and describe a living myth from which the Kabbala developed. Such a description is missing from the extensive work dealing with rabbinical beliefs, because even serious talmudic scholars have been unable to altogether avoid the influence of those preconceived notions that describe rabbinical Judaism as legalistic and opposed to mysticism and myth. The first to spread this libel, which many Jews construed as praise, were the Christians, starting with Paul. Therefore, most scholars dealing with mythical descriptions such as the ones following, often see them as only explicit or implicit forms of a message belonging in the human realm, failing to combine them into a complete, credible myth (though support for various forms of the talmudic myth has indeed been voiced over the last few years). I have chosen the opposite path and granted priority to celestial beings for, as we shall see, the rabbis thought that human religious behavior must spring from the mythical essence of divinity. I believe that this claim is self-evident and the onus of proof is on those claiming that the rabbis were "flippant," so to speak, precisely when they came to describe their God.

The first example will serve to link various genres of talmudic-midrashic literature, as well as show the affinities between this literature and Kabbala. It is from the Babylonian Talmud, Berakhot 7a:

> R. Ishmael b. Elisha says: I once entered into the innermost part [of the Sanctuary] to offer incense and saw Akathriel Yah, the Lord of Hosts, seated upon a high and exalted throne. He said to me: Ishamael, My son, bless Me! I replied: May it be Thy will that Thy mercy may suppress Thy anger and Thy mercy may prevail over Thy other attributes, so that Thou mayest deal with Thy children according to the attribute of mercy and mayest, on their behalf, stop short of the limit of strict justice! And He nodded to me with His head.

Several scholars felt this passage was incompatible with their own approach. In a paper attempting to define and limit the scope of the mystical element in rabbinical literature, Ephraim Urbach, the most comprehensive scholar of rabbinic thought in our time, dismissed it as part of the *Hekhalot* literature and of the "mysteries of the Chariot watchers, who were far from the ways of the first *tannaim*."[21] This passage is indeed related to the tradition of *Hekhalot* literature, as can also be inferred from the names of its two protagonists: the divine one (Akatriel Yah . . .) and the human one (Rabbi Ishmael ben Elisha, the High Priest), as Urbach pointed out. *Hekhalot* literature resembles kabbalistic literature on various counts, and precisely for this reason, we shall not be devoting special attention to it in this essay, where we are concerned with the mainstream midrashic tradition and the continuum linking it to Kabbala. I have chosen this passage to show that noting its closeness to *Hekhalot* literature is not, in and by itself, sufficient to remove it from the realm of rabbinical literature. In the following pages, we will compare it with others of professed "midrashic" quality and thus further our understanding of its special features as well as its links with the other examples.

True, the preceding passage has a quasi-kabbalistic character unusual for the Talmud: God's attributes[22] seem to be independent entities, "suppressing" and "prevailing" over each other and actually controlled by a man, Rabbi Ishmael, just as the Kabbala speaks about the ten *sefirot* that the kabbalist can affect. However, it is immediately apparent that the image of God is not wholly kabbalistic. A personal God requesting a blessing is revealed to Rabbi Ishmael beyond the attributes, whereas no God is found in the Kabbala outside the *sefirot*, as the emanating *Ein-Sof* is neither a personal image nor the object of a religious relationship.[23] Evidence of this difference can also be found in the kabbalists' exegeses of this passage: not satisfied with the slight overlap between the attributes and their own *sefirot*, they made "Akatriel" himself part of the scheme, and precisely as the lowest *sefira*, which is beneath the attributes.[24]

But are the attributes indeed independent entities, separate from God? Let us consider this question by looking at another talmudic passage, which appears immediately before the previous one:

> R. Johanan says in the name of R. Jose. . . hence [you learn] that the Holy One, blessed be He, says prayers. What does he pray?—R. Zutra b. Tobi said in the name of Rab: "May it be My will that My mercy may subdue My anger, and that My mercy may prevail over My [other] attributes, so that I may deal with My children in the attribute of mercy and, on their behalf, stop short of the limit of strict justice." (Berakhot 7a)

This passage is much more in line with the general features of talmudic style. There is no "Akatriel" and no "Rabbi Ishmael the High Priest" from *Hekhalot* literature but rather an ordinary statement by a famous *amora*, without hinting at human influence on the divine attributes. Although Rabbi Ishmael's blessing is reproduced literally, in this passage it appears as a prayer that the Holy One, blessed be He, prays by Himself, to Himself and for Himself. Can we still adhere to a description of the attributes as independent entities mechanistically linked? Were this the case, God should have acted directly on the attributes rather than pray to Himself "May it be My will. . ." and, most certainly, so should Rabbi Ishmael, whose blessing too begins with "May it be Thy will. . ." Whereas at first we could have ignored this formula, which seemed a polite form of address to God that masks direct human interference with the divine attributes, we now find that God Himself requests "May it be My will" and the euphemistic argument cannot be applied to Him.

We may infer from this "self-prayer" that the attributes are only psychological characteristics typical of human beings, who are prey to their instincts and need to struggle in order to overcome feelings such as pity and anger. True, the attributes occasionally appear as independent entities, but the rabbis also depicted the *yetser ha-ra* [evil inclination] as a fly dwelling between the two entrances to the heart (Berakhot 61a), and the collective *yetser ha-ra* of the people of Israel as a young fiery lion coming forth from the Temple's Holy of Holies (Yoma 69b).

But... may we speak of God's evil inclination? Indeed we may. We can understand Rabbi Ishmael for choosing not to: It is disrespecful to mention His evil inclination to Him even as we are blessing Him, and the term does not suit the exalted tone of the passage. However, we find this explicit phrase elsewhere:

> R. Joshua b. Levi said: Why were they called men of the Great Assembly? Because they restored the crown of the divine attributes to its ancient completeness. [For] Moses had come and said (Deuteronomy 10:17): "The great God, the mighty and the awful." Then Jeremiah came and said: Aliens are destroying His Temple. Where are, then, His awful deeds? Hence he omitted [the attribute] the "awful."[25] Daniel came and said: Aliens are enslaving his sons. Where are His mighty deeds?[26] Hence he omitted the word *mighty*.[27] But they came and said: On the contrary! Therein lie His mighty deeds that He subdues His inclination, that He extends long suffering to the wicked. Therein lie His awful powers: For but for the fear of Him, how could one [single] nation persist among the [many] nations! But how could [the earlier] rabbis [meaning Jeremiah and Daniel] abolish something established by Moses? R. Eleazar said: Since they knew that the Holy One, blessed be He, insists on truth, they would not ascribe false [things] to Him. (Yoma 69b)

The usage "His inclination" was unacceptable to some of the copyists, who wrote "His wrath" instead, whereas the Gaon of Vilna opted for "His will," but this usage still appears in the main printed edition. Evidence of its accuracy is also furnished by the parallel verse in Avot 4:1: "Who is a hero? He who subdues his inclination."[28] Indeed, the same verb appears as well in Rabbi Ishmael ben Elisha's blessing ("That Thy mercy may subdue Thy anger") and from the parallel version of this passage it is clear that no external suppression was intended there either. Moreover, even the use of "prevail" adopted by Rabbi Ishmael ("Thy mercy may prevail over Thy other attributes") lacks a mechanistic connotation regarding the attributes. In the Aramaic version of the Bible we find "his mercy prevailed" as a translation of "his affection was kindled" (Genesis 43:30)—spoken of Joseph, a human being.

The Jewish myth changed between the biblical and the rabbinical periods and the passage from Yoma, attributed to the period of the Great Assembly, shows awareness of this change. In the biblical period God still had external enemies although, indeed, none as great and powerful as He: "Who is like Thee, O Lord, among the gods?" (Exodus 15:11). God could not be vanquished by His enemies but, nonetheless, it was still God's glory to defeat them and He was praised by the men of the Bible for His past and future victories: "I will sing to the Lord, for He has triumphed gloriously: the horse and his rider He has thrown into the sea" (Exodus 15:1) or "On that day the Lord with His sore and great and strong sword shall punish Leviathan the flying serpent, and Leviathan that crooked serpent; and He shall slay the crocodile that is in the sea" (Isaiah 27:1). This is not the approach of the Midrash, where both the human enemies and the monsters of the sea have been brought low and are not seen as worthy adversaries. The war with the Leviathan becomes Gabriel's task, and the battle ends following God's intervention (Baba Bathra 74b–75a): "Gabriel is to arrange in the future a chase of Leviathan. . . . And if the Holy One, blessed be He, will not help him, he will be unable to prevail over him." Indeed, there are still angels and a celestial retinue who argue sometimes with their Creator, mainly because they envy mortals, but their whole nature is to serve. God's arguments with them might lead Him to hesitate, but not to external war. Outwardly (as is already the case in several biblical instances), God is Almighty; His real wars are only waged within Himself.

Therefore, according to this passage, when Jeremiah and Daniel felt that God appeared to have been defeated by His enemies, they ceased His praises since they were false and "they would not ascribe false [things] to Him" or, in the version of the Jerusalem Talmud, "flatter Him."[29] After all, these praises continue those of Moses (Deuteronomy 10:17): "a great God, a mighty, and a terrible, who favors no person, and takes no bribe." The men of the Great Assembly thus changed the prophets' ways and reverted to the full wording: "a great God, a mighty and a terrible."[30] Why the reversal? We could explain it in the spirit of the biblical myth and ascribe it to the political and religious improvements in the wake of the Return to Zion but, for the rabbis, this would be out of character. Indeed, unlike the prophets, the men of the Great Assembly could never imagine God's defeat at the hands of His enemies, but neither would they consider it an heroic deed for God to defeat them. In order to be called a *hero*, God must overcome. What, then, must He overcome? The men of the Great Assembly introduced their psychological myth and "restored the crown of the divine attributes to its ancient completeness": They restored the myth of God's heroism. To the extent that the biblical God was a hero, He is now a hero of heroes because "Who is a hero? He who subdues his inclination." What does this mean? It means extending "long suffering to the wicked" (an expression also found in the Sanhedrin passage later, p. 18), when God lets His enemies rule over His house and His people and seems defeated.

It is noteworthy that the Jerusalem Talmud expresses reservations about this myth as well and ascribes it, though in a more subtle form and without the words "His inclination," to the prophet Jeremiah. Unlike Daniel, Jeremiah did say "mighty" because, according to the Jerusalem Talmud version: "He should be called mighty, that He sees His house destroyed and is silent." However, the men of the Great Assembly did not follow Jeremiah because, for abstract theological reasons, they opposed all mythology—man is incapable of grasping God's ways or, in their words: "Does flesh and blood have the power to measure these things?!" The rabbis in the Babylonian Talmud also expressed views in this spirit when they dealt elsewhere with the formula of "great, mighty and terrible God." Angry at those attempting to add a chain of adjectives to these three, in the spirit of the *Hekhalot* literature, the rabbis stated that even these, "had not Moses our Master mentioned them in the Law and had not the men of the Great Assembly come and inserted them in the prayer, we should not have been able to mention them."[31]

Saadia Gaon's approach is worth noting in this context. He also compared the words of Jeremiah and Daniel to the biblical verse and commented on the absence of "mighty and terrible." Although this comparison was obviously inspired by the Talmud, he totally ignored the rabbinical pronouncements in this regard and settled the issue in totally nonmythical fashion![32]

During the biblical period, when God still had external enemies, He could request help from man, at least in ancient rhetorical devices such as?

> And He saw that there was no man,[33] and was astonished that there was no intercessor; therefore His arm brought salvation to Him; and His righteousness, it sustained Him. For He put on righteousness as a breastplate, and a helmet of salvation upon His head and He put on the garments of vengance for clothing, and was clad with zeal as a cloak, according to their deeds, so

will He repay, fury to His adversaries, recompense to His enemies; to the islands He will repay recompense. (Isaiah 59:16–18)

What help can God expect from flesh and blood creatures? Verbal encouragement, as in the words of the prophet: "Awake, awake, put on strength, O arm of the Lord; awake as in the ancient days, in the generations of old. Art Thou not it that has cut Rahav in pieces, and wounded the crocodile? Art Thou not it which dried the sea, the waters of the great deep; that made the depths of the sea a way for the ransomed to pass over?" (Isaiah 51:9–10)

But what is Rabbi Ishmael's role? Is the expectation that man should help God also found in the rabbinical period? How can man interfere with God's attributes? The talmudic God too asks man for help, real and crucial help, even if many talmudic scholars are uncomfortable with this request. Help again appears as verbal encouragement, despite the fact that God struggles against His own attributes. As human beings need help and support in their struggle against their passions, so does God, and this parallel is explicitly mentioned when summarizing the passage on Akatriel and Ishmael: "Here we learn that the blessing of an ordinary man must not be considered lightly in your eyes" (elsewhere the Talmud learns the same rule from stories about biblical figures).[34] That is, we may learn from God's request about human nature and about the proper conduct toward humankind in general since, despite claims to the contrary, the ethos of the rabbis is grounded on their myth but does not replace it.[35]

Rabbi Ishmael's blessing even entered the liturgy and is included in the morning prayer after the reading on the binding of Isaac; to encourage God further, Abraham is presented to Him in the prayers so that his memory may be preserved in reward for his actions, and also as a paragon for the subdual of passion:

Master of the world! Even as Abraham our father held back his compassion in order to do Thy will with loyal heart, so may Thy mercy hold back Thy anger from us; let Thy mercy prevail over Thy attributes. Lord our God, deal with us kindly and mercifully; in Thy great goodness, may Thy fierce wrath turn away from Thy people, Thy city, Thy land, and Thy heritage. . .

Doubts may still remain as to whether this is not an unusual motif in rabbinical literature that only appears here because of the mentioned links between the Akatriel story and *Hekhalot* literature.

The following parallel passage, of impeccable midrashic credentials, should help to allay them:

> R. Joshua b. Levi also said: When Moses ascended on high, he found the Holy One, blessed be He, tying crowns on the letters [of the Torah]. Said He to him, "Moses, is there no [greeting of] Peace in thy town?" "Shall a servant extend [a greeting of] Peace to his Master!" replied he. "Yet thou shouldst have assisted Me," said He. Immediately he cried out to Him, (Numbers 14:17) "And now, I pray thee, let the power of the Lord be great, according as thou hast spoken." (Shabbath 89a)

Although this passage resembles the Akatriel-Ishmael story in content, in its literary approach it is diametrically opposed. In that case, as usual in *Hekhalot* literature, the dominant tone is mystical and formal, creating a distance between God and His creatures. Akatriel and Ishmael, a product of this literature, feature as protagonists. In this case, the protagonists are familiar and close to every Jew—the Holy One, blessed be He, and Moses. There is a close link between the identity of the protagonists and the contents of the stories: The first tells of a High Priest who enters the innermost part of the sanctuary to offer incense, when God officially addresses him and requests a blessing. The second tells of an intimate conversation between God and Moses, conducted as a psychological contest full of cunning and misunderstandings.

In the Akatriel-Ishmael story, as in other accounts of ascents to Heaven from *Hekhalot* and apocalyptic literature, God's nature is revealed in the very statement about His attributes or about celestial entities. Ostensibly, this is the main "content" of the story. But here, in the personal myth, God's psychological dilemma is also sharply expressed in the "background story," the story of the meeting between Moses and God. God tries to protect His honor as Lord and Master while trying to obtain Moses' help, and His request for a blessing thus seems like an admonition, seemingly phrased in simple, popular language: "Moses, is there no [greeting of] Peace in thy town!?" Is it not the custom to extend peace greetings where you grew up!? Moses truly believes that God is protecting His honor and does not understand that, in fact, He is asking for his help. Therefore, Moses' reply is in the spirit of God's admonition: "Shall a servant extend [a greeting of] peace to his Master?" God then sees that hints will not suffice—He humiliates Himself and makes His request explicit: "Yet thou shouldst have assisted Me." Only now does Moses understand what is being asked of him and he blesses God in the words of the verse, wishing that His power, which is identical with His attributes of mercy, may grow.

God's attributes of mercy appear in the next biblical verse, which the Talmud reader is supposed to have completed in his mind: "And now, I pray Thee, let the power of my Lord be great, according as Thou hast spoken, saying, The Lord is long suffering, and great in love. . ." The mention of His attributes of mercy attests that, in this case as well, it is intended to have mercy "prevail over His attributes"; however, identifying His attributes of mercy with "His power" may point to their actual nature as characteristics of God rather than separate entities, as could have been understood from the Akatriel story.

The very mention of the attributes through a biblical quote helps to soften the formal style and the mythical overtones of Rabbi Ishmael's phrasing ("Thy mercy may prevail over Thy other attributes"); by contrast, the understatement characterizing the encounter between God and Moses accords the myth a more personal and primitive bent. The story of Akatriel seems to be nothing but a formal, exalted formulation and a conceptualized abstraction of this primitive myth, intended to hide God's "human weaknesses" under a cloak of distant glory in order to adjust it to the mystical style of *Hekhalot* literature. The alternative—turning the story of Akatriel into a personal myth—is inconceivable. We do occasionally find in *Hekhalot* literature expressions of an intimate bond between God and His worshippers, often to the chagrin of the ministering angels; the contrast created after the breach in the cloak of distance makes this bond seem even more powerful. We will see in section III that, in rabbinical *midrashim* too, the angels fulfill a similar literary role).

In the more aloof version of the Akatriel-Ishmael story the mystic's influence on the divine attributes seems to be a quasi-magical or, more accurately, a quasi-theurgic act; however, in the personal story, it appears more likely that Moses influences his God through his words of encouragement. This idea is found explicitly in an earlier version of this story, where Moses' words to God ("And now I pray Thee, let the power. . .") are compared with the cries of support with which spectators encourage athletes in the arena:

> "enhances strength" (Job 17:9). . .applies to Moses who enhanced the strength of the Almighty, as when he said "And now, I pray Thee, let the strength of the Lord be enhanced. . ." so that the measure of mercy [may] prevail over the measure of justice. . . A strong man was exercising with a block of stone that came from a stonecutter. A passer-by saw him and said: "Your power is

marvelous. You are strong and brave," as is written: "And now, I pray Thee. . ." R. Azariah, citing R. Judah bar R. Simon, said: Whenever righteous men do the Holy One's will, they enhance the strength of the Almighty. Hence Moses' plea, "And now, I pray Thee. . ." On the other hand, when men do not do His will, then, if one dare say such a thing, (Deuteronomy 32:18):[36] "The Rock that begot thee, thou dost weaken."[37]

In a sentence preceding this passage, the Midrash suggests another option: " 'enhances strength. . .' is the Holy One who enhances the strength of the righteous to enable them to do His will." Indeed, in the account of Moses' ascent to heaven cited in the Shabbath passage (p. 16), the parties were also ambivalent. God and man are meshed and need each other. It is not only God who needs to be encouraged by Moses to abandon justice and embrace mercy, but Moses too needs God's prodding to become aware of the need for mercy, first through a hint ("Is there no [greeting of] peace in thy town?") and then explicitly ("Yet thou shouldst have assisted Me"). This appears even more clearly in another talmudic version of the encounter between God and Moses, where Moses speaks of the attribute of mercy relying on the same biblical verse, but God makes it explicitly clear that it is He who holds the copyright on the idea of mercy:

When Moses ascended on high, he found the Holy One, blessed be He, sitting and writing "long suffering." Said he to Him, "Master of the World! Long suffering to the righteous?" He replied,[38] "Even to the wicked." He urged, "Let the wicked perish!" "See now what thou desirest," was His answer. "When Israel sinned," He said to him, "didst thou not urge Me, [Let Thy] long suffering be for the righteous [only]?" "Master of the World!" said he, "but didst Thou not assure me, Even to the wicked!" Hence it is written, "And now, I pray Thee, let the power of my Lord be great, according as Thou hast spoken, saying." (Sanhedrin 111a–111b)

In this passage, the relationship between God and Moses seems more complex and delicate than the biblical one. This dialogue would not fit the style of the biblical myth, which is more aloof and unequivocal. In the biblical context, Moses seems to be consistently on the side of mercy, as it is said (Psalms 106:23): "Therefore He said that He would destroy them, had not Moses His chosen one stood before Him in the breach, to turn away His wrath, lest He should destroy them." We even find God imploring Moses (Deuteronomy 9:14):

"Let Me alone, that I may destroy them, and blot out their name from under heaven: and I will make of thee a nation mightier and greater than they" but Moses does not leave Him alone and, as we shall see later, "ignores God's command." As usual, the Talmud added a daring mythical picture:

> R. Abbahu said: Were it not explicitly written, it would be impossible to say such a thing. . .[This formula serves to license the pursuit of a very bold line in the development of the biblical myth. Although this direction is already latent in a literal reading of the text, it entails an exaggerated concretization of the phrase "let Me alone"] this teaches that Moses took hold of the Holy One, blessed be He, like a man who seizes his fellow by his garment and said before Him: Master of the World, I will not let Thee go until Thou forgivest and pardonest them. (Berakhot, 32a)

The Zohar developed this idea through the use of kabbalistic symbolism. As usual, it amplified the myth while leaving its personal intensity undiminished, and described Moses as embracing the King, wrestling with Him and pinning Him down by His arms.[39] According to Exodus 33:34, when God would not come up in the midst of His people Moses forced Him to reveal to him the secret of His attributes of mercy, through which He might be brought to change His decrees. This biblical description already seems to contain all the seeds of the blunt myth on which the *Selihot* ritual is grounded:

> R. Johanan said: Were it not written in the text, it would be impossible for us to say such a thing; this verse teaches us that the Holy One, blessed be He, drew his robe round Him like the reader of a congregation and showed Moses the order of the prayer. He said to him: Whenever Israel sin, let them carry out this service before Me, and I will forgive them. . .A covenant has been made with the thirteen attributes that they will not be turned away empty handed. (Rosh Hashana 17b)

In talmudic sources however, Moses is ambivalent in his commitment to the attribute of mercy, as we saw earlier. The reasons will become clearer as we delve further into Moses' character in the Talmud, where we find another description of his meeting with God:

> Rab Judah said in the name of Rab: When Moses ascended on high he found the Holy One, blessed be He, engaged in tying

crowns to the letters. Said Moses, "Master of the World, Who stays Thy hand?" He answered, "There will arise a man, at the end of many generations, Akiba b. Joseph by name, who will expound upon each tittle heaps and heaps of laws." "Master of the World," said Moses; "permit me to see him." He replied, "Turn thee round." Moses went and sat down behind eight rows [and listened to the discourses upon the law]. Not being able to follow their arguments he was weakened, but when they came to a certain subject and the disciples said to the master "Whence do you know it?" and the latter replied "It is a law given unto Moses at Sinai," he was comforted. Thereupon he returned to the Holy One, blessed be He, and said, "Master of the World, Thou hast such a man and Thou givest the Torah by me!" he replied, "Be silent, for such is My decree." Then said Moses, "Master of the World, Thou hast shown me his Torah, show me his reward." "Turn thee round," said He; and Moses turned round and saw them weighing out his flesh at the market stalls. "Master of the World," cried Moses, "such Torah, and such a reward!" He replied, "Be silent, for such is My decree." (Menahot 29b)

This famous passage, widely regarded as the archetype of the relation between the Written and the Oral Law, replicates the situation presented in the two previous ones (pp. 16 and 18). In itself, the very appearance of a story in three different versions is proof of its "mythical validity," close to that of a personal legend and far from the rank of an "article of faith." This passage opens like the one in Shabbath and Moses encounters God as He is engaged in tying crowns to the letters but, whereas in the passage in Menahot the crowns are the story's substance, in the Shabbath passage the crowns are never mentioned again. However, were we to join to the Shabbath passage the "long suffering" quote from Sanhedrin (p. 18), the meaning of the crowns in the former would become clearer. Crowns are added to letters, in the same way that the attribute of mercy is added to justice, but Moses cannot grasp this. In Menahot he is presented as a slightly inadequate man; he not only fails to grasp the meaning of the crowns, needing to be "telescoped" into the future, but he also fails to understand the discussions between Rabbi Akiba and his students, till "he is weakened." It is interesting to note that the Talmud chose to use the very expression used in reference to God.[40] Moses is "comforted" when hearing the argument quoted in his name, but his sense of justice compels him to return to God and request that the Torah be given through Rabbi Akiba, a wiser man. However, God claims that justice is not at stake—"Be silent, for such is My decree"—and even repeats this answer when relating to Moses' stronger appeal—"Such Torah, and such a reward!"—which he had voiced when witnessing Rabbi Akiba's painful death.

Moses is also portrayed elsewhere in the Talmud as refusing to accept that God can depart from the principle of justice:

> R. Johanan further said in the name of R. Jose: Three things did Moses ask of the Holy One, blessed be He, and they were granted to him.... He asked that He should show him the ways of the Holy One, blessed be He, and it was granted to him. For it is said "Show me now Thy ways" (Exodus, 33:13). Moses said before Him: "Master of the World, why is it that some righteous men prosper and others are in adversity, some wicked men prosper and others are in adversity?" He replied to him: "Moses, the righteous man who prospers is a righteous man the son of a righteous man; the righteous man who is in adversity is a righteous man the son of a wicked man. The wicked man who prospers is a wicked man son of a righteous man; the wicked man who is in adversity is a wicked man son of a wicked man." (Berakhot 7a)

Although God somehow answers Moses' question, the Talmud finds this response unacceptable and corrects it a few lines later: "a righteous man who prospers is a perfectly righteous man." However, others felt that Moses' question had not been answered at all and, rather than being a problem of justice, this issue belongs in the realm of God's arbitrary right of clemency:

> Now this [saying of R. Johanan] is in opposition to the saying of R. Meir. For R. Meir said: "Only two [requests] were granted to him, and one was not granted to him." For it is said (Exodus 33:19): "And I will be gracious to whom I will be gracious," although he may not deserve it, "And I will show mercy on whom I will show mercy," although he may not deserve it.

Unlike Moses, Rabbi Akiba himself never complained about the injustice of his painful agony, as the Talmud tells us elsewhere:

> When R. Akiba was taken out for execution, it was the hour for the recital of the *Shema* (Deuteronomy 6:4), and while they combed his flesh with iron combs, he was accepting upon himself the kingship of heaven. His disciples said to him: "Our teacher,

even to this point?" He said to them: "All my days I have been troubled by this verse (Deuteronomy 6:5): 'with all thy soul,' [which I interpret] "even if He takes thy soul." I said: "When shall I have the opportunity of fulfilling this? Now that I have the opportunity shall I not fulfill it?" He prolonged the word *Ehad* [One] until he expired while saying it. A *bat kol* [heavenly voice] went forth and proclaimed: "Happy art thou, Akiba, that thy soul has departed with the word *Ehad!*" The ministering angels said before the Holy One, blessed be He: "Such Torah, and such a reward? [He should have been] 'from them that die by Thy hand, O Lord' (Psalms 17:14). He replied to them: 'their portion is in life' (ibid). A *bat kol* went forth and proclaimed, "Happy art thou, R. Akiba, that thou art destined for the life of the world to come." (Berakhot 61b)

Moses thus ranked among the angels; they had also asked about Rabbi Akiba's death "Such Torah, and such a reward?" and had received an answer from God—reward is in the world to come. Rabbi Akiba himself, however, does not demand justice from God and sees his agony as an expression of His love (the full verse that troubled Rabbi Akiba reads: "And thou shall love the Lord thy God . . .and with all thy soul . . ."). Rabbi Akiba seems to view his death as an expression of God's love. "His ways," His mythical ways, are better known to Rabbi Akiba than to Moses, the man of justice; the only answer to which Moses is therefore entitled about Rabbi Akiba's death is "Be silent, for such is My decree." This death is not in the rational realm, and you, who cannot penetrate the mystery of God's passion and love, must accept it as capricious and arbitrary.

This description of Rabbi Akiba is also supported by other sources. In a book[41] I devoted to the talmudic passage "Four entered the *pardes*" (Hagiga, 14b–15a), I show that Rabbi Akiba—who is here considered the perfect mystic and whose ascent to heaven resembles that of Moses—is described as the antithesis of Elisha ben Avuyah, the "other," whose very demand for formal justice causes his downfall. In my analysis of the prophet Jonah, I show that he too is one of those who share in God's mysteries and oppose the idea of justice, as does Abraham, who is tested in order to prove this.[42]

I would not have dared to suggest this interpretation of God's love, had the Talmud not done so before me:

Raba (some said R. Hisda) says: If a man sees that painful sufferings visit him, let him examine his conduct. . . . If he examines and finds nothing [objectionable] let him attribute it to the neglect of the study of the Torah.... If he did attribute it [thus] and still did not find [this to be the cause] let him be sure that these are the chastenings of love. For it is said (Proverbs 3:12): "For whom the Lord loveth He correcteth." Raba, in the name of R. Sahorah, in the name of R. Huna, says: "If the Holy One, blessed be He, is pleased with a man, He crashes him with painful sufferings, for it is said (Isaiah 53:10): "And the Lord was pleased with [him, hence] he crushed him by disease." Now, you might think that it is so even if he did not accept them with love. Therefore it is said (ibid): "To see if his soul would offer itself in restitution." Even as the trespass offering must be brought by consent, so also the sufferings must be endured with consent. (Berakhot 5a)

The rabbis deal extensively with the virtue of suffering, and scholars have summarized their views.[43] However, the lofty stage of "chastenings of love" that are reserved only for individuals such as Rabbi Akiba and "God's servant" in the verse from Isaiah, has not been sufficiently clarified. Despite R. Ami's view, which resembles that of Job's friends—"There is no suffering without iniquity" (Shabbath 55a)—the chastenings of love are not related to any sin, as is clear from the beginning of the passage as well as from a saying in the following page: "Leprosy...they are an altar of atonement, but they are not chastenings of love" (Berakhot 5b). The "love" in the "chastenings of love" is not the love of the sufferer but the love of God, who is their source and reason (except for the indirect suffering caused by the envy of those who are jealous of this love; see, e.g., Zohar I:182b). The sufferer is indeed meant to give love in return, like Rabbi Akiba, but merely raising the possibility that he might not—"even if he did not accept them with love"—emphasizes again that the main lover is God.

A comparison with the kabbalistic explanation of "chastenings of love" is in place here. The Zohar (I:181a) claims that the "love" in "chastenings of love" refers to the *Shekhina*, called *Ahava Zuta* [minor love], who is pained by its separation from the male divinity, that includes the *Ahava Raba* [great love] - apparently implying the *sefira* of *hesed*. Humanity is also hurt by these sufferings—those born on the moon's wane are fated to suffer with it and to be renewed with the new moon, for the moon is a symbol of the *Shekhina*.

Rather than a negligible view of God's love, this description is an integral and important part of the overall Jewish myth, though it is not easily found since God's honor requires its concealment. We shall see in the final section that this description fits the figure of the biblical God as it emerges elsewhere in the Talmud. Thus, we shall see that God sometimes causes the righteous to suffer because He longs to hear their prayers (Yebamoth 64a), whereas the statement "the righteous are seized [by death] for the [sins of the] generation" (Shabbath 33b) seems to rely on a similar assumption, which in Christianity was transformed into the sacrifice of the "son of God." We find in the *Midrash Rabba* on Song of Songs 6:2: " 'My beloved is gone down to his garden, to the beds of spices'. . .'My beloved' refers to the Holy One, blessed be He; 'to his garden' refers to the world; 'to the beds of spices' indicates Israel; 'to feed in the gardens' indicates synagogues and houses of study and 'to gather lilies' to take away the righteous in Israel." More bluntly and dramatically, this idea is conveyed by "a certain child" (an anonymous child can apparently say more) in the eulogy to Rabba son of R. Huna: "In His wrath against His world, God robbed it of its souls and rejoiced in them as in a new bride; He who rides upon the clouds gladdened in the coming of a pure and righteous soul" (Moed Katan, 25b).

Rabbi Akiba's example gave strong impetus to this mythical trend in Jewish tradition, because Jewish martyrs throughout history saw it, alongside the binding of Isaac, as a model. Following his example, they died with the *Shema* on their lips as a testimony of their faith.[44] The story of R. Akiba's death is woven into the myth of "the Ten Martyrs," which appears in many versions—some midrashic, some in the *Hekhalot* literature, and some as *piyutim* (ritual songs). This myth became part of the very core of Jewish religion and any attempt to describe it would be beyond the scope of this essay, so I shall only touch on a number of relevant points and briefly trace its development in kabbalistic literature.

In the book *Bahir*, which is considered the first text of this literature, Moses' question appears as follows:

> Said Rabbi Rehumai: "This I have learned; when Moses asked to know the ways of God and said (Exodus 33:18) 'Show me Thy ways,' he asked to know why some righteous men prosper and others are in adversity, some wicked men prosper and others are in adversity, and they did not tell him." "You say they did not tell him? Rather, they did not tell him what he asked. Can you possibly believe that Moses did not know this secret? But thus did Moses say: 'I know the ways of the powers but I do not know how the Thought unfolds in them, I know that in the Thought is truth, but I do not know its parts, and I ask to know.' And they did not tell him."[45]

In Exodus 33, Moses makes two requests: the first, in verse 13, "show me Thy ways," and the second, in verse 18, "show me Thy glory." He was granted the first, and thus said: "I know the ways of the powers"; he was denied the second, and thus said: "I do not know how the Thought unfolds in them." The word *glory* [literally, honor] stands for God's essence; as a dignified person is addressed as "your honor" rather than "you," God's essence here is called "the Thought" (as in the talmudic quote: "Be silent, this is My decree" or, literally, "Be silent, thus it has entered My Thought) and therefore Moses said: "I know that in the Thought is truth." Similarly, in *Hilkhot Yesodei ha-Torah* 1:10, Maimonides expounded the word glory in the Exodus verse as "He sought to have a clear apprehension of the truth of God's existence" and stated: "It is beyond the mental capacity of a human creature, composed of body and soul, to obtain in this regard clear knowledge of the truth" (unlike Saadia Gaon who translated "your glory" as "your light"; i.e., the created Glory).

The book *Bahir* looks on Moses' problem as one typical of kabbalists: he understands God's attributes, which have become quasi-mechanical entities—"the ways of the powers"—acting each in its own destined way and bringing either good or evil. But God's essence, or His personal Thought, cannot be predicted, and we cannot understand "why some righteous men prosper and others are in adversity, some wicked men prosper and others are in adversity." This distinction between attributes and essence is kabbalistic and not talmudic, but is an adequate conceptual formulation of the difference noted above between Moses' quasi-mechanistic perception of God's attributes and Rabbi Akiba's personal approach.

Nonetheless, it is noteworthy that the book *Bahir* is aware of a divine personal essence transcending the attributes and the *sefirot*, attesting to this book's special status between Midrash and Kabbala. Although later kabbalistic literature also reveals this awareness,[46] it tends to emphasize elements of mechanical regularity. Kabbalists went even further than the request denied to Moses and explained, although in great secrecy, the unfolding of Divine Thought that caused the death of the Ten Martyrs, as well as the details of God's cruel love for Rabbi Akiba. This was not merely a spiritual love, but the expression of a divine need that was sexual and physiological. The death of Rabbi Akiba and his friends, as well as that of others after them, raises the *mayin nukbin*, the liquid that enables the mating of the male and female elements in the Divine.[47] *Kiddush hashem* [the sanctification of the name] seems to have been derived from *kiddushin*—marriage. Moreover, the phrase *thus it has entered My Thought*, through which God expressed His love, assumes technical significance, and the death of the Ten Martyrs became a myth of catharsis, namely, repairing the worlds by purifying the Divine Thought from its dross—an old Jewish idea that, according to Moshe Idel, developed under the influence of Persian religion. The Ten acquired cosmic significance as representing the *sefirot*, which they purify throughout history, and for this purpose, the myth of the Ten Martyrs was merged with the myth of the destruction of the worlds and the death of the Edomite kings.[58] In this instance, the Jewish religion adopted a course not unknown in the history of religion and included human beings in a divine myth.[49] However, it retained their essence as flesh and blood creatures and conceived them as reincarnated souls, from the days of Joseph's brothers, for whose sin the Ten were sentenced to death according to the midrashim,[50] through Rabbi Simeon bar Yohai's friends in the *Idra* of the Zohar, all the way to Rabbi Isaac Luria and his disciples.

Already in the book *Bahir*, in a passage immediately following the one just cited, we are told that "some righteous men prosper and others are in adversity, some wicked men prosper and others are in adversity" due to their actions in previous incarnations. The book *Bahir* may have ascribed this explanation to the "ways of the powers" that became known to Moses rather than to the "unfolding of the Thought," if there is any correspondence at all between these two passages in the book, but other kabbalists merged the two and turned the death and reincarnations of the Ten into a way of purifying the divine Thought.

This relationship between Rabbi Akiba and Moses is also woven into the details of the kabbalistic myth and into Lurianic Kabbala in particular, where it attained its full development. Rabbi Akiba indeed ranks higher than Moses in this myth (a statement generally true, although the opposite is occasionally the case due to the intricacies of reincarnations and soul sparks). Moses is placed in the *sefira* of *tiferet*, which is a "corporeal" rank, and his mating is corporeal and through *yesod*, whereas Rabbi Akiba is placed in the *sefira* of *bina* and mates through a kiss, a more exalted and spiritual love transmitted through the mouth. Thus, it is no mere coincidence that Rabbi Akiba is the main figure in the "Oral Law," which is perceived as ranking higher than the "Written Law," obviously represented by Moses.[51] It is from the Talmud that the kabbalists inferred that Moses had not reached the *sefira* of *bina* (Rosh Hashanah 21b): "Fifty gates of *bina* [understanding] were created in the world and all were given to Moses save one," though this might be another case of a midrashic idea that attained technical development in the Kabbala. When we compare this statement to the previous passage where Moses was denied understanding of "why is it that some righteous men prosper...," as well as with the mystery of Rabbi Akiba's sufferings, we may conclude that the fiftieth gate of *bina* is the key to these questions, and it was granted to Rabbi Akiba. Some kabbalists refer to the gate denied to Moses as "the gate of silence,"[52] perhaps pursuant to "Be silent, for such is My decree." Compare, "the mystery of 'these are the kings who ruled in Edom,' namely, in the place of silence [from the Hebrew *dom* for be silent] for this is My decree."[53] This may clarify the use of *Masa Duma* ["the burden of Duma" (Isaiah 21:11)] in reference to the "sacred religion of Edom," which is how Jacob Frank referred to his conversion to Christianity, whose true meaning must remain secret.[54] For Luria, as usual, the ontological myth assumes the guise of reincarnation: he saw himself as Moses and his disciple Rabbi Hayyim Vital as a reincarnation of Rabbi Akiba.[55]

III. Talmud and Kabbala:
The Essence of the Divine Attributes

We shall continue the analysis of the divine attributes as they are reflected in other passages of rabbinical and kabbalistic literature. This analysis will reveal different nuances in the definition of these attributes as well as in their relationship to God and will clarify and illustrate the character of the talmudic myth, whose flexibility can only attest to its vitality. The divine attributes are sometimes depicted as external instruments, with God pondering which to select:

> The Lord God—This may be compared to a king who had some thin glasses. Said the king: "If I pour hot water into them, they will burst; if cold, they will contract [and snap]." What then did the king do? He mixed hot and cold water and poured it into them, and so they remained [unbroken]. Thus said the Holy One, blessed be He: "If I create the world only with the attribute of mercy, its sins will be great; only with the attribute of justice, the world cannot exist. Hence I will create it with the attribute of justice and with the attribute of mercy and may it stand." (Genesis Rabba 12:15)

This description was congenial to the kabbalists, who relied on it for some of their ideas, such as the destruction of earlier worlds because of unmitigaged justice. In the Kabbala this concept is not used metaphorically but refers to real worlds that had actually been destroyed, such as the kingdom of Edom. But this kabbalistic notion may simply be bringing to full fruition an idea already latent in this midrash, which expounds God's "full name," the Lord God, as found in the Genesis 2 version of the Creation. Then, as usual, it interprets *Lord* as the attribute of mercy and *God* as the attribute of justice, though it must obviously have been aware of the story of Creation as told in Genesis 1, where only the name *God* appears. (As is well known, biblical source criticism is founded on these distinctions and on reiterations of the divine name). The author may also have assumed that a world created earlier and founded on the attribute of justice, had not survived; indeed, a passage in Genesis Rabba 3:7 states "that the Holy One, blessed be He, went on creating worlds and destroying them until He created these ones." Further on, however, this midrash ascribes the destruction of the worlds to God's arbitrary will rather than to His external attributes: "this pleases Me, but those did not please Me." Although a similar notion appears in the Kabbala too, kabbalists leave room for God's judgment and the destruction of the worlds takes place inside the divine Thought.[56]

Elsewhere, the divine attributes appear not as God's qualities but as His different dwellings, and another description speaks of different chairs God sits on when passing judgment.[57] The spirit of this description is close to the Kabbala, which suggests the theory of the *sefirot* as vessels but without seing them as the divine essence. In its original meaning, *mida* [attribute] denotes a measuring container; if this is meant to point to the nature of the attributes, we may assume that a fixed regularity characterizes their functioning:

> It was taught in R. Meir's name: " 'For behold, the Lord comes out of His place' (Micah 1:3)—He moves from one attribute to the other. He leaves the attribute of justice and enters the attribute of mercy for Israel...." R. Samuel b. Nahman: "If the Holy One, blessed be He, meant to bring good—'God is not a man that He should lie' (Numbers 23:19), and if He meant to bring evil—'Has He said and He shall not perform? Or has He spoken and shall He not make it good?' (ibid)[58]

This view was later contended by those claiming that God's actions are not dictated by the set functioning of the attributes but by His relations with man:

> And the sages said: "Was it not a man that turned God's words as if they were not?!—'Lord, why does Thy wrath burn against Thy people' (Exodus 32:11). 'Nor the son of man, that He should

repent' (Numbers 23:19)—"Was it not the son of Amram who made God repent?!"—'And the Lord relented of the evil which He thought to do to His people' (Exodus 32:14).

This is also the direction followed by the Babylonian Talmud: "R. Eliezer said, Why are the prayers of the righteous likened to a pitchfork?[59] To teach thee that just as the pitchfork turns the corn from place to place in the barn, so the prayers of the righteous turn the mind of the Holy One, blessed be He, from the attribute of cruelty to that of compassion." (Sukkah 14a).

This passage too draws a parallel between "places" and "attributes," although here the attributes are clearly personal. They are part of "the mind of the Holy One" and, instead of alluding to them by their technical names, as "the attribute of justice and the attribute of mercy," the reference is psychological—"the attribute of cruelty and that of compassion"—and suggests the righteous can affect these through their prayers. But human influence extends here only to the attribute of justice, as is evident from this passage as well as from the rabbis' references to Moses in the previous one. The attribute of mercy functions in its set way, as we saw earlier in the promise given to Moses: "A covenant has been made with the thirteen attributes that they will not be turned away empty handed" (Rosh Hashanah 17b). It is possible that this covenant was not conceived in purely magical terms, and it may leave room for a personal approach to God (see the wording of the *Selihot* prayer, "Remember today the covenant of the thirteen attributes," which overlooks the contradiction between the request to remember and the preset regularity of the covenant). It is indeed suggested elsewhere that the attribute of mercy might also be abolished and by the very same R. Samuel bar Nahman who had prescribed exactly the opposite rule:

R. Samuel b. Nahman said: "Woe to the wicked who turn the attribute of mercy into the attribute of judgement. Wherever Lord is employed it connotes the attribute of mercy, as in the verse, 'The Lord, The Lord, merciful and gracious.' (Exodus 34:6) Yet it is written, 'And the Lord saw that the wickedness of man was great,' (Genesis 6:5) 'And the Lord repented that He had made man,' (ibid.: 6) 'And the Lord said: I will blot out man.' (ibid.: 7) Happy are the righteous who turn the attribute of judgment into the attribute of mercy. Wherever God is employed it connotes the attribute of judgment—'Thou shall not revile God,' (Exodus 22:27) 'The cause of both parties shall come before God.' (ibid.: 8)[60] Yet it is written, 'And God heard their groaning and God

remembered His covenant,' (ibid. 2:24) 'And God remembered
Rachel,' (Genesis 30:22) 'And God remembered Noah' (ibid. 8:1)."
(Genesis Rabba 33:3)

Rather than presenting God as moving from one attribute to
another, here the attribute itself changes: the attribute of mercy shows
justice and the attribute of justice shows mercy. We may interpret this
in two ways: either each attribute has its own ontological personality,
transcending the qualities of mercy and justice, or this is no more than
a description of God's moods and He is called by the justice name *God*
even if He changed His mind at the last moment, and by the mercy
name *Lord*, even if He is suddenly filled with wrath against the
wicked. Although the kabbalists grew up on this notion, they were
incapable of such flexibility:

> You may at times find in verses of mercy the name God which
> indicates justice. . . . And also in verses of wrath the name Lord
> which indicates mercy. . . . Since a righteous man deserves well,
> then why was his judgment crooked, and a wicked one, does he
> deserve mercy? He should be destroyed. But the depth of these
> questions is only given to the masters of worship [namely, the
> kabbalists].[61]

In the personal myth, the assumption that the attribute of mercy
would always remain while the attribute of justice could be eliminated
was formulated differently, but this myth too speaks of the contrary
option as a possible exception:

> For R. Aha b. R. Hanina said: "Never did a good word go forth
> from the mouth of the Holy One, blessed be He, of which He
> retracted for an evil one, save the following, where it is written,
> (Ezekiel 9:4) 'And the Lord said unto him, Go through the midst
> of the city, through the midst of Jerusalem, and set a mark upon
> the foreheads of the men that sigh and that cry for all the
> abominations that be done in the midst thereof. . .' The Holy
> One, blessed be He, said to Gabriel: "Go and set a mark of ink
> upon the foreheads of the righteous, that the destroying angels
> may have no power over them, and a mark of blood upon the
> foreheads of the wicked, that the destroying angels may have
> power over them."[62] Said the attribute of justice before the Holy
> One, blessed be He, "Master of the World, wherein are these
> different from those?" "Those are completely rigteous men,
> while these are completely wicked men," replied He. "Master

of the World," it continued, "they had the power to protest but did not." "It was revealed and known to them that, had they protested, they would not have been heeded." "Master of the World," said he, "if it was revealed to Thee, was it revealed to them?" (Shabbath 55a)

The opening passage refers only to God, who may "retract" at will, although it later becomes clear that He retracts because of the attribute of justice. However, the attribute of justice here is not a mechanistic structure but rather a personality in its own right, persuading its master with logical arguments. It is clear from the opening statement ("Never did. . .") that persuasion is not guaranteed success and that, at times, God will not change His views. Indeed, in a similar instance elsewhere in the Talmud, the attribute of justice makes the very same claim ("Wherein are these different from those?" [Israel and the nations of the world]) and God rejects its plea.[63]

The personal nature of the attribute of justice is enhanced by its identification with the angel Gabriel, who appears at the opening. As the plot unfolds, it becomes clear that the attribute of justice is reacting to the mission God assigned to Gabriel; in another version of the same story, "the angel of death" appears instead of Gabriel, strengthening this identification even further.[64] In its final response, the attribute of justice is quoted as "Said he" [the angel, of masculine gender on Hebrew), rather than "Said she" [the attribute, of feminine gender in Hebrew].[65] This is not the only instance of an interchange between the attribute of justice and the angels. In Sanhedrin 103a, "the Holy One, blessed be He, made Manasse a kind of opening in the Heavens against the attribute of justice, in order to accept him in his repentance," whereas parallel sources claim that the angels, and not the attribute of justice, blocked the windows so that Manasse's prayer would not be heard in Heaven.[66]

On the one hand then, the attribute of justice is identified with the angel (we shall return to this later), and on the other hand, it is only a divine psychological characteristic, or God's evil inclination. In *Avot de-Rabbi Nathan*, God's spiritual qualities are portrayed as angels who minister to the throne of glory: "Seven attributes minister before the throne of glory, to wit: wisdom, righteousness, justice, mercy and compassion, truth and peace."[67] These attributes closely resemble the homonymous kabbalistic *sefirot*. There is a further dimension: the attribute and the angel are also limbs of the divine body. Several talmudic references to this parallel are pointed out later, but this image is better known from the Kabbala, and is already found in the book *Bahir*:

The Holy One, blessed be He, has seven sacred shapes which also appear in man, as is said (Genesis 9:6) "for in the image of God made He man," (Genesis 1:27) "in the image of God He created him; male and female He created them." And they are these: a right and left thigh, a right and left hand, a body with a circumcised member[68] and a head, to wit, six. And you had said seven? The seventh is His wife, as is said (Genesis 2:22) "and they become one flesh," and she had been taken from His side. . .[69]

These seven shapes and limbs are undoubtedly the divine attributes, as can be inferred from other passages in the book *Bahir*. In a parallel statement (82), they are spoken of as "the powers in Heaven" of the seven human limbs, and the attribute of justice is also described as one of the limbs—God's hand:

And what is Satan? It teaches us that the Holy One, blessed be He, has an attribute named evil to the North of the Holy One, blessed be He. . . . And what is this attribute?[70] It is the shape of the hand, with many extensions,[71] and all are named evil, evil. . . . And all of man's evil inclination comes from there. And why was it given to the left? Because he may not rule anywhere except in the North. . .(162–163)

Although the attribute of justice does not appear as God's hand in the Talmud, the attribute of mercy indeed does:

R. Simeon b. Lakish said in the name of R. Judah Nisiah: What is implied by the verse (Ezekiel 1:8) "And they had his hand of a man under their wings?" *Yado* [his hand] is written [instead of *yede*, the hands of]: this refers to the hand of the Holy One, blessed be He, which is spread out under the wings of the living creatures [the angels that bore the Divine Chariot] in order to accept penitents and shield them from the attribute of justice." (Pesahim 119a)

From, in the phrase *from the attribute of justice* at the end of this passage is a translation of the Hebrew *mi-yad* [from the hand of], hinting perhaps at a literal hand. But it seems more likely that the attribute of justice is represented by the shielding wings of the living creatures blocking access to heaven, through which God passes His hand in order to make way for penitents, as in the opening He had made for Manasse against the angels.[72] In kabbalistic literature, the attribute of mercy and the attribute of justice appear as the right and the left hands.

As the attributes in the Talmud, the shapes in the book *Bahir* are not only God's limbs but also His angels. Thus, the attribute of justice is called *Satan* and further on assumes an extremely personal form. This is true as well for generic references: the concept "sacred shapes" in the book *Bahir* is also a name for the angels, as emerges from their role as keepers of the Garden of Eden and in charge of the nations of the world (95,98.) These references are clearly to the same shapes, since the author of the book *Bahir* uses the seven limbs to bring the full count of angelic shapes to seventy two.[73]

Though these ideas are explicitly stated in the book *Bahir*, in essence they appear much earlier. Beside the talmudic hints we have considered, there are exact parallels to the *Bahir*'s statements on the shapes of God as His attributes and as His angels in ancient Jewish literature, in the Dead Sea Scrolls, and in the Apochrypha. Similar images also appear in Gnostic and Patristic works which were influenced by the Judaic literature of the times, and even in the *Shi'ur Koma* literature, which is concerned with the description of God's limbs and also perceives them as angels.[74] However, it seems that in the *Shiur Koma* literature the perception of the limbs is more basic and binding, resembling the sefirotic frameworks in the Kabbala, whereas in the Talmud it is merely another aspect of the dynamic personal myth, as further quotations will make clear.

Before proceeding with the textual discussion, let us pause to consider the significance of the talmudic finding. A serious question emerges: Given that the talmudic myth allows for changes and nuances, what is the meaning of turning spiritual attributes into places and chairs,[75] or even into angels and limbs? I believe this approach is rooted in the ambivalent rabbinical relationship to God. On the one hand, the rabbis felt a close intimacy with God, which enabled them to deal in meticulous detail with the mysteries of His attributes. On the other hand, they feared for the King's honor. It is to this end that angels were created, since it is easier to speak of them than of God; angels help to keep the suitable distance, and this is also their role in *Hekhalot* literature. However, as created, external beings, the angels fail to express the depth of the divine dilemma. The obvious question is this: since God is Almighty, why should He listen to the angels? How can these created beings prevent God from acting on His will? These questions are also relevant to the talmudic use of places and chairs, which can express only ways of enacting God's decrees rather than the spiritual struggles that preceded them.

It is to fulfill the contradictory demands posed by the need to guard God's honor without diminishing the importance of His internal struggles that the angels were identified with the limbs, which enjoy an intermediate status: they are not as close as the spiritual attributes but are not as separate and distinct as the angels. This dilemma, wherein manifestations of intimacy alternate with concealment and distance, characterizes not only those who formulate the talmudic myth, but also the God emerging from it. We already noted this in the Akatriel-Ishmael story discussed in the previous section, and we shall find further echoes of it in the following passages.

Evidence of the difference between God's limbs, which are His angels, and God's essence, can also be found elsewhere: "What is meant by 'the day of vengeance is in mine heart' (Isaiah 63:4)? R. Johanan said: I have revealed it to my heart, but not to my limbs. R. Simeon b. Lakish said: I have revealed it to my heart, but not to the ministering angels." (Sanhedrin 99a)

The two views appear as alternative formulations of the same idea. Although both R. Johanan and R. Simeon b. Lakish equate between the limbs and the angels, they avail themselves of different myths. R. Simeon b. Lakish's statement that God refrains from revealing the secret of the end of days to the angels is linked to the well-known motif of the angels' jealousy of mortals. As the angels had opposed the creation of Adam, the giving of the Torah to Moses, and the ascent of the four *tannaim* who entered the *pardes*,[76] so do they oppose redemption. They may rely for their opposition on the principle of justice, which assumes the children of Israel are unworthy of redemption (in their standard phrasing, quoted earlier—"wherein are these different from those?"), as the angels are often merely another manifestation of the celestial attribute of justice or, in more general terms, of the rational aspect of God's essence. R. Johanan's saying, however, is concerned with God's internal spiritual struggle. God conceals "the day of vengeance" in His heart, that is, in His unconscious (we shall have more to say about God's heart later).[77] He is afraid to bring it to conscious awareness and reveal it to His limbs or let it pass His lips, because expressing it verbally would turn a diffuse feeling into a conscious, defined plan. As Rashi commented: "I did not utter anything my limbs may hear, but this secret was hiding in my heart." This interpretation is confirmed by a parallel version, wherein the limbs are replaced by the mouth: "R. Samuel taught in the name of R. Judah: Should a man tell you when redemption is to come, do not believe him, as it is written 'the day of vengeance is in my heart.' If the heart has not disclosed it to the mouth, how can the mouth disclose it to others?!"[78]

Why this fear of revealing "the day of vengeance" to the limbs? It is hardly possible that God fears the limbs may reveal His plans to the nations of the world. First, the limbs or the angels do not act against His will, and second, who could prevent God from acting as He wishes, even were His plan to be revealed? There is another reason. The feeling of vengeance should preferably remain in God's heart since an explicitly stated plan for revenge may rouse divine doubt and hesitation and call forth contradictory claims from the attribute of justice and the attribute of mercy that, as stated, are identified with the angels and the limbs. This is an authentic reason since, as we shall see later, God indeed has profound doubts about redemption and His vacillations at times foil all attempts to bring it about, as was understood by R. Johanan[79] when he spoke of the heart and the limbs. There is a further reason, related to the first: Exposing feelings, such as the desire for vengeance, is not in keeping with the King's honor, and He therefore hides it. This interpretation is clearly confirmed in the following passage:

> "But if ye will not hear it, My soul shall weep in secret for the pride." (Jeremiah 13:7) R. Samuel b. Inia said in the name of Rab: The Holy One, blessed be He, has a place and its name is "Secret." What is the meaning of "for the pride"? R. Samuel b. Isaac said: For the pride of Israel that has been taken from them and given to the nations of the world. R. Samuel b. Nahmani said: For the pride of the Kingdom of Heaven. But is there weeping before the Holy One, blessed be He? And R. Papa said: There is no grief before the Holy one, as is said (Chronicles I 16: 27): "Honor and majesty are before Him; strength and gladness in His place." There is no contradiction: the one case means inwards and the other outwards. And outwards there is no weeping? And yet it is written (Isaiah 22:12): "And on that day did the Lord God of hosts call to weeping, and to mourning, and to baldness, and to girding with sackcloth"—The destruction of the Temple is different, for even the angels of peace wept, as is said: (Isaiah 33:7) "Behold, the mighty ones cried outside, the angels of peace wept bitterly." (Hagiga 5b)

God does not hide His feelings in His heart, but in a secret place, one concealed even from the angels. Indeed, the feelings in this passage are not feelings of compassion for Israel but rather feelings of vengeance against the nations of the world, but this is irrelevant for our purposes. Two reasons were advanced for this concealment: "For the pride of Israel that has been taken from them and given

to the nations of the world" and "For the pride of the Kingdom of
Heaven." The two reasons are juxtaposed and lexically parallel, and
the reader may mistakenly assume that they are also parallel in their
contents,[80] but I believe that this juxtaposition is a deliberate
camouflage to protect the pride of the Kingdom of Heaven and avoid
the statement: "for the pride of the Kingdom of Heaven that was
taken." God indeed fears the scorn of the Gentiles—as in the next
passage—but these misgivings are not serious. The pride of the
Kingdom of Heaven cannot be taken away by any rivals, after the men
of the Great Assembly "restored the crown of the divine attributes
to its ancient completeness."[81] The pride of the Kingdom of Heaven
is cited here as a reason for hiding, not for weeping. Public weeping
would hurt God's pride and, for this reason, He cries in "Secret";
namely, "inwardly" and not "outwardly"[82] as do the angels. The day
of the destruction of the Temple is an exception; on that day, God
agreed to forego His honor and weeping in public was allowed.

The dialectic tangle regarding the breach of honor entailed by
weeping is developed in the parallel version below, which confirms
our interpretation:

> At that time [the destruction of the Temple] the Holy One, blessed
> be He, wept and said: Woe to me! What have I done? I caused
> my *Shekhina* to dwell below on earth for the sake of Israel; but
> now that they have sinned I have returned to my former
> habitation. Heaven forfend that I should become a laughingstock
> and mockery to the nations. At that time Metatron came, fell
> upon himself and said before Him: Master of the World, let me
> weep but do Thou not weep. He replied: If you do not let Me weep
> now I will repair to a place where you are not allowed to enter
> and I will weep, as it is said: "But if you will not hear it, my
> soul shall weep in secret for your pride." (Jeremiah 13:17).
> (Lamentations Rabbati, proem 24)

In this passage, the situation is inverted: wishing to protect God's
honor, the angel offers to weep in His place and God refuses,
threatening to weep in secret. In the rest of this chapter, it is again
God who wishes to forego His honor because of Israel's grief (although
the chapter recounts the day of the Temple's destruction, a day on
which the talmudic passage quoted earlier also agreed to waive the
rules of honor). Thus, we see God undressing and girding only
sackcloth on His loins to teach the angels the laws of mourning. In
a picture not unlike the mad King Lear, God cries: "Woe to the King
who succeeded in His youth but failed in His old age." "Were it not

written it could not have been said," says the Midrash when referring to the angels who mourned for God "like a man whose dead is lying before him," a precedent for those claiming that God died in Auschwitz.

"Secret" is an internal "place" for God (similar to the Zoharic usage of the word *place*). However, for the same reason, God also tends to hide in other places:

> It has been taught: R. Jose says, I was once traveling on the road, and I entered into one of the ruins of Jerusalem in order to pray. Elijah of blessed memory appeared and waited for me at the door till I finished my prayer. He said to me: Peace be with you, my master! I replied: Peace be with you, my master and teacher! And he said to me: My son, why did you go into this ruin? I replied: To pray. He said to me: You ought to have prayed on the road. I replied: I feared lest passersby might interrupt me. He said to me: You ought to have said an abbreviated prayer. I then learned three things from him: One must not go into a ruin; one may say the prayer on the road and if one does say his prayer on the road, he recites an abbreviated prayer. He further said to me: My son, what sound did you hear in this ruin? I replied: I heard a divine voice, cooing like a dove, and saying: Woe to the children, on account of whose sins I destroyed My house and burnt My temple and exiled them among the nations of the world! And he said to me: By your life and by your head! Not in this moment alone does it so exclaim, but thrice each day does it exclaim thus! And more than that, whenever the children of Israel go into the synagogues and the houses of study and respond: "May His great name be blessed," the Holy One, blessed be He, shakes His head and says: Happy is the king who is thus praised in His house! Woe to the father who had to banish his children, and woe to the children who had to be banished from the table of their father! (Berakhot 3a)

Why does Elijah come and why does he admonish R. Jose for having entered the ruin rather than saying a short prayer? Are these commandments that important? Even if they are, is there no connection between them and the divine voice in the second part of the story? I believe the divine voice is the reason for the ban on entering the ruin and the other related prescriptions: it is forbidden to enter and intrude upon the solitude and weeping of God. Other reasons are advanced later for the ban on entering the ruin: "There are three reasons why one must not go into a ruin: because of suspicion, because of falling debris, and because of demons," but this is a new passage

attached because of a thematic association and there is no evidence
that these were Elijah's reasons. Perhaps, this passage is intended
as camouflage, since explicitly stating a prohibition against breaching
the King's honor would in itself constitute a breach.

God is not always careful to hide when weeping over His children,
and His grief and sorrow can engulf the earth and affect the whole
universe. A natural phenomenon called *zewa'ot* is usually interpreted
to mean earthquakes, but the talmudic description, as well as the
comparable Arab term,[83] seem to point to an association with thunder
and lightening or with meteors hitting the earth:

> R. Kattina was once going along the road, and when he came
> to the door of the house of a certain necromancer, there was a
> rumbling of the earth. He said: Does the necromancer know what
> this rumbling is? He called after him, Kattina, Kattina, why
> should I not know? When the Holy One, blessed be He, calls to
> mind His children, who are plunged in suffering among the
> nations of the world, He lets fall two tears into the ocean, and
> the sound is heard from one end of the world to the other, and
> that is the rumbling. Said R. Kattina: The necromancer is a liar
> and his words are false. If it was as he says, there should be one
> rumbling after another! He did not really mean this however.
> There really was one rumbling after another, and the reason why
> he did not admit it was so that people should not go astray after
> him. R. Kattina, for his own part, said: [God] clasps His hands,
> as it says (Ezekiel 21:22) "I will also smite my hands together,
> and I will relieve my fury." R. Nathan said: [God] emits a sigh,
> as it says (Ezekiel 5:13) "I will relieve my fury and I will be
> comforted." And the Rabbis said: He treads upon the firmament,
> as it says (Jeremiah 25:30) "He shall give a shout, as they that
> tread the grapes, against all the inhabitants of the earth." R.
> Aha b. Jacob says: He presses His feet together beneath the
> throne of glory, as it says (Isaiah 66:1): "Thus saith the Lord,
> the heaven is my throne and the earth is my footstool." (Berakhot
> 59a)

Before us is a myth in the full sense of this term, and one of
the most elemental kind: It is meant to explain natural phenomena
and is intentionally put in the mouth of a Gentile necromancer and
wizard. The rabbis agreed with him, and it was only for the sake of
appearances that they contested his views, to prevent others from
being led astray by him. As for the issue itself, they do not disagree
with the wizard any more than they disagree among themselves

(God's tears for the suffering of exile are also mentioned in Hagiga 5b), and the main difference is in the mythical style, which also affects the contents. Contrary to the wizard's self-reliance, the rabbis are careful to back their statements with biblical verses. It is interesting to compare this myth with its later versions in the Kabbala and note the erosion of its elemental character: the tears rolling into the sea are no longer meteors or lightening and have become the foundations of the principle of justice, which undergo meticulous analysis, sweetened in the sea of the *sefira* of *malkhut* or the *sefira* of *hokhma*.[84]

The rabbinical explanation of the night watches resembles that of the *zewa'ot*: "R. Isaac b. Samuel says in the name of Rab: The night has three watches, and at each watch the Holy One, blessed be He, sits and roars like a lion and says: Woe to the children, on account of whose sins I destroyed My house and burnt My temple and exiled them among the nations of the world" (Berakhot 3a).

Here as well, there is a full, complete myth; Rab even adopts the necromancer's style and fails to rely on any verse.[85] In a superficial reading, this might appear as no more than a suitable story about the sorrows of exile rather than a true myth touching on God's essence. After all, God is omnipotent and Israel was exiled by His will; should He so desire, He could return them without weeping, sighs or roars. I tend to see this as a real myth, well anchored in the image of the talmudic God for whom, as He is portrayed in many places, Israel means everything and it is hence no wonder that He suffers in their grief. In the next section we shall see that God not only empathizes with the sufferings of His people, but is enslaved when they are enslaved and their redemption is His redemption. Redemption is truly difficult for God, due to psychological difficulties and profound doubts. The following passage shows that it is not necessarily the attribute of justice that prevents redemption and, at times, it might be the attribute of mercy:

> It is written (Jeremiah 30:6) "Ask now, and see whether a man travails with child? Why then do I see every man with his hands on his loins, as a woman in travail, and all faces are turned to paleness?" What is meant by "I see every man" [*gever*]? Raba b. Isaac said in Rab's name: It refers to Him to whom all strength [*gevura*] belongs. And what is meant by "all faces are turned to paleness?" R. Johanan said: God's heavenly family and God's earthly family,[86] [Rashi expounds these as the angels and Israel] when God says: These are the work of My hands and these are the work of My hands [Rashi expounds these as the Gentiles and Israel] how shall I destroy the former on account of the latter? (Sanhedrin 98b)

The thrust of this passage is to explain the meaning of the "pangs of the Messiah," which the Talmud mentioned and described a few lines before. There too, "pangs" were perceived in their original sense as related to pregnancy and birth and their duration was therefore established as nine months, but the mother was not named. In this passage, the mother is clearly God Himself, the only one about whom it may be said: "Him to whom all strength belongs" (Compare with Song of Songs Rabba 1:11: "On King Solomon" [*Shelomo*]—on a King to whom peace [*shalom*] belongs.") We follow Rashi's exegesis of this passage with no fear of R. Meir Ha-Levi (Ramah), who warned those who adopt this interpretation that they "will be called upon to answer for it."[87] In the passage from Isaiah 66:7–9, which is probably the background for the preceding talmudic statement as well as the source of the expression *pangs of the Messiah*, God is the father though the mother is "Zion." In the Kabbala, this matter became part of a large and impressive myth wherein the doe, which is the *Shekhina*, delivers the Messiah with the help of a serpent that bites her womb.[88] In the Talmud the birthpains represent God's profound doubts, an internal psychological drama that revolves around the price of Israel's redemption, once more unlike the Ramah's exegesis *ad locum*, who claims that God is struggling with the created attribute of mercy, which differs from His essence. Evidence may be advanced from the famous parallel version stating that God rebuked the ministering angels when the Red Sea parted saying: "The work of my hands is being drowned in the sea, and you chant hymns. . . because the Holy One, blessed be He, does not rejoice in the downfall of the wicked" (Megilla 10b). That is, God Himself is merciful, and His opponents in this case are the angels, who represent the attribute of justice.

In both these stories the situation is the same, and both are quoted in Rabbi Johanan's name, who uses the expression *the work of My hands* in the same sense. Indeed, in a later, midrashic version of the story,[89] the rulers of Egypt and Israel quarrel over the drowning of the Egyptians, and only after the victory of the ruler of Israel did God act in accordance with the attribute of justice, which is not portrayed as a divine spiritual quality but as a chair on which He chooses to sit. The myth of God as alternating between the chair of justice and the chair of mercy appears frequently in rabbinical literature.[90] These descriptions should not be seen as mutually contradictory nor should one be read through the perspective of another; all are legitimate variations of the living talmudic myth and reflect the tendencies and personal tastes of each author. In the following pages, we shall give further consideration to the limits of potential flexibility in a myth of this kind.

God's hesitations and doubts as described in the Talmud reflect those of the rabbis themselves: A suffering, doubting God is proper and fitting for a suffering and doubting people like the Jews. In the pages following the earlier Sanhedrin passage the Talmud cites all possible views on redemption, from those who await it all their lives and see it as a cosmic ideal beyond nature, to take place at a fixed time, all the way to those who say: "There is no Messiah for Israel, as they have already enjoyed him during the reign of Hezekiah" (Sanhedrin 98b). Between these extremes there are many intermediate stages, such as the view that "The only difference between this world and the days of the Messiah is in the enslavement to foreign powers" (Sanhedrin 99a) or that which sees redemption as concerning only respectable householders and not learned scholars: "All the prophets prophesied only in respect of him who marries his daughter to a scholar, or engages in business on behalf of a scholar or benefits a scholar with his possesions, but as for scholars themselves, 'the eye has not seen, O God, beside Thee' (Isaiah 64:3)" (Sanhedrin 99a).

There are also some highly paradoxical statements about redemption: One claims that the very yearning for the Messiah forbids us to think about him, as our thoughts keep him away: "Three come when the mind is diverted: Messiah, a finding, and a scorpion" (Sanhedrin 97a). The contrary view also appears—awaiting the Messiah is its own reward; this expectation will never be fulfilled and its only value is in the performance of a commandment. (Compare this to the question, Did you hope for salvation? which the soul is asked after death—Shabbath 31a.) According to this view, even God awaits the Messiah, but in the context of an internal psychological struggle that makes its fufillment impossible. This struggle resembles the one in the previous passage; though we are not explicitly told there whether the struggle has been or will be decided, it would seem it is still pending, given that God has been debating this question since Jeremiah's time. (Note the use of the past tense: "when the Holy One, blessed be He, said.") On the other hand, in the next passage the negative answer is almost explicit: God's problem in the previous passage was His mercy, whereas here the source of the delay is the attribute of justice:

> What is meant by "it speaks [va-yafeah] concerning the end and does not lie?" (Habakkuk 2:3). R. Samuel b. Nahmani said in the name of R. Jonathan: Blasted [tipah] be[91] the bones of those who calculate the end. For they would say, since the prede-

termined time has arrived, and yet he has not come, he will never come. But wait for him, as it is written (ibid.) "if it seem slow, wait for him." Should you say, we wait for his coming, and He does not, therefore Scripture says (Isaiah 30:18): "And therefore will the Lord wait, that He may be gracious to you, and therefore will He be exalted, that He may have mercy upon you." And since we wait for him and He waits for him, what delays [his coming]? The attribute of justice delays it. But since the attribute of justice delays it, why do we await it? To be rewarded [for hoping], as it is written (ibid.): "Happy are all that wait for him." (Sanhedrin 97b)

The question "But since the attribute of justice delays it, why do we await it?" assumes that the delay is eternal. The answer does not dispute this, nor does it set a time limit for the delay caused by the attribute of justice.[92] Those "who calculate the end" and say "he will never come" are cursed not because they lied but because they said what they said and ceased waiting. The prophet Habakkuk said in fact the opposite: He not only said "if it seem slow, wait for it," but also "because it will surely come, it will not delay." However, the rabbis quote only the first half of the verse, reading it as a declaration rather than a condition. This was also Maimonides's view, who was influenced by this talmudic passage when formulating his own article about the coming of the Messiah.[93]

IV. Talmud and Kabbala:
Keneset Israel

The following passage illustrates the action of the attribute of justice, how it prevents God from bringing redemption and who its opponents are:

"For the increase of the realm and for peace without end" (Isaiah 9:6). R. Tanhum said: Bar Kappara expounded in Sephoris, Why is every *mem* in the middle of a word open, whereas this is closed? [In the word *marbeh* (increase), the Hebrew letter *mem* is closed, as it should be were it the final letter of the word.] The Holy One, blessed be He, wished to appoint Hezekiah as the Messiah, and Sanherib as Gog and Magog; whereupon the attribute of justice said before the Holy One, blessed be He: Master of the World! If Thou didst not make David the Messiah, who uttered

so many hymns and praises before Thee, wilt Thou appoint
Hezekiah as Messiah, who did not sing your praise despite all
the miracles which Thou wroughtest for him? Therefore it [the
mem] is closed. Immediately, the earth said to Him: Master of
the World! Let me sing before Thee instead of this righteous man
and make him the Messiah. So it broke into song before Him,
as it is written (Isaiah 24:16): "From the uttermost part of the
earth have we heard songs of glory to the righteous." The prince
of the world said to Him: Master of the World! Fulfill the desire
of this righteous man. A heavenly voice cried out (ibid.): "It is
my secret, it is my secret." Said the prophet (ibid.): "Woe to me,
Woe to me." How long [must we wait]? The heavenly voice cried
out (ibid.): "Traitors have dealt treacherously; traitors have dealt
very treacherously." Said Raba, and others say R. Isaac: Until
there came spoilers, and spoilers of the spoilers. (Sanhedrin 94a)

The attribute of justice is especially harsh here. The sin that
it condemns—refraining from hymns and praises—is not even
mentioned in the Bible and is nowhere considered an offense, except
in Lurianic Kabbala where singing praises serves to "raise the *mayin
nukbin*" [the female waters] and to repair the world. The attribute
of justice infers this is an offense only on the basis of a petty a fortiori
argument: "If Thou didst not make David. . ." [a fortiori arguments
are generally called *din*, as *midat hadin*, the attribute of justice]. Even
so, an exceptionally harsh punishment is imposed on the basis of this
argument—preventing redemption, perhaps not only in Hezekiah's
times but forever, as indicated by the expression "until there come
spoilers, and spoilers of the spoilers." This expression pertains not only
to two generations of traitors and thieves but perhaps "for all times,"
a hypothesis that the following statement may strengthen: "R. Hillel
said: There is no Messiah for Israel, since they have already enjoyed
him during the reign of Hezekiah" (Sanhedrin 98b). R. Hillel's
mention of Hezekiah and the context of the discussion following
indicate that the allusion in the preceding passage is to this
statement.

The one attempt to oppose the attribute of justice, unfortunately
to no avail, is not made by the attribute of mercy but by the earth.
True, the earth appears in the expounded verse, but is it indeed an
adequate adversary for the attribute of justice? Some of these doubts
will be allayed if we see that, in this passage, the earth is identical
with the "prince of the world." The paragraph "Master of the World!
Fulfill the desire [*tsiviono*] of this righteous man" only paraphrases
the words of the earth, with the root *tsevi* serving as a connecting

link: "Immediately, the earth said to Him: Master of the World! Let me sing before Thee instead of this righteous man and make him the Messiah. So it broke into song before Him, as it is written (Isaiah 24:16): 'From the uttermost part of the earth have we heard songs, glory [*tsevi*] to the righteous.'" I believe that this identification between the earth and the prince of the world is also dictated by the plot, in which there is no room for two separate figures, one "the earth" and the other "the prince of the world." The title *prince of the world* also suits the "earth," because the Rabbis use the term *world* in a meaning approximating that of "the earth" in biblical language.

The prince of the world seems a more adequate adversary for the attribute of justice because he is an angel ["prince"], a shape that, as we saw, is at times assumed by the attribute itself. Furthermore, in his appointed role as caretaker of the world, we may assume that the prince wishes the Messiah to come, even more so if we refer to earlier traditions (not explicitly mentioned in the Talmud), which identify the "prince of the world" with Michael, "the prince of Israel," and then with Metatron,[94] the protector of "the rights of Israel" and responsible for punishing the Gentiles.[95]

Having established that the "earth" and the "prince of the world" are identical, it will be easier to find traces of this mythical personality in other rabbinical passages mentioning "the earth." Thus, for instance,

> "Behold, I will destroy them with the earth" (Genesis 6:13). R. Huna and R. Jeremiah said in R. Kahana's name: Even the three handbreaths of the earth's surface which the plough turns was washed away. It is as if a royal prince had a tutor, and whenever he did wrong, his tutor was punished; or as if a royal prince had a nurse, and whenever he did wrong his nurse was punished. Similarly, the Holy One, blessed be He, said: "Behold, I will destroy them with the earth," I will destroy them and the earth with them. (Genesis Rabba 33:7)

True, the tutor and the nurse are only metaphors for the earth, but when the earth stands for a tutor and a nurse who are punished together with their charge, it transcends its concrete, material meaning. Most important, we found almost the same parable in the same *midrash* (Genesis Rabba 27:4) and in the same context—the cooperation of others in the destruction of humanity during the Flood—but this time "God's heart" appears instead of "the earth": "'And it grieved Him at His heart' (Genesis 6:6). R. Berekiah said: If a king has a palace built by an architect and when he sees it, it displeases him, against whom is he to complain? Surely against the architect!"

God's heart appears here as a separate entity, mediating between Him and Creation. (Indeed, in a parallel version—in Genesis Rabba 8:3—the divine heart stands for "an agent," and it is claimed that heaven and earth were God's two advisors in the Creation.) God creates the world through His heart and punishes it when Creation fails. A mediating entity evokes immediate associations with Gnosticism, the heretical Christian sect of the time, whose main tenet is the distinction between a Supreme God and a Creator known as the Demiurge. In Gnosis, *earth* is also a name of a celestial power. Moshe Idel cited Gnostic sources on the earth and showed the similarities between them and kabbalistic writings dealing with this symbol.[96] Although these similarities are unquestionable, they do not stem from a direct connection between Gnosis and Kabbala but rather, as Idel stated, from the Jewish sources of Gnosticism. Here I will deal with the mainstream trends in kabbalistic development; that is, with its origin in the talmudic myth.

The notion of the heart as a mediating entity between God and the world, identical with the prince and the earth, is not all we may infer from the talmudic sources previously quoted. God's "heart," like the human heart, is inseparable from Him, and Creation is said to have taken place through God's heart only because the rabbis believed that, for humankind too, the heart represents the creative aspect, as in "a discerning heart" (Berakhot, 61a) As God's heart is portrayed as an agent, so is the human heart.[97] God's heart is indeed identical with the earth, which is the prince of the world and, like the attribute of mercy, acts to bring the Messiah but, as we saw earlier,[98] messianic times are directly connected to God's heart without mentioning "the earth." The heart there is God's "unconscious," which is portrayed as part of His spiritual essence and unlike the angels who are the limbs, as God concealed from them the secret of the end of days and revealed it only to His heart. Althought this statement confirms the validity of the link we posed between the heart and messianic times, it also upsets the identification between heart, "prince of the world" and "earth."

However, this contradiction is only apparent, reflecting a level of conceptual rigor inappropriate to the living talmudic myth—a myth lacking in self-reflection and of undefined ontological validity. The angels can be perceived simultaneously as external entities serving God and as His limbs or His attributes. Similarly the heart, God's internal spirituality as against angels and limbs, can be perceived in another context as "prince of the world," despite the latter's angelic character, or even as identical with the earth. In an ancient parallel version of this statement, God's Son replaces the heart. I am referring to Jesus' statement in the New Testament (Matthew 24:36; Mark 13:32): "But of that day and hour no one knows, not even the angels of heaven, nor the Son, but the Father only." Contrary indeed to the talmudic heart, here the secret is not even revealed to the Son; nevertheless, his role is that of an intermediate entity, more worthy of knowledge than the angels. Thus, this myth appears in many variations, even if we choose to disregard the last passage due to its different literary source.

This flexibility is lost in the kabbalistic myth. I have claimed before that the *mytholegoumena* was not invented by the kabbalists, who only confined it within the conceptual framework of the ten *sefirot*, and the following is a prominent example. The last *sefira* is called *malchut* or *Shekhina*, a concept that developed gradually from an immanent aspect of divinity that rested in the Tabernacle onto the distinct, divine personality of the kabbalists.[99] But even the kabbalists preserved some of the *Shekhina*'s elemental quality as an inseparable aspect of God and thus used it to define the duality we encountered in the Talmud. On the one hand, the *Shekhina* is part of the divine world, the ten *sefirot* the Zohar refers to as the world of union or *alma de-yihuda*, and on the other hand, it is the beginning of a world of separation.[100] The *Shekhina* is one of divinity's supernal stones, which the "builders" [the higher *sefirot*] had rejected as "worthless," and which then became "the cornerstone" of the nether world.[101] Kabbalists ascribed to this *sefira* all the preceding *midrashim* about "the earth," as well as other examples of rabbinical literature dealing with similar myths.[102] This *sefira* is therefore called "earth" (or "the land of Israel")[103] as well as "prince of the world" or the angel Metatron.[104] Included in this *sefira* are other *midrashim* too, such as the ones on the heart, the nurse, the agent, and the architect.[105] Although the kabbalists did not resolve the duality apparent in midrashic descriptions of God's heart, they allocated this duality (or better, multiplicity) a special and stable "place"—the *sefira* of *malchut*. This allocation may also be seen as a way of formalizing the duality and raising its level of ontological validity.

The most important symbol of the *Shekhina* in Kabbala is that of God's consort. A wife, unlike a man's heart, is an independent person, but an almost organic fusion occurs when she mates with her spouse and the two together create one "being."[106] The difference between the two types of sources is mainly one of emphasis: Whereas the Midrash speaks of the *Shekhina* as an integral part of God's personality, which may also be perceived as the "prince of the world," for the Kabbala this is essentially a separate figure. However, the extent of this separation may vary, and the *Shekhina* may alternately appear as God's partner or as His "heart." In any event, there is an unquestionable continuity between Midrash and Kabbala, and the latter cannot be seen as a new creation. We shall also show later that neither was kabbalistic erotic imagery created ex nihilo, but is rather the culmination of a gradual process of development.

The *Shekhina* is also known in Kabbala as *Keneset Israel*. It dwells [*shokhenet*] within the people of Israel, is saved when they are rescued, and grieves when they suffer. This symbol can easily be linked to these midrashic and talmudic myths, such as those dealing with the image of "the earth" punished for human sinfulness during the flood and asking for the coming of the Messiah, and its national features become even sharper when it is called "the land of Israel." Moreover, the *Shekhina* in Kabbala is also the city of Jerusalem. It thus inherits the ancestral notion of a "heavenly city," which was widespread in early Christianity and in Gnosis and also appears in talmudic literature,[107] as well as other national motifs in rabbinical literature to be reviewed later. Already in the midrashic sources, the mutual relationship between God and Israel is in every case attended by a mythical entity; all the kabbalists had to do was to identify all these entities and unite them in the figure of the *Shekhina*.

Moreover, in Pesahim 118b the Talmud even contrasts *Keneset Israel* and the Jewish people, and makes *Keneset Israel* look very similar to its kabbalistic meaning.

One of the *Shekhina*'s most important names among the early kabbalists was *atara* (crown). As recent research shows,[108] this symbol was derived from mythical ideas found in the literature and times of the Rabbis, such as wreathing the divine crown from the prayers offered by His people (Hagigah 13b) and the phylacteries laid by God, in which it is written "And who is like Thy people Israel, a singular nation in the earth" (Berakhot 6a). Another and no less important symbol is the moon. The waning and waxing of the moon points to the role of Israel,[109] and I believe that this motif too is already found in rabbinical literature. Thus, for instance, in the famous myth about the waning of the moon:

> R. Simeon b. Pazzi pointed out a contradiction [between verses]. It says (Genesis 1:16) "And God made the two great lights," and it says (ibid.) "The greater light...and the lesser light." Said the moon unto the Holy One, blessed be He: "Master of the World! Is it possible for two kings to wear one crown?" He answered, "Go then and make thyself smaller." "Master of the

World!" cried the moon. "Because I have suggested that which is proper must I make myself smaller?" He replied, "Go and thou wilt rule by day and by night." "But what is the value of this?" cried the moon. "Of what use is a lamp in broad daylight?" He replied "Go. Israel shall reckon by thee the days and the years." "But it is impossible," said the moon, "to do without the sun for the reckoning of the seasons, as it is written (Genesis 1:14): 'And let them be for signs, and for seasons, and for days and years'" "Go. The righteous shall be named after thee as we find, Jacob the Small, Samuel the Small, David the Small." On seeing that it would not be consoled the Holy One, blessed be He, said, "Bring an atonement for Me making the moon smaller." This is what is meant by R. Simeon b. Lakish when he declared, "Why is it that the he-goat offered on the new moon is different, in that it is written concerning it (Numbers 28:15): 'unto the Lord'? Because the Holy One, blessed be He, said, 'Let this he-goat be an atonement for Me making the moon smaller'." (Hullin 60b)

Even at the literal level, the connection between the moon and Israel in this myth is already clear. To compensate the moon for its waning, God ruled that Israel shall reckon their days by it instead of by the sun, as do the Gentiles, and lunar eclipses are therefore considered a bad omen for Israel in the Talmud.[110] Furthermore, God ruled that the righteous of Israel shall be named after the moon. One of them is King David (according to Samuel I, 17:14: "And David was the youngest [smallest]," his links with the moon are discussed later). The second is no other than the people of Israel, who are the ones intended by the only occurrence of the expression appearing in Amos 7:5: "How shall Jacob stand? For he is small."

A sacrifice is offered with the new month to atone for this divine sin, suggesting that the waning of the moon is the cause and symbol of Israel's misfortunes. This was the usual kabbalistic interpretation of this talmudic myth,[111] though with a characteristic difference. According to the Kabbala, the waning of the moon was devised with a certain purpose or reflects some immanent fault in the structure of the supernal worlds, whereas the Talmud adopts a personal myth. The moon's claim "Is it possible for two kings to wear one crown?" bothered God, who inadvertently answered "Go then and make thyself smaller." God understood immediately that He had been unfair but could not retract His words, despite the destructive consequences henceforth to the people of Israel. In exactly this fashion, King Xerxes in the book of Esther regrets his promise to Hamman to harm Israel but cannot withdraw it, and it is noteworthy that in talmudic literature, King Xerxes is compared to the King of the world.[112]

This connection between the moon and Israel recurs often in the Midrash. Thus, we are told in Exodus Rabba 15:26 that during the reign of king Solomon [Shelomo], the true [*shalem*] king who built the Temple, "the moon's disc was full." This notion is pervasive in Kabbala and was further enhanced by the identification between Solomon and the *sefira* of *yesod*.[113] A stronger expression of the connection between the moon and Israel appears in the following statement, in the benediction over the new moon formulated by the Babylonian *amora* Rab Judah (Sanhedrin 42a): "The moon He ordered that it should renew herself as a crown of beauty for those whom He sustains from the womb." Rashi comments: "The Holy One, blessed be He, told the moon that it should renew itself as a crown of beauty for those whom He sustains from the womb [namely, Israel[114]]; the moon is a sign to them that, as they reckon her days by it[115] they shall also renew themselves in their exile like the moon." The kabbalists readily extended this interpretation to the renewal of the *Shekhina*,[116] although it is worth noting that the comparison of the moon to God appears already in the Talmud:

> Said R. Johanan: Whoever pronounces the benediction over the new moon in its due time welcomes, as it were, the presence of the *Shekhina*, for it is written here (Exodus 12:2): "This month" and it is written there (Exodus 15:2): "This is my God and I will praise Him." In the school of R. Ishmael it was taught: Had Israel earned no other privilege than to greet the presence of their Heavenly Father once a month, it were sufficient. Abaye said: Therefore we must recite it standing. (Sanhedrin 42a)

The traditional benediction over the new moon concludes with the phrase "David king of Israel lives and will endure," linking King David with the moon. The source of this concluding formula is in Rosh Hashanah 25a, where it had served as a secret code for the sanctification of the month: "Rabbi said to R. Hiyya, Go to En Tob [a place where the court would meet for this purpose] and sanctify the month and send me the password 'David king of Israel lives and will endure.'"

Rashi created a link between King David and the moon through the verse in Psalms 89:38: "It [his throne] shall be established forever like the moon" though, in the previous verse, David's throne had actually been compared to the sun. It seems that David's link to the moon is stronger than the one suggested by Rashi; we saw earlier that David, who was "the smallest," had been named after the moon. This time perhaps the Zohar, in its addition of a messianic motif, is closest to the original spirit of the talmudic statement: "When the moon is renewed, David king of Israel lives and will endure" (Zohar I:192a). The mystery surrounding the intercalation of the month and the year in the Talmud ["the secret of the intercalation"], of which this password is part, may attest to it. Decisions about the calendar were considered an expression of sovereignty and the rabbis insisted on these issues being settled only in the land of Israel, in defiance of the the Roman authorities that had apparently tried to abolish this symbol of Jewish statehood.[117]

These rabbinical perceptions developed gradually, until they attained their full kabbalistic significance. The kabbalistic idea does appear almost fully grown in the following statement by the pietist movement in Ashkenaz, which scholars have acknowledged as the transitional link between rabbinical literature and Kabbala:[118]

When Israel is forced into apostasy, the moon wanes,[119] as it is written (Jeremiah 31:14): "Rachel weeping for her children." And why was the woman compared to the moon? To tell you that, as the moon waxes for half a month and wanes for half a month, so the woman is close to her husband for half a month and lonely in her impurity for half a month. And as the moon is accessible at night, so is the woman, as it is written:[120] "In the evening she would come" (Esther 2:14).[121]

In this passage, the moon is also granted female sexual characteristics, first and foremost in the comparison between the monthly cycle of the woman and that of the moon. Apparently, the original source for this comparison is the following passage:

The women heard but did not consent to give their earrings to their husbands [in order to make the golden calf]. . . . And the Holy One, blessed be He, gave the women their reward in this world, that they should observe the new moons more stringently than men and rewarded them in the world to come, that they are destined to be renewed like the new moons. (Pirke de-Rabbi Eliezer, 45)

Jews in medieval Ashkenaz were apparently impressed by this passage, and this is the source for the custom[122] whereby women refrain from work on the days of the new moon. R. Isaac b. Moshe from Vienna, the author of the Or Zarua' and one of the leading Ashkenazi halakhists in the twelfth and thirteenth centuries who knew nothing about Kabbala, added another explanation:[123] "Every month the woman immerses, is renewed and returns to her husband as beloved as on her wedding day. As the moon is renewed each month and they yearn to see her, so the woman is renewed every month to her husband and he yearns for her as if she were new, and that is why the day of the new moon is a holiday for women."

But the passage in *Sefer Hasidim* [The Book of the Pious] went a step further. It combined this link between the moon and the woman with that between the moon and Israel, and the waning of the moon and the impurity of the woman were thus united with the destiny of Israel. The kabbalists did exactly the same and identified both these faults with the fault in the *Shekhina—Keneset Israel*.[124] Another important similarity between these two sources is in the figure of Rachel and in the use of the verse "Rachel weeping for her children"; as far back as *Sefer Hasidim*, Rachel symbolized *Keneset Israel*, and this is also the kabbalistic usage.[125]

However, there is one difference between the *Sefer Hasidim* and the Kabbala. The moon and the female may symbolize *Keneset Israel* but not the *Shekhina* as a divine entity though, as I showed earlier,[126] the main kabbalistic innovation pertaining to the concept of the *Shekhina* is not related to its mythical content but to the crystallization of a formula that changed its ontological status. This is also the case here. A well-known prophetic metaphor likens the people of Israel to God's bride though the ontological status of these comparisons varies, even in the Bible. The statement (Jeremiah 2:2) "I remember in thy favor the devotion of thy youth, thy love as a bride" is not the same as the detailed descriptions in Ezekiel 16 and 23 or as the first chapters in Hosea, where the prophet resorts to symbolic erotic acts. The rabbis went a step further when they expounded all the love poems in Song of Songs as expressions of the love between God and *Keneset Israel*, and a consecutive reading of Song of Songs Rabba creates great difficulties for those committed to an exclusively allegorical interpretation. Other rabbinical passages, such as the description of the Temple's cherubs as a pair of lovers drawing close and separating according to the relation between God and His people, only strengthen the difficulties entailed by this interpretation.[127]

The biblical God is single. Genesis 1:27 indeed states: "So God created mankind in His own image, in the image of God He created him; male and female He created them." From here, we might conclude with the kabbalists[128] that God's image is both male and female, as is further implied by the plural usage of the previous verse: "And God said, Let us make mankind in our image, after our likeness."

However, even if this were the early literal approach, there is no trace of it in later biblical consciousness. Celibacy is a difficult condition, as may be inferred from the statement by God Himself in Genesis 2:18: "And the Lord God said, It is not good that the man should be alone"; in order to repair this situation God created the woman and, in a celestial parallel, made Israel His consort.[129] I believe this interpretation is the source of the erotic allusions in the prophetic "parables" on Israel, as well as of the rabbinical attitudes reflected in the *midrashim* on *Keneset Israel* and other utterances, such as God rejoicing in the souls of the righteous as in a "new bride."[130] These statements closely resemble the kabbalistic approach linking the personified image of *Keneset Israel* in rabbinical literature (or the biblical "virgin daughter of Israel") with the *Shekhina,* God's consort.

Even without the erotic overtones, the people of Israel were the foremost concern of the talmudic God, as is clear from the talmudic myths dealing with God's anguish over the Exile discussed in the previous section. No one portrays an alienated divinity indifferent to our destiny. All the mythical descriptions deal with God's attitude to His creatures and, first and foremost, to the people of Israel. It is precisely the mutual relationship between human and God that constitutes the very contents of the Jewish myth, as is even manifest in God's name (see Rashi's commentary on Exodus 3:14, based on Berakhot 9b.) These descriptions lent further credence to the kabbalistic portrayal of the *Shekhina* as *Keneset Israel.* Although the use of this symbol limited and clearly defined the contents of these myths, it also strengthened their mythical validity and enabled their conceptual formalization. For the kabbalists, God suffers not "only" in empathy with Israel, but because of a rift in the divine essence that severs the *Shekhina* from the higher *sefirot.* Whereas the Talmud attributes the pain to God in general, the Kabbala focuses it on the *Shekhina*; the pain also affects the *sefira* of *tiferet* (as well as the related *sefira* of *yesod*) that affects the *Shekhina* from above and is portrayed as its partner, because water cannot go through a blocked channel and, if it is a tree (the Tree of Life), it withers.[131] Thus, divorce also afflicts the evicting husband, "his visage is marred" and he "is lost."[132]

In Kabbala, this rift is called "the exile of the *Shekhina,*" a notion that also derives from a talmudic myth:

> It has been taught: R. Simon b. Yohai said: Come and see how beloved are Israel in the sight of God, in that to every place to which they were exiled the *Shekhina* went with them. They were exiled to Egypt and the *Shekhina* was with them, as it says. . . .

And when they will be redeemed in the future, the *Shekhina* will be with them, as it says (Deuteronomy 30:3): "Then the Lord thy God will return thy captivity." It does not say here *ve-heshiv* [He shall bring back] but *ve-shav* [He shall return]. This teaches us that the Holy One, blessed be He, will return with them from the places of exile. (Megilla 29a)

Different variations of this idea appear in rabbinical literature.[133] From other passages it is clear that not only does God accompany Israel in its exile, but that its anguish is His anguish and that He is saved through its salvation as, for instance, in the description of the *hossanas* ritual as it appears in the Jerusalem Talmud (Sukkah 4:3). According to one of the views cited in the Mishnah, those circling the altar say: "May me and Him be saved," which is expounded in the Gemara as meaning that God Himself needs to be saved with His people, and many verses attesting to His enslavement in all places of exile are advanced as evidence. The *piyut* [ritual song] *ke-hosha'ta*, which is recited during the ceremony of the *hossanas*, is based on this interpretation. Also, in Exodus Rabba 30:31, God is not the savior but is "saved" (according to the original Hebrew version of Zechariah 9:9) and in *Pesikta de-Rav Kahana* 17:5, the redemption of Israel will come together with the redemption of God's right hand (probably an allusion to the *Shekhina*), which is bound as long as Israel is enslaved.

This myth too underwent a similar process. The expression "the *Shekhina* went with them" served in kabbalistic literature to identify between the exiled God and the *sefira* of *malkhut*, the exile being the separation of *malkhut* from "the Holy One, blessed be He" [the *sefirah* of *tiferet*], though the Talmud explicitly sees them as identical. The exile of the *Shekhina* is also portrayed in the Kabbala in more conceptualized terms: While in exile, the *Shekhina*'s link to God is mediated through the princes of the nations whereas, under normal circumstances, the *Shekhina* would have served to mediate the divine emanation to the princes, who would have been Her subordinates.[134]

We found another talmudic myth worthy of the name *the exile of the Shekhina*:

R. Judah b. Idi said in the name of R. Johanan: The *Shekhina* made ten journeys, as is stated: from the ark cover to the cherub, and from one cherub to another, and from the cherub to the threshold, and from the threshold to the court, and from the court to the altar, and from the altar to the roof, and from the roof to the wall, and from the wall to the town, and from the town to the mountain, and from the mountain to the wilderness,

and from the wilderness it ascended to its own abode, as it says
(Hosea 5:15): "I will go and return to my place."...Correspond-
ingly, the Sanhedrin wandered to ten places of banishment...
(Rosh Hashana 31a)

A similar vision appears in the Midrash:

"And they heard the voice of the Lord God walking in the garden
in the cool of the day." (Genesis 3:8) R. Abba b. Kahana said:
Not *mehallekh* [walking] but *mithalekh* is written here, which
means that it repeatedly leaped and ascended. The real home
of the *Shekhina* was in the nether sphere; when Adam sinned
it departed to the first firmament; when Cain sinned, it ascended
to the second firmament; when the generation of Enosh sinned,
it ascended to the third; when the generation of the Flood sinned,
to the fourth; with the generation of the tower of Babel, to the
fifth; with the Sodomites, to the sixth; with the Egyptians in
the days of Abraham, to the seventh. But as against these there
arose seven righteous men: Abraham, Isaac, Jacob, Levi, Kohath,
Amram, and Moses, and they brought it down again to earth.
Abraham [brought it down] from the seventh to the sixth...
(Genesis Rabba 19:7)

The kabbalists integrated this picture too into their broader
myth. When the channels are repaired, God's stature is complete and
reaches the earth; and when they are blocked through fault of human
action, the *Shekhina* rises and returns to its source in the world of
emanations.[135] The early kabbalists' descriptions of the *Shekhina*'s
exile are not always consistent: at times the *Shekhina* descends into
exile and at times it ascends. However, as kabbalistic doctrine was
perfected, descriptions of the *Shekhina*'s exile also sharpened into
more rigid conceptual frameworks.[136] This process culminated in the
complicated divine machine of Isaac Luria, wherein every picture
found its place. Certain aspects of the *Shekhina* descended and are
in exile, whereas others returned to their source and even the Holy
One, blessed be He, called *Ze'er Anpin* in Lurianic Kabbala, at times
returns to its mother's womb in the *sefira* of *bina* (which in Lurianic
Kabbala signifies the slavery in Egypt).[137] The ascent of the *sefira* of
tiferet is easily portrayed as the completion of the rift caused by the
descent of *malkhut*. Thus did the Kabbala preserve both the concepts
and the images of the talmudic myth, and its chief innovation was
changing the character and the ontological status of this myth.

V. The Biblical Background
and Its Implications

This description of the talmudic and kabbalistic myth as essentially God's internal struggle over the fate of Israel, may seem inappropiate to those whose knowledge of Judaism is derived from other sources. I believe this description simply traces the development and the change in the biblical image of God that, eventually, affected Jewish religion at all levels. Obviously, it is beyond the scope of this essay to delve into the wide field of biblical research. I will only outline the biblical God's characteristic features as they appear, in different forms and with varying emphases, in several biblical sources. My focus will be on those narrative sections of the Bible that were the basis for the talmudic and kabbalistic passages discussed in the previous sections.

One of the the salient features of biblical stories is that they portray history as dependent on the character and moods of God, whose attitude to His creatures is ambivalent, compounding love, on the one hand, and hatred and jealousy, on the other. God created and sustains humankind; to mitigate His loneliness and find expression for His love and His kingdom, He chooses those who are worthy because, in the words of a medieval kabbalistic proverb, "there is no King without a people." But, since Creation, God has been jealous of His creatures, whose separate existence abolished His exclusivity; He is afraid that human beings may compete with Him and deny Him the awe and honour due to Him as a king, or that they may not requit His love suitably, through absolute devotion and even self-sacrifice. However, God understands that consummating His jealousy would entail the destruction of Creation and He gives those He has chosen precise instructions aimed at assuaging His anger and jealousy while perpetuating their continued separate existence.

This is the impression usually left by a literal reading of the Bible, and there is nothing new in it. Since ancestral times, most of those who have read the Scriptures literally have perceived God's image in this fashion, even when they found it antithetical to their views. As a result of this literal approach, some came to hate the biblical divinity (like the Gnostics of Marcion's school, snake worshippers, and Cain's worshippers) or to oppose biblical religion (like Julian the Apostate, who tried to revive Greek paganism, and felt biblical religion was too mythical for his taste![138] Others grappled consciously with the literal level and, to save the Scripture's authority, interpreted it according to philosophical systems (such as Philo and

Maimonides). Not so the rabbis; they had no problem at all with the biblical myth and added much of their own to it when delving into the essence of God and describing it in myths such as the ones we reviewed in the previous chapters. The rabbinical myth is more daring and explicit than the biblical one; the Bible approaches its myth with extreme awe and reverence, endowing with higher ontological validity. As we showed earlier, when seeking to understand God's attributes the Rabbis resorted to personifications, which were later consolidated and systematized in kabbalistic literature. The biblical approach, on the other hand, consistently presents one divine image; when a noun like *Wrath* is used as a substitute for God Himself, it is only as a form of speech appropriate mainly to dignitaries like kings, whose honor requires us to speak of their actions rather than their essence. Indeed, deferring to God by referring to His actions (such as *Might* or *Shekhina*) rather than to His name, abetted the mythical concern with the attributes at a later stage, although the final result defeated the original intention of abstaining from dealing with God's "personality."

We may, therefore, resort to rabbinical exegeses to understand the biblical myth and, in itself, their "homiletical" quality does not negate their hermeneutical value. Through its use of a different genre and due to its greater freedom, the rabbinical myth often amplifies and actualizes the implicit potential of the biblical stories. A discerning and discriminate reader knows how to choose a *midrash* and use it, as Rashi clearly shows in his biblical commentary, which has been espoused by the people as a reflection of their own consciousness. Rashi too accepted myth at face value and without any ideological justifications; such mythical simplicity is not found even in kabbalistic literature, wherein myth is already self-conscious and reflective, as well as to a certain extent polemical.[139] Rashi tended to sharpen the mythical-psychological aspects and even the sexual ones in unexpected situations or where the Bible, out of deference, limits itself to a hint. Thus, Genesis 2:18: "It is not good that man should be alone; I will make him a help to match him," is usually interpreted to mean that it is not good for a man to be without a woman; Rashi, however, ascribes this complaint to God's situation when threatened by a competitor: "That it should not be said that there are two entities: God above, alone without a mate, and the one below without a mate." Even if we choose to ignore Rashi's commentary and expound this verse as relating only to the anguish of man's loneliness, there is ample evidence of the Creator's problem in this regard. When saying "it is not good that man should be alone," God may be attesting to His own experience when moved to create man,[140] although in this chapter there is no dearth of doubts and regrets about His Creation (as usual in rabbinical and apocalyptic literature these doubts became arguments with the angels, who opposed the creation of man).

This apprehension is clearly revealed in the prohibition to eat from the tree of knowledge. Indeed, the reason for this prohibition is only explained by the snake (Genesis 3:5): "for God knows that on the day you eat of it, then your eyes shall be opened and you shall be as God, knowing good and evil," but it is also confirmed by God, who used it to justify the expulsion from the Garden of Eden (ibid., 3:22): "And the Lord God said, Behold, the man is become like one of us, knowing good and evil: and now, what if he put forth his hand, and take also of the tree of life, and eating, live for ever." The rabbis developed this theme even further and attributed to the snake the claim that God feared man would develop the ability to create worlds after eating from the tree of knowledge, as every artisan hates his fellow craftsmen, and His suspicions were confirmed when man knew his wife and begot children.[141] The rabbis believed that these were also the grounds for banning individuals from pursuing mystical concerns on their own, particularly in the *Sefer Yetsira* [the Book of Creation] and in the creation of the *Golem*.[142]

This is the beginning of the long human saga in which human beings disobey God's will, He punishes them and selects those individuals beloved to Him. The reason for God's anger is not always explicit, though the quintessential sin would appear to be rebellion. The sin of the flood generation is vaguely stated as "wickedness," "evil" (Genesis 6:5), or "violence" (ibid. 6:11), but apparently, the main offence was that stated at the beginning of the chapter: the sons of God took the daughters of man for their wives and the daughters bore the mighty men of renown who threatened God's standing. This issue is stated more explicitly in the story about the tower of Babel, from which we we may also draw inferences about the generation of the flood. The builders of the tower made their intentions clear: "And they said, Come, let us build us a city and a tower, whose top may reach to heaven; and let us make us a name [compare "man of renown" earlier] lest we be scattered abroad upon the face of the whole earth" (Genesis 11:4). God is concerned about this design: "And the Lord said, Behold, the people is one, and they have all one language, and this they begin to do: and now nothing will be withheld from them, which they have schemed to do" (ibid., 11:6).

The sin of addressing another divine entity beside God, which is discussed later, may be adding betrayal to the sin of rebellion. This may explain God's anger over the sons of God taking the daughters of man, as against "But Noah found favor in the eyes of the Lord . . . and Noah walked with God" (Genesis 6:8–9). God wants His chosen,

His loved ones, those who walk with Him, for Himself alone. Thus "And Hanokh walked with God: and he was not; for God took him" (Genesis 5:22). Thus Abraham, who is called His lover (see Isaiah 41:8), who is not taken to Heaven but is told to leave his country, his kindred, and his father's house and belong only to God (Genesis 12:1) and is then commanded: "Take now thy son, thy only son Isaac, whom thou lovest, and get thee into the land of Moriah; and offer him there for a burnt offering upon one of the mountains which I will tell thee of" (Genesis 22:2). I believe that the reason for this command may be God's suspicion that Abraham is turning away his love from Him toward his only son.

Because of His love for the patriarchs, God chose their children—Israel—to be His people. Love is now demanded from the whole people: "Hear, O Israel: The Lord our God; the Lord is one. And thou shalt love the Lord thy God with all thy heart, and with all thy soul, and with all thy might" (Deuteronomy 6:4–5). I think that Rabbi Akiba, in seeing this as a demand to give up his soul,[143] was not far from the spirit of this verse. However, this demand cannot be accommodated with the social and political existence of a whole people; the people maintained this demand as an ideal and tended to rely on the merits of the ancestors' love and devotion, and particularly on the binding of Isaac, rather than impose the duty of sacrifice on every individual. Even if only on some individuals, this ideal did have an effect and the call for sacrifice was never abolished, which is the reason for the ambivalent biblical attitude toward human sacrifices.[144] The verses intimate that, originally, the sanctification of the firstborn required that they be sacrificed, and only following a later development of biblical law were the people told to redeem them;[145] similarly, the tribe of Levi was singled out for the task of worship only after its members "consecrated" themselves against their families (Exodus 32:29).

The struggle over this question continued throughout the period of the First Temple; some would immolate their sons to the *Moloch*, which is not idol worship but a kind of sacrifice to God,[146] whereas others refrained from doing so. One of the prophets believed that burning children is a vile practice, but God commanded it to punish the people of Israel (Ezekiel 20:24–26), and another cries, in God's name: "I did not command them, nor did it come into my heart,"[147] as he said about all other sacrifices.[148] Still another prophet knew this practice to be an an accepted custom, as valid as other sacrifices, all of which he opposed (Micah 6:6–8). Indeed, many animal sacrifices (specially sacrifices of atonement) are substitutes for human sacrifices. There are many signs, among them the famous description by Philo of Byblos,[149] indicating that the practice of circumcision is another example of this type of substitution. Nevertheless, and despite these historical developments, vows of human sacrifice could not be rescinded,[150] and continued to influence God.[151] These ambivalent feelings about human sacrifice can later be traced in a similar ambivalence toward *Kiddush ha-Shem* [martyrdom].[152] *Kiddush ha-Shem* has remained a law pertinent only to individuals and is not to be commanded, as we saw in section II regarding Rabbi Akiba, on the grounds that the behavior of the commanded man must reflect the spirit of the commanding God.

The reverse side of love is jealousy, in heaven as on earth. For this reason idolatry is considered as the foremost biblical sin. Scripture often expounds it in this way, as in the second of the Ten Commandments (Exodus 20:3-6), where God calls Himself "jealous," the idol worshippers "those that hate me," and their opposite "those that love me." It also explains the widespread use of "whoring" for describing the yearning after other gods, a common usage in the Bible, often accompanied by long and explicit descriptions of defilement with foreign gods as opposed to loyal marriage to the God of Israel. The intensity of this image (accompanied in Hosea by symbolic acts), takes it beyond its exclusive metaphoric quality. A priori, this is indeed not a metaphor—the verb *to whore* seems to be one of the original terms for idolatry rather than a colorful substitute for another.

It is appropriate to mention the Zohar in this context, which excels in bringing to the surface elemental and archaic mythical feelings and applying them to the kabbalistic framework. The Zohar strongly emphasizes the necessary link between love and jealousy, in heaven as on earth, and even dares to use celestial jealousy to strengthen love. The Zohar found a hint in the following verse (Genesis 6:18): "But with thee I will erect my covenant"; according to the Zohar, the covenant refers to the male sexual organ, and the verse expresses the idea that the love of the righteous for the *Shekhina* arouses God's jealousy, and He is thus moved to mate with her.[153]

Apparently, monotheism itself is only an elaboration of the idea of God's jealousy, which preceded and created monotheism: the efforts to appease the jealous God eventually generated the idea that other gods simply do not exist. This idea, unknown to figures such as Jephtah and David,[154] started to take shape among the prophets toward the end of the First Temple and became established in the writings of Deutero-Isaiah and Malachi, apparently under the influence of Persian universal religion.[155] The prevalence of ontological monotheism (namely, acknowledging the reality of only one God, as opposed to religious monotheism, which commands the worship of only one God and is obviously fundamental to biblical religion from its inception) in later Judaism, eventually weakened the idea of jealousy that had engendered it: if there are no other gods, there is nobody to be jealous of.

Alongside jealousy is wrath; it is in fear of God's wrath that Jewish religion and many of its commandments, mainly those aimed at appeasing and soothing Him—called *signs*, such as circumcision,[156] *tefillin*[157] and *mezuzah*[158]—took shape. We have previously mentioned circumcision in another context, but there is no contradiction. The distinction between the soul's attributes entails an abstraction, and in reality, they are intertwined; this is also the case for religious reactions to God's attributes, as well as for "love substitutes," such as atonement sacrifices, that can also act as defense mechanisms against the anger God expresses when He fails to receive His due. This link between love and defense mechanisms appears most sharply in the Zohar, when the right meditation is assigned to the *nefilat appayim* (prostration) ritual at the end of the prayer. By prostrating, the worshipper delivers himself to his death and thereby saves himself from the *Shekhina*, who actually wishes to kill him. God must be "seduced," but wholeheartedly and without deceitful thoughts![159]

Occasionally, protection is needed not from God's wrath but from Satan or other harmful agents. However, as we saw in Section III, Satan is at times merely an amplification of the divine attribute of justice. Even those cases that originate in nonmonotheistic mythologies or are part of universal demonology are gradually integrated by religious consciousness into a specifically Jewish mythical scheme. The status of evil in Kabbala is therefore hard to define, because the same system appears at times as dualistic and at times as monistic;[160] in fact, the very attempt at definition may be inappropriate, as the struggle between these impulses is immanent to the Jewish myth, like it is to the divinity itself. Thus, some of the sacrifices, such as the scapegoat[161] or the *millu'im* [consecration] offerings,[162] are described in both rabbinical and kabbalistic literature as bribes to Satan. However, kabbalistic literature at times perceives all sacrifices in this fashion: only the intentional meditation [*kavvana*] accompanying sacrifices rises to Heaven, whereas the sacrificial flesh symbolizes the rejection of evil.[163] This rejection is at times expounded as part of the process of building the complete "divine stature," when everything will be in its proper place,[164] and the Zohar therefore finds fault with those who "abstain from evil" and do not give the *sitra ahra* [the other side] its due. According to the Zohar, the "act of Creation," that is, the emanation of the divine, can be described according to the "mystery of the great crocodile," which is the *sitra ahra* or Satan.[165]

God's wrath resembles not only that of a jealous lover but also that of a king angry at his rebellious subjects, as He is also the king of His people. Since religion's inception, fear of punishment appears side by side with awe of His majesty. This awe is in a relentless struggle with the intimate love for God, particularly in the hearts of those mystic followers who felt themselves torn between two religious duties: the wish to be near, to know and to enter the mysteries of the divine, against the duty to defer to the king and respect His aloofness.[166] The latter inclination grew stronger in *Hekhalot* literature, which tended to raise God to inaccessible heights while placing the world of the *Hekhalot* as a mystical object within grasp, in contrast to the talmudic myth, as reviewed in Section II. Awe of His majesty opened the way for the absorption of philosophical, antimythical ideas into Judaism, though with an important reservation: philosophy could be a part of Judaism as long as it fought against all other myths while strengthening that of God's kingdom as an object of awe and love (as is clear from Maimonides' writings). But, when following its own inner logic, philosophy also revealed the mythical foundations of God's kingdom and made God into an abstract idea, it turned against its original Jewish purpose and ceased being an organic part of Jewish religion (e.g., Spinoza). This was an unacceptable development for, in Zoharic terms, this religion is wholly founded upon the covenant and the grace between the *Adam Tata'a* [the man below] and the *Adam Ila'a* [the Man Supreme.]

──────── APPENDIX: Messianism in Maimonides ────────

Compare this talmudic passage with the wording of the twelfth of Maimonides' thirteen articles of faith concerning the coming of the Messiah. These articles appear in Maimonides's *Commentary on the Mishnah*, at the beginning of the tenth chapter of Sanhedrin, while the passage from Sanhedrin 97b is from the Gemara to M. Sanhedrin 10:1 discussed by Maimonides. The gist of Maimonides's twelfth article is the same Habakuk verse found in the talmudic passage that, in my view, influenced Maimonides' view.

The twelfth article is messianic times, which means to believe in his coming and not to say that he is delayed and, if he is delayed, wait for him; no time is to be set for him, and Scripture is not to be expounded in order to disclose when he is due to come. The rabbis said—blasted be the bones of those who calculate the end. And to believe in greatness and love and to pray for his coming.[167]

Contrary to the talmudic passage, Maimonides does account for the phrase *it will not delay* at the end of the verse, but takes it out of its literal context and formulates it as "not to say that he is delayed," implying "not to argue or complain about his delay" in the Arabic original. *It will not delay* ceases to be a factual statement about the coming of the Messiah and becomes a religious demand imposed on the believer; Maimonides's formulation thus supports the talmudic exegesis of the verse "if he is delayed." This approach was adopted by the author of the famous medieval paraphrase printed in Ashkenazi prayer books, who worded "the thirteen articles" as a credo: "And although he is delayed"; however, it is doubtful whether this was the interpretation of those who turned this article of faith into a Zionist song.

Maimonides's language confirms this interpretation. Accurately translated, his twelfth article would read as follows: "That he should believe in him [with a belief that entails] greatness [or praise] and love"[168] or "To believe in him [entails] praise and love." Rather than the Messiah, the believer or his belief is praised, because the word *love* makes no sense otherwise. This version is unlike the one adopted by the accepted translation, where *honor* replaced *love* and a few words were added in an attempt to make sense of the passage: "And he should believe in him that he precedes in greatness and honor all the kings that have ever been."[169]

Hence, for Maimonides, awaiting the Messiah is a virtue with its own reward, unrelated to his actual coming. In the same spirit, in Laws of Kings 11:1, Maimonides accused of heresy[170] not only those "who do not believe in him" but also those who "do not look forward to the coming of the Messiah."[171] Moroeover, in Laws of Kings 12:2, Maimonides stated that one should not busy oneself with legends describing detailed events to take place in messianic times, "since they lead neither to the fear of God nor to the love of Him," thus implying that the only purpose of messianic belief is fear and love.[172] This idea is also emphasized in the *Epistle to Yemen*, which stresses that reckoning the end and attaining worldly success are unimportant in relation to the eternity of the people and the Torah and to the expectation of redemption. Indeed, the prevalent spirit in this Epistle, aimed at comforting the masses, is more lenient toward those busy reckoning the end. It even engages on some of these calculations on its own but lends them less credibility, viewing them rather as instrumental in fostering perseverance in the expectation of the Messiah. The Habakuk verse is therefore given a different interpretation.[173] Messianic times are important as an ideal: hoping for them and attempting to bring them about affect religious life in this world. Hence, Maimonides ascribed worldly and natural features to messianic times, which enable attempts to realize the messianic ideal but do not guarantee their success. Writing the *Mishneh Torah* as the constitution of the ideal state, should be seen as one such attempt.

Maimonides did not rule out the possibility of fufilling messianic expectations and even described two contradictory scenarios. In Laws of Kings 11 the King Messiah is portrayed as a warrior in King David's image, who will bring about messianic times through coercion and war, whereas in the *Commentary on the Mishnah*[174] he is portrayed in the image of King Solomon, who will attain messianic aims through persuasion and after attaining world recognition. (See Laws of Repentance 11:2 and in *Guide of the Perplexed* III:11, though Solomon's name is not mentioned.) The second description cannot be dismissed as unrealistic, because it suits the purpose of human existence according to Maimonides (as explicitly stated in the *Guide*, ibid.). Moreover, because in Maimonides's view the world will never be destroyed (see *Guide of the Perplexed* II:27–29), we may assume that the potential latent in man's purpose will eventually be actualized, as is claimed by Aristotelian philosophy.[175] However, there is apparently no urgency in this expectation and its realization entails a very lengthy process. We may infer this from Maimonides's statement that messianic times will be very long "since the wise [referring to Plato][176] said that when a sublime combination is attained, it will be very hard to split it apart."[177]

But the core of redemption for Maimonides is not its actual realization. This is also clear from his description of messianic times that, in addition to realistic aspects, includes a utopian dimension.[178] Although he was influenced in this regard by the Sanhedrin passage, Maimonides changed it according to his own view: He softened the statement about the impossibility of attaining redemption and, obviously, dismissed the mythical explanation—the indictment of the attribute of justice. These changes not only reflect Maimonides's theories of the divinity. In his view, messianic times would come only after human beings change their nature, cease their squabbles and hatreds over material scarcity and replace them with the knowledge of God (see mainly the short and moving chapter in *Guide of the Perplexed* III:11). What claims will the attributes of justice and mercy raise then? Even if this expectation fails to be realized, awaiting the Messiah is enormously significant for human life and, on this point, there is no difference between Maimonides and his talmudic source.

2

The Kabbalistic Myth
as Told by Orpheus

Erikapaios appears at times as one of the names of Phanes, the father of the gods in the Orphic pantheon.[1] It seems that Hebrew speakers should have no difficulty identifying this name as simply a combining form, joining together the Hebrew words *erekh appayim* [long suffering] and a Greek suffix. Robert Eisler had already pointed this out in his book,[2] indicating that the Aramaic version of *erekh appayim—arikh anpin—*is also the name of the supreme divine entity in the Zohar.

Eisler's book appeared more than seventy years ago, and the research on Kabbala has since made long strides, but I have not found any reference to this identification, either to confirm it or refute it. This seems puzzling because, if it is indeed accurate and the supreme kabbalistic "countenance" is already mentioned in early Orphic theogony, this should certainly affect our approach to the origins of the kabbalistic myth. Why, then, have Eisler's hypotheses been completely overlooked? An answer to this question may be found in the words of Gershom Scholem, the leading kabbalistic scholar. In his youth, Scholem had met Eisler and even considered cooperating with him, but changed his mind soon after. This is how Scholem describes Eisler in his autobiography, *From Berlin to Jerusalem*:

> Eisler was the son of a Jewish millionaire from Vienna. By his own testimony, his education had taught him to despise Judaism, and he converted about the age of twenty. He was an extremely talented man, alert, energetic, and ambitious. His scholarly interests were very broad, he was eloquent and gifted with considerable literary ability. In 1909, in his late twenties, he had published a two-volume work intriguingly titled *Weltenmantel und Himmelszelt* [Cosmic Cloak and Heavenly Canopy], extremely daring in its far-fetched hypotheses and packed with incredible erudition, marking its author as a very original historian of religion but also as one distracted from solid

discourse by his wild fancy. There were no experts capable of evaluating this book, which transcended the bounds of all known disciplines but many, familiar with specific sources or with a particular topic, had rejected his analysis or questioned his conclusions (as I did when delving into his discussion of Kabbala that, to my great surprise, took up considerable space in his book).... He was moved to begin his study of Kabbala by the French translation of the Zohar, which I mentioned earlier. Eisler used this translation extensively, praised it highly and built many theories on it, which turned out to be groundless. He had apparently begun his efforts to establish the society [for the promotion of research on Kabbala] in 1916, and had undoubtedly invested a great deal of energy in this project. He was also well aware of the methodological problems raised by the study of Kabbala, though he knew little Hebrew and no Aramaic.... It did not take me long to realize the serious shortcomings of his deficient Hebrew. His independent research in the field of Kabbala included a great discovery about the true author of the *Sefer Yetsira*...what he told me appeared to rely on flimsy evidence and his kabbalistic hypotheses in *Weltenmantel und Himmelszelt* roused in me—who had only then decided to seriously take on the yoke of rigorous philological discipline— many doubts and even a shudder. "You must think I am a sad case as a philologist, pitiful really," he once said, without spite. His rich and inventive imagination surmounted all the hurdles of historical criticism. He cannot be accused of lacking original ideas, and sometimes even enticing ones, in fields as varied as protosemitic inscriptions in Sinai, Greek mysteries, the origin of the Gypsies and, for many years, early Christianity, all sharing one common feature: They were brimming with unsolved questions, leaving wide scope for the manipulations of his genius. Anyone hearing him lecture was captivated by his rhetorical gifts. Anyone reading his writings was rendered speechless by the wealth of his quotations and his references to the most astonishing and remote sources. I have never seen any comparable acrobatics in the world of scholarship. Still, he also had influential scientific admirers, such as Solomon Reinach in Paris and Sir Gilbert Murray in Oxford. His opponents said of him, in an almost open anti-Semitic quip, that he was a speculator who had strayed into the field of science. In short, he was unique and special in his own way. But no publisher who had ever printed one of his books was willing to enter into any further dealings with him, for very good reasons: He would rewrite the book while reading the proofs until it ended up at least twice as long, and every publication ended in a row.[3]

Clearly, Scholem's disregard of Eisler's work does not suggest indifference but rather the opposite. When starting out, Scholem was indeed "captivated" and "rendered speechless by the wealth of his quotations," and Eisler's "original ideas" were "sometimes even enticing" (as the impressive collection of books by Eisler in Scholem's library might well attest). But Scholem, "who had only then decided to seriously take on the yoke of rigorous philological discipline," divorced himself completely, whether consciously or unconsciously, from enticing ideas arousing "many doubts and even a shudder." The ambivalence Scholem felt toward Eisler may have had a share in this—he could not forgive him his apostasy and his virulent opposition to Zionism, though he was magnetized by his tempestous spirit, his brilliance and charm. However, Scholem may have glimpsed a suspicious frivolity, as in the anecdote he quotes about Eisler's library, where cognac bottles were hidden behind bindings marked *Erotica et Curiosa*. The main point is clear: Scholem despised scholars of Eisler's ilk, who dispensed with systematic and rigorous philological methods in the research of Kabbala and its inner development. Rather than a discipline in its own right, these scholars saw Kabbala as a no-man's land, for which browsing and flimsy knowledge, based on secondary sources and translations, should suffice to understand kabbalistic concepts and even to find their origin or compare them with other religious phenomena far removed in time and place. All this, displaying great virtuosity and neglecting those facts that could indeed be discovered about Kabbala's spiritual and historic background.

The young Scholem rebelled against this climate of "anything goes," which describes the state of the art in kabbalistic scholarship when he began to show interest in it. Hence, he firmly opted for another course: the inner, meticulous research of kabbalistic literature. Against this background, it is easier to understand his inclination to view Kabbala as a closed and unique religious phenomenon, to be interpreted immanently, as well as his tendency to make limited use of extra-kabbalistic sources to elucidate the kabbalistic phenomenon.

This approach has proved extremely useful to kabbalistic research and has indeed put this science on its feet. We now have an apparatus for confirming or refuting claims and hypotheses, and the name of Kabbala cannot be taken in vain. Scholem and his disciples have developed a fairly elaborate description of kabbalistic doctrine, its development, and its various schools; although this description can always be improved on, emended, and changed, there is now a frame to contend with. Clearly, the role of kabbalistic scholars today is to continue along this road, which is still infinitely long and wide as well as full of interest and surprises, but the important question is whether scholars can still be satisfied with it or conditions are already ripe for breaking the present mold and suggesting more general hypotheses about the origins of Kabbala and its place within Judaism. The more we know of kabbalistic texts and the inner development of their ideas, the sharper are the questions that cannot be answered within this frame. These questions concern the origin of mythical-kabbalistic patterns of thought and the "raw material" of kabbalistic myths. The conventional wisdom, claiming that kabbalistic myths first appeared in the twelfth and thirteenth centuries, is indeed exceptionally well supported: there is no precedent for these ideas before this time and the onus of proof is therefore on whoever wishes to predate them. In Gershom Scholem's words:

> These are the four generations at the beginning of Kabbala [R. Jehudah ben Barzilai, R. Abraham ben Issac, R. Abraham ben David, and R. Isaac the Blind]. Before them, it does not exist. No one knows about it, as attested by the commentary on the *Sefer Yetsira* by R. Jehudah ben Barzilai from Barcelona. The argument *in silentium* is valid in his regard...[4]

However, there are some serious drawbacks to this description. Is it so simple to assume that a detailed and preeminently mythical kabbalistic doctrine appeared at the heart of antimythical Judaism— as Judaism is described by advocates of this position—when its monotheistic character was still being refined by Maimonides and his disciples? That this new phenomenon evoked almost no opposition and, within a relatively short time, overwhelmed most of the Jewish religious consciousness? That its first appearance occurred not in peripheral circles but among the main bearers of the rabbinic tradition, such as R. Abraham ben Izhak, Nahmanides, and R. Solomon ben Adret? Moreover, that they chose to refer to these mythical elements as *Kabbala*, namely, a received secret tradition? Is the assumption that this name indeed reflects a factual truth so much harder to accept than its opposite, and should the onus of proof indeed be on its proponents?

I might not be saying this were I certain that no allusions anticipating kabbalistic myths are ever found in ancient texts. However, quite to the contrary, it seems to me that many such hints appear in talmudic and midrashic literature; if we were not to interpret them too minimalistically and were undeterred from expounding them in a kabbalistic spirit, they might shed new light on the rabbis' spiritual and religious world. Most of the scholarship on the rabbinic period has not proceeded along these lines although Yitzhak Baer, known for his illuminating studies, wrote the following on the mishnaic sages:

> Clearly, Halakha and what is called *Aggada* cannot be separated, since both attest to the links between the celestial and the mundane. Later mystics were justified in searching for hidden mysteries when expounding Halakha and *Aggada*. Every *halakha*, from its conception, conceals a great deal of mythical-mystical symbolism, whereas *Aggada*'s main aim is to reveal the glory of the Creator's actions toward His creatures and the ways in which He leads His world through His divine attributes and powers and through His commandments, His elect, and His followers.[5]

Through this deeper approach to the sources, Baer sought to acquit the Jewish religion of the time of Jesus from the libelous charges of "legalism" raised by a long line of Christian scholars and unwittingly adopted by many Jewish scholars. The latter felt that this arid description of rabbinic tradition was not only historically true but also vindicated Jewish religion and purified it from its negative elements. So widespread was, and still is, this view (even among rabbis and "halakhic men" of later generations, who strikingly differ from Soloveichik's *Halakhic Man*)[6] that it affected even Gershom Scholem. Scholem in fact supported the opposite view, claiming that the mythical-mystical dimension which he had deemed to be the life force and the mystery behind the survival of Jewish religion, must be returned to Jewish history,[7] but he carefully refrained from applying this principle to any period preceding the mid-Middle Ages. Scholem indeed discussed the origins of Kabbala in occult doctrines and in rabbinic statements from the talmudic period, but he drew a sharp and clear distinction between these two mystical phenomena. He analyzed only the overt level of ancient texts and never suggested retrospective inferences; he even tended to interpret as restrictively as possible expressions that, ostensibly, could be seen as anticipating the later spirit of Kabbala.[8] As for Halakha, Scholem devoted many essays and studies to its description, focusing on the dialectic tension between Halakha and Kabbala.[9] Baer dedicated his book *Israel Among the Nations*, from which I quoted earlier, "to Gershom Scholem, in loyal friendship," though he clearly went far beyond Scholem in his method.

True, Baer stated only a general principle without showing how it should be applied to Halakha's concrete details, but it seems that even if we were to make it more explicit, it probably would still not suffice. Rabbinic statements are not the only source for learning about the Jewish religion of their time. It is a plausible assumption that rabbinic statements will not, in fact, be a particularly rich source for mythical traditions, both because of their unsystematic, exegetic character and because of the esoteric approach they usually adopted regarding these questions, as explicitly stated in the following halakhic ruling: "The laws of incest may not be expounded to three persons, nor the story of creation before two persons, nor the subject of the chariot before one person alone, unless he be a sage and comprehends of his own knowledge" (M. Hagigah 2:1). Moreover, many Jewish mythical utterances failed to enter canonic traditional Jewish literature.

The relevant corpus has grown extensively over the last few years. It seems that the Apocrypha, Hellenistic literature, the writings of Philo and Josephus, the Dead Sea Scrolls, and the New Testament, or even explicit quotes from Jewish sources found in patristic or pagan writings, no longer seem sufficient. Judaism exerted enormous spiritual influence in the Hellenistic period, and a great deal of Jewish material is also found in the writings of non-Jews. Thus, the prevailing view in the latest research on Gnostic sects is that they were mainly the outcome of an inner Jewish development (despite the metaphysical anti-Semitism permeating their writings)[10] and had not, as previously assumed, originated in Persia or Egypt. We might add that, among the texts discovered at Nag Hammadi, some were written by Jews and carry many Jewish connotations.[11] This is not the case only regarding Gnostics who relied on the Bible or the New Testament; Jewish traces are aboundantly found in "purely" pagan myths created during this "syncretistic" period, such as in the writings attributted to Hermes Trismagistus[12] and, as we shall see, also in those attributed to Orpheus.

In the future, a great deal of valuable scholarship will veer in this direction, and I believe that many sources of the kabbalistic myth will be found to be deeply implanted in all branches of ancient Jewish literature. In addition to spreading its influence, Jewish religion also absorbed elements from its surroundings. Those who fail to acknowledge these external influences resemble those given the inner keys but not the outer ones, in Y. Baer's paraphrase of the rabbinic parable. Mutual influences at times will be encountered, particularly in the context of the ongoing bond between Judaism and Christianity.[13] This suggested break in the frame of kabbalistic research is not only a vision for the future. It has already begun, particularly through the studies of Moshe Idel, and most of my argument up till now has relied on my conversations with him. In his studies, Idel has mentioned ancient sources for several kabbalistic ideas, such as the kabbalistic conception of the Torah[14] and the sources of evil[15] and even of the *sefirot* above the *sefirot*[16] as well as of the image of man above the *sefirot*[17] and even the *Shekhina*. I have also discussed similar concepts elsewhere and have pointed to antique sources for the Zohar, among them the Gnostic sources of the dualistic myth appearing in some of the *Idrot*.[18] This myth will also concern us now, when we return to search for its origins, this time in Orphic sources.

I might appear to be suggesting the notion that ancient writings from several remote sources, such as the Gnostic and Orphic traditions, were available to the author of the Zohar, who then proceeded to assemble them to create his own myth. Although it is known that the Zohar weaves together many rabbinic and medieval strands when forging its special texture, I am far from making this assumption. My hypothesis is different: I suggest that there was an ancient Jewish myth, which the author of the Zohar used as his building material. This myth was not totally preserved in ancient Jewish literature, and we know of it mainly through the Zohar, though parts of it appear in various ancient texts, either Jewish or reflecting Jewish influence. These texts can bear out that this is indeed an ancient myth without impairing its Jewish credentials, though this myth was also affected by its contact with other religions. Thus, for instance, Gnostic writings from the school of Simon Magus confirm that the "dual-antinomian" facet of the *Idra* relies on very old sources indeed, and I have dealt with this before; the Orphic myth will substantiate the "theogonian" aspect, which is the subject of this essay.

If I refer to my assumption as a *hypothesis*, it is not because I hold any doubts about the validity of the comparison between the *Idra* and Orphic writings, which I shall demonstrate later. I simply intend to stress that, even if accurate, the approach I am suggesting is still limited in its scope—there are wide gaps in our knowledge and about a thousand years elapsed between the Orphic myth and the Zohar. We do not know exactly where the myth was during all this time or how it reached the author of the Zohar: Was this tradition written in a secret scroll[19] or was it perhaps transmitted orally? There are many problems, which I mean to emphasize rather than blur—unlike Eisler, who heeded the scholarship of his times—because this seems to offer the only hope of a solution in the future. The gaps in our knowledge should not, in any event, deter us from stating what we already know: "it is not [incumbent] upon thee to finish the work, but neither art thou free to refrain from it" (Avoth 2:16). Further on, I shall cite several allusions to this myth found in prekabbalistic Jewish literature, which might point to a certain continuity over time. Moreover, this would not be the only instance of a Jewish myth whose origin becomes known to us through a non-Jewish version (developed mainly in Alexandria), and then emerges in medieval Kabbala.[20]

Before I turn to the concrete aspects of my argument, I would like to qualify the possible effects of this type of research on our views about the Zohar and Kabbala in general. Claiming ancient sources for the Zohar does not imply that the Zohar is an ancient text. Its time and place have already been ascertained by scholars: Castile in the second half of the thirteenth century. However, its author (or authors) did not create ex nihilo, but rather found clues that were then impressed with their own stamp. It is this free spirit, as well as the choice of a pseudo-epigraphic style, that facilitated the use of other sources in addition to the classic Jewish ones. The author (or authors) wove together these various sources into a uniquely wondrous and multifaceted single whole. Although in a different way, this is also true of the Lurianic myth, which emerged out of a process of profound contemplation of the Zohar and reconstructs its views where unexplicit.[21] However, on certain questions, Luria also seems to have had access to other knowledge, not based on the Zohar, which Orphic and patristic writings prove to be very old, as I shall also attempt to show later.

Let us now move on to examine the Orphic texts. At what stage in its long development can Orphic religion be said to have had contact with Judaism? These contacts can hardly be traced back to the beginnings of Orphism, around the sixth century B.C.[22] The first quotations from Orpheus found in classical Greek texts (among them Plato),[23] point to certain basic similarities between the Orphic and Hebrew myths. But this resemblance, which I shall discuss later, belongs in the realm of Semitic influences on Greek culture and myth during the prebiblical era. Scholars[24] acknowledge that this influence was especially prominent in the realm of theogony, not only Orphic theogony but also Hesiod's more famous one.[25] Both these theogonies can indeed be considered variations on one theme, and this basic resemblance between the Orphic and Semitic myths later enabled Orphic religion to incorporate Jewish motifs. These motifs appear in Orphic quotations found in writings dating from the early Christian era, mainly in those of neo-Platonic philosophers—who found the Orphic myth suited their needs and was particularly useful in their controversy with Christianity[26]—and in patristic writings. However, the first contact between the two religions must be dated earlier, closer to the onset of the Hellenistic era that, as we know, was characterized by "syncretism" and religious turmoil. It apparently occurred in Egypt, a center for both Hellenistic Judaism and Orphic religion, as well for other Hellenistic currents of thought that had integrated Jewish elements. Moreover, it is also there that the name *Erikapaios* was first used in a context possibly attesting to its Jewish origins.

I claim that Orphic believers, who had adhered from ancestral times to a myth resembling the Jewish one, adopted certain facets of the Jewish myth following their acquaintance with Alexandrian Jews in the last centuries of the pre-Christian era. This Jewish myth, although contemporary Jewish sources only hint at it rather than document it systematically, remained alive within Judaism until its literary crystallization in mediaeval Kabbala, mainly in the Zohar. Hence the resemblance between the Orphic and kabbalistic myths— the topic of this essay—that will now be examined in detail.

We will begin with the name *Erikapaios*, which was indeed our starting point, as I believe that a strong case can be made for the Hebrew origins of this name and its resemblance to *erekh appayim*. This case cannot be dismissed by simply alleging "phenomenological" affinity, to be explained perhaps through a model such as the Jungian theory of archetypes, as would have been possible were we only facing parallel mythical descriptions. Linguistic affinity, further supported by a similarity in the mythical contents, conclusively points to a historical linkage. It was indeed the linguistic resemblance that first made me wonder about the parallels between the Orphic and kabbalistic myths.

Scholars have long been perplexed by the root of the name *Erikapaios*,[27] and naturally, most of them attempted to derive it from Greek etymology. The prevailing view is that *Erikapaios* means "swallowed in the morning" or "swallowed early," hinting at the story of his having been devoured by Zeus. However, this explanation seems not only bizarre substantially, but is also questionable linguistically. There is no such word as *kapaios* in Greek, and it is hard to derive it from the verb *kapto* or *katapino*. Robert Eisler pointed this out in his own discussion on Erikapaios, and even added that the word *kapos*, in the sense of "wind"—though enlisted by some scholars to suggest that *Erikapaios* means "spring wind"—does not exist and appears in dictionaries as no more than a *lusus grammaticorum*. On the other hand, the Hebrew ethymology of *erekh appayim* is very adequate and retains the original form of the word.

Furthermore, even in antiquity, it had already been argued that the name *Erikapaios* was an Oriental import. Thus, John Malalas, the sixth century C.E. Antiochian historian, derives the name *Erikapaios* from the language spoken in his region. In a passage that we shall compare further on to the text of the Zohar, John Malalas stated that *Erikapaios* means "life giver"—*Zo'odoter* (and in a parallel version we also find the meaning "life"—*Zoie*).[28] True, this is not the literal meaning of the name *erekh appayim* but could be seen as an acceptable description, as God "breathed into his nostrils the breath of life" (Genesis 2:7). This description parallels the Zohar's portrayal of *arikh anpin* (III:130b, *Idra Rabba*), which has two nostrils, one breathing "life" and the other "life of life," "life of life" into *ze'eir anpin* and "life" into the messianic king.[29]

The name *Erikapaios* does not appear in the ancient sources of Orphism, and the evidence at hand is from a later period.[30] The quotations in neo-Platonic literature and in patristic writings, and even an anthology of Orphic hymns where one is devoted to this god, all date from the early Christian era;[31] this hymn indeed uses another one of his names—*Protogonos* [the first-born or the eldest son]—but also uses the name *Erikapaios*. However, the first reference to Erikapaios appears earlier, in slightly altered form, in a syncretic papyrus including Orphic elements from the third century B.C., found in the Gurob area in Egypt. This papyrus was later used as cardboard wrapping for a mummy and was greatly damaged; only about two words in each line have been preserved and, on this basis, scholars have concluded that the text speaks of an initiation ceremony or an introduction to the religion's mysteries. The name *Erikapaios* appears in one of them, in the phrase *Irikepaige, soisom me*; namely, "Irikepaigus, save me!"[32]

Even a cursory look at this combination and its context can serve to support the notion of Hebrew influence. Not only does the name *Erikapaios* seem Hebrew, but so does the phrase in which it appears for the first time: "*Erekh appayim*, save me" (or "*hoshia' na*"). Pleas such as this—including an appeal to God and the phrase "save me" or "save us, we pray Thee"—are common in the Book of Psalms and were almost ritualized formulas during the time of the Second Temple.[33] This formula was also the basis for the *Hosannas* and for the ritual hymns recited over *Simhat Torah* [The Rejoicing of the Torah Festival]: "God of the winds, save us, we pray Thee." The name *long suffering* seems particularly adequate in these circumstances, because it refers to God's attribute of mercy.

Indeed, the cry "save me" is occasionally present in Greek pagan cults, and in the papyrus we mentioned it even appears (line 5) in connection with another deity, but it is not as common as in Judaism. Moreover, one could assume that, in this papyrus too, the ritual formulas for appealing to other gods had been influenced by Jewish rite. Such influences can be discerned in another contemporary Egyptian papyrus, which seems to be a pagan adaptation of a Psalms chapter in Aramaic written in Egyptian demotic script.[34]

Another phrase, in the next line, lends further support to the hypothesis of Jewish influence on the ritual formulas of the Gurob papyrus. The next readable words after "Irikapaigus, save me" are *Heis Dionysos*; namely, "Dyonisos is one." This Dyonisos is apparently the god Erikapaios, as they were often identical in Orphism.[35] It is almost superfluous to point out that this phrase too calls to mind a famous Jewish religious motto: "God is One." Indeed, such monotheistic formulations appear elsewhere in later Orphic religion,[36] although we cannot rule out the option of Jewish influence on them as well. Neither can one ignore the ritual phrase common in the cult of Serapis, the official Egyptian deity of the times, *Heis Zeys Serapis* [Zeus Sarapis is one],[37] although I suggest we do not overlook the possibility that this formula also reflects the influence of Alexandria's powerful Jewish community. It is indeed the case that Jews, as well as the contest between the God of Israel and Zeus Sarapis, are often mentioned together with these formulas.[38] The rest of the documents found together with the one mentioning Erikapaios for the first time indeed deal with legal issues concerning Jewish controversies.[39]

Let us now mention briefly some of the main motifs in Orphic theogony related to Erikapaios and compare them with kabbalistic texts. In a certain version of Orphic theogony, the supreme divine principle is called *ageless time—Chronos ageraos—*or *infinite time—Chronos Apeiros*. Scholars had already sensed that these concepts did not originate in Greece but rather in the East. Hieronymus and Hellaenicus, the Orphic sources that the neo-Platonic philosopher Damascius cited for these concepts, were also from the Levant and seemed to have relied on an Alexandrian tradition (this Hieronymus was apparently the same one Josephus cites as the author of a history book on the Phoenicians).[40] Persian sources have also been mentioned for these concepts, and as Shlomo Pines has recently confirmed to me, this attribution seems justified. However, a Jewish myth could have been integrated here during the Hellenistic period: The biblical term *The Ancient of Days* (Daniel 7:9; 13), as well as the term *Attika Kaddisha* [the Holy Ancient One], which in the Zohar refers to the supreme divine entity, could also be advanced as expressing the idea of eternal time. Moreover, in line with Eisler (pp. 470–473), the concept of "infinite time" could be seen as parallel to the kabbalistic *Ein-sof.*

This comparison will seem more valid once we have examined the other parts of the myth. In the same Oriental source quoted by Damascius, ageless time is described as a three-headed dragon: one is a bull's head, the other a lion's head, and between them is a god's head—obviously shaped as a human head—with winged shoulders.[41] The general picture of time as an animal-headed monster—though not necessarily these particular animals—originates in Persian Zurvanism; however, I believe that Jewish influences can be discerned here too. Eisler (p. 473) had already pointed out that the Zohar also describes the supreme divine principle as three headed, relying for evidence on the famous statement at the beginning of the *Idra Zutta* (Zohar III:288a). As usual, Eisler quoted from the French version of the Zohar, which is rendered untranslated in his German book; this parallel is indeed on solid ground and can be taken even further. Eisler was satisfied with pointing to the correspondence between the numbers—three heads in the Orphic myth and three in the Zohar (there are additional instances in the Zohar where these three are discussed, such as I:19a)—but there are similarities in the mythical content as well. The Zohar does not explicitly mention a bull's head, a lion's head, and a man in the middle, but it does so describe the three principles ruling the world of the male *sefirot* below these heads (see I:19a; III:274a). An eagle's head is added for the *sefira* of *malkhut* that, though missing in the parallel Orphic myth, might possibly be suggested there by the wings on the dragon's shoulders. We could certainly infer from the lower *sefirot* to the supreme three heads, as these heads are the source of the *sefirot* and the Zohar regularly assumes that consequences will resemble their causes. Exactly in this fashion, the Zohar's author finds these four heads at lower levels of being, and particularly in the divine chariot that is below the *sefirot* (not surprisingly, as this account is taken from the description of the chariot in Ezekiel 1:10). It is possible that the Zohar glossed over this description and, out of reverence, refrained from portraying the three supreme heads explicitly—they are part of the higher spheres and it is unseemly to describe God in the image of animal heads.

This linkage between the quality of the three supreme heads and the principle of the *sefirot* below them would be strengthened if we were to acknowledge that the Zohar bases its description on the famous responsum attributed to R. Hai Gaon and belongs in the *Iyyun* circle.[42] In this responsum, the three supreme entities (or *Ha-Tsahtsahot* [The Brightness], as the kabbalists—who approach this responsum as the crucial source on this question—usually refer to them) are called *heads* or, more exactly, *heads of heads*. This responsum also reveals these heads as the supreme sources for the attributes of love, stern judgment, and compassion or, respectively, for the *sefirot* of *Hesed, Gevura*, and *Tiferet*, depicted in the Zohar as three heads: a lion, a bull, and a man in the middle.

This parallel, which specifically relates to three animal heads, is just too explicit to be a coincidence. Neither can the argument that the Jewish sources are from later periods be cited in this case, because the three animals appear already in Ezekiel's description of the divine chariot and fulfilled an important role in Jewish mystical and apocalyptic literature.[43] It is precisely the presence of animal heads at the beginning of the theogonic myth, as well as their particular order—a man in the middle and the eventual neglect of the eagle's head in favor of the other three—that create the parallels between the Orphic myth and the Zohar. These parallels could attest that these varied dimensions in the meditations on the divine chariot do not begin in mediaeval kabbalistic circles but have ancient Jewish sources.

Until now we have dealt with Chronos, the first cosmic principle in Orphic religion. Let us now turn to the second—Phanes-Erikapaios—which is our main concern. A similar picture emerges from ancient iconography, and even from the writings of Hellaenicus and Hieronymus and the neo-Platonic philosopher Proclus.[44] Phanes also has three heads (a ram, a deer, and a lion in the middle). G. Quispel, the well-known scholar of Gnosis, showed that this image originated in Alexandria and spread from there to other Oriental religions, such as Mithraism. However, this symbol was not at all strange to contemporary Judaism and, in the icons, it is occasionally identified with the god *Yehu Adonai*.[45] Quispel further proved that the image of the god Phanes was part and parcel of several Jewish schools of thought in the Hellenistic period. This figure is the first creator of the world in the Orphic myth—although not the present world, which was created later by Zeus—and served as model for the Demiurge found in some classic Gnostic-Jewish writings that were totally unaffected by Christian influences.[46]

Hellenistic Jews were familiar with this image of Phanes and were greatly influenced by it. Its similarities with some Zoharic allusions could thus be explained by assuming that ancient Jewish texts lost to us reached the author of the Zohar. However, there is something missing in Quispel's description: It is hard to assume a unidirectional connection. As Jewish thought was influenced by certain features of the ancient god Phanes, so did Jewish features influence the description of Phanes in the Hellenistic period; it is the blend between them that created the famous figure of Gnostic-Jewish writings. Oriental influences on Orphic religion in general and on its Alexandrian manifestation in particular are almost a truism in the research of Orphism; moreover, we have also pointed to Jewish influences in the name *Erikapaios–erekh appayim*, in the ritual formulas accompanying its first appearance, and even in images from Ezekiel's divine chariot.

In my view, the dualistic perception characteristic of *erekh appayim* is Jewish in origin, and its meeting with Orphism only gave it a further dimension. This notion was popular in "heterodox" circles during the rabbinic period and was described at length in A. F. Segal's book about the the two powers in Heaven.[47] The dualistic approach was particularly widespread among Alexandrian Jews and, as Quispel pointed out after Segal, a great deal of Philo's doctrine is devoted to its rejection.[48] Unlike these two authors however, I do not believe that dualism originates in the Hellenistic period, because its sources seem even older than the Bible. I shall not deal here with this issue—which by far exceeds the intentions of this essay and has occupied scholars at great length—and shall only allude to the famous ancestral Caananite myth of Ugaritic literature: The supreme god abdicates power in favor of his sons led by Baal, the creator of heaven and earth. As is well known, this myth has parallels in ancient Greek theogonies originating in the East—both those by Hesiod and by Orpheus—and can also be glimpsed in several places in the Bible, despite constant attempts to repress it. One such instance is Psalms 91, which was originally a hymn consecrating those who had abandoned the protection of the Almighty to abide under the shadow of the Lord, as shown by Tur Sinai.[49] Another is the appearance of *The Ancient of Days* in Daniel 7, who delegated his government to another divine figure. Unlike the view of later Christian tradition, a literal reading of this text would indicate that the second figure is the God of Israel rather than the Messiah (Christians later returned to this interpretation when they ascribed divine attributes to their Messiah). This is not a human figure but rather one with the likeness of a man, and He emerges from the clouds as God often does in the Bible, steering his heavenly chariot;[50] this image of God in His chariot was envisioned by the prophet as "the likeness as the appearance of a man" (Ezekiel 1:26). *The Ancient of Days* is indeed another name for the *arikh anpin* of the Zohar. At the end of this essay, I shall refer to further instances in rabbinic literature pointing in this direction, possibly serving as transitional stages between the ancient myth reflected in Orphic writings and the Zohar.

Let us now return to the comparison between Orphic theogony and the Zohar; even if dualistic theory first appeared in Judasim during the Hellenistic period, it could still be seen as affecting the Zohar.

The next stage in Orphic cosmogony—indeed the theogony—is the egg stage. The primeval elements crystallized in the image of a cosmic egg cradling the god Phanes (who is Erikapaios). All the sources emphasize its androgynous essence, because it was meant to create the world through self-impregnation. When mature, it cracked the shell and shone with a great light, as suggested by his name: Phanes - shines. This myth appears in all descriptions of Orphic theogony and is famous as the Orphic element par excellence: The absence of a cosmic egg in Hesiod's theogony is indeed its main difference with the Orphic one. When this myth appears in the writings of a classic Greek author, as in Aristophanes' *The Birds*, scholars refer to it as an Orphic element. In the Hellaenicus and Hieronymus sources quoted previously, it was three-headed Chronos, the god of time, who formed the egg; however, Chronos is not mentioned in later Orphic sources, where it is claimed the egg emerged spontaneously at the first stage of cosmic creation, during the turmoil involving the four primordial elements. As we shall see later, one of the four elements, air, has a special relation with the egg.

All scholars discerned a link between this myth (or between Greek theogonies in general) and parallel myths in the East, particularly in Egypt and Phoenicia.[51] Several sources attest to the myth of the cosmic egg as an element of early Canaanite religion: Philo of Biblos' study of Phoenician religion,[52] Mochos' description as quoted in Damascius' writings[53] and, as Eisfeldt showed, the allusions found in Ugaritic texts.[54] Some scholars have claimed that traces of this myth could also be discerned in the biblical story of creation. They derived the verb *merahefet* [hovered] in the verse "and a wind from God hovered over the surface of the water" (Genesis 1:2), from a root meaning "to brood," according to its meaning in Syrian and in Deuteronomy 32:11. Others, and first and foremost M. D. Cassuto, were opposed to this etymology[55] but Eisfeldt, and Quispel after him, have lent it strong credence,[56] relying mainly on the parallels between the beginning of Genesis and the Canaanite and Orphic myths. As Phanes is the light shining forth from the Orphic egg, so is light the first biblical creation after "a wind from God hovered over the surface of the water." Moreover, the biblical egg—if there is such a thing—is hatched by the "wind from God," just as in the parallel myths the egg is related to the wind or to the element of air. According to Mochos' Phoenician description, at first there was air (*aer* or *aither*), from which *ulamus* (resembling the Hebrew *olamim*, namely, eternity or world) came forth, an androgynous creature that impregnated itself and begot both an egg and another creature named Quasorus. Quasorus cracked the egg and, from both halves, created heaven and earth.

However, the Orphic egg is even more intimately linked to the element of air. In Aristophanes' comedy *The Birds*, the cosmic egg is called *hypenemion oion*; namely, "an egg carried by the wind" or "a wind egg."[57] According to Hieronymus' Orphic theogony, Chronos begot Air (*Aiether*), Confusion (*Chaos*) and *Erebos* (resembling the Hebrew *erev*, namely, evening or darkness). In a parallel version, found in fragments of the *Rhapsodies*, Chronos begot Air, Depth, and Darkness, and the similarities between this picture and Genesis 1:2 can hardly be ignored. These two Orphic sources share in the view that Chronos carved the egg from *Aiether* (air), and the hatching of the egg at Phanes' birth is sometimes described as splitting the air.[58] John Malalas, in the fragment cited on the meaning of Erikapaios' name, does not mention the egg explicitly but claims light split the air and illuminated the earth and all creation. The name of this light is Matis, meaning counsel; Phanes, meaning light; and Erikapaios, life giving.

I believe that the *tannaim* were also aware of this interpretation of Creation. Ben-Zoma said in Genesis Rabba 2:4: "I was contemplating the Creation [and have come to the conclusion] that between the upper and nether waters there is but two or three fingerbreadths. For it is not written here 'and the wind from God blew' but 'hovered,' like a bird flying and flapping its wings, its wings barely touching [the nest over which it hovers]." The wind from God during the first day of Creation is thus compared to a chick hatching from the egg; the egg's two halves—the waters above and the waters below—were still attached to each other, because the two halves were divided only when Heaven was created in the second day. This seems to be the original picture, predating the parallel version in Hagiga 15a where the wind from God is compared to "a dove which hovers over her young without touching [them]." The latter image—where the wind from God hovers between the two halves of the water rather than as a dove hovering over her young—appears less adequate. (The version of the Jerusalem Talmud, Hagigah 2:1, 77b, cannot be used as supporting evidence: "It is said here 'hovering' and it is said there [Deuteronomy 32:11]: 'As an eagle stirs up its nest, hovers over its young'. Just as the 'hovering' which is spoken of there [implies] 'almost touching but not quite,' so the 'hovering' spoken of here is 'almost touching but not quite.'" The purpose of bringing evidence from the eagle is only to establish the exact meaning of the verb *hover*, and has no bearing on the content of the image, as is also the case in Tosefta Hagigah 2:6.) The *tannaim* indeed claimed that Ben Zoma's quest came to a bad end, though they challenged its form rather than its substance (see later, note 67).

It is indeed possible to doubt the presence of an egg myth in Genesis 1 (though I am inclined to support it), but the parallels between this Orphic myth and the beginning of the Zohar (I:15a) rest on firmer ground. The statement in Zohar I:15a opens both the creation story and the book as a whole, because the preceding pages—entitled Preface—were placed there by the printers for lack of a better place. The initial phrase—"At the very beginning"—is intended as an exegesis of the first word in Genesis; therefore, if this passage were to include the egg myth, as I intend to show, the author of the Zohar (just like Ben Zoma) should be added to the list of scholars who found this myth at the beginning of the Torah. I shall quote this passage literally, and the parallel versions will concern us only when directly relevant.

"In the beginning" (Genesis 1:1)—At the very beginning the king made engravings in the supernal purity. A spark of blackness emerged in the sealed within the sealed from the mystery of *Ein-Sof*, a mist within matter, implanted in a ring, no white, no black, no red, no yellow, no color at all. When he measured with the standard of measure, he made colors to provide light. Within the spark, in the innermost part, emerged a source, from which the colors are painted below, and it is sealed among the sealed things of the mystery of *Ein-Sof*. It penetrated, but did not penetrate, its air; it was not known at all until the pressure of its penetration a single point shone, sealed, supernal...[59]

In general lines, this description assumes that the first creation is an entity that split[60] the "supernal purity," or is itself called *supernal purity* or *a spark of blackness*, or *a spark of blackness* is the engraver. At any rate, a single point endeavored to emerge from this entity and, for this purpose, attempted to penetrate it. "It penetrated, but did not penetrate" until it finally succeeded in shining outside.

Although it is not explicitly mentioned, a hatching chick can easily be recognized in this description. The Zohar somehow attempted to conceal this mythical picture under the cloak of more speculative concepts, but this is indeed the picture expounded by later kabbalists.[61] Another symbol from the animal world appears further on in this passage from the Zohar, when the next stage of emanation is described as a silkworm wrapping itself in its covers. The author may have hinted at an egg in the words *purity* or *spark*. *Purity* is related to whiteness—an adequate name for an egg—and in Arabic the words egg and white are indeed derived from the same root (though it is to be assumed that white derives from egg rather than the opposite).

As for *spark*, in Aramaic this word means both "candle" and "eggplant," and the association between this vegetable and eggs appears in many languages. Moreover, the sound of the word *buzina* [spark] slightly resembles the Hebrew word *beiza* [egg], the more so if we note that the Zohar frequently substitutes *buzina* for *buziza*, and this word indeed carries several connotations in the Zohar. I have devoted a lengthy and detailed study to its various forms and combinations, particularly to the phrase *botzina de-kadrinuta* [a spark of blackness] in the previous passage,[62] and these comments are meant to add a further dimension. These ambiguities of meaning are typical of the Zohar and the word *botsina* [spark] illustrates this well, even without the suggested association to the egg. If the "spark of blackness" in this passage does not refer to the entity being split but stands rather for the splitting agent, then it should be interpreted— as indeed it was—as a light of some sort, according to the usual meaning of the word, *spark*. This interpretation preserves the parallel with the Orphic myth of Phanes—a light shining forth from the egg.

In this passage, the Zohar describes a chick hatching from its egg and also reveals their origin. The egg is called *air*, just like the Orphic egg, and the point-chick not only emerges from it but also lights and shines, just like Phanes! As for the ommission of the word *egg*, this is also the case in classic Orphic texts; as I pointed out earlier, the explicit mention of the egg is also omitted in Malalas' description, who wrote only "the light split the air" [*to ptos rhexon ton Aithera*].

G. Scholem[63] has already shown that there are parallel versions of this Zoharic passage in the writings of the *Iyyun* circle. For instance, this is how the *midrash* of Simeon the Just portrays the emanation of *hokhma* from *keter*: "Before any creature was created, the first air was alone. . . the power of the Holy One, blessed be He, was concealed inside Him and was not noted until the air was penetrated, his splendor was seen and his glory revealed." Scholem claimed that the Zohar's author was influenced by writings from the *Iyyun* circle, but this assumption is unnecessary and it seems that the status of the Zohar is equal to that of the writings of the *Iyyun* circle (Scholem had also noted the book *Ma'ayan Ha-Hokhma* [Source of Wisdom] and another work). All knew of the egg myth tradition, but the mythical element became even more blurred in the writings of the *Iyyun* circle. In the latter's writings, its only remnant is the splitting of the air and the appearance of light, while in the Zohar the description includes the penetration and the bursting of the point within the supernal purity. However, even the expression "the air was penetrated and his splendor was seen" in the preceding passage, is totally implausible without the notion of the Orphic egg.

Moreover, Scholem claimed that both the *Iyyun* circle and the Zohar took this notion from a celebrated line in Ibn Gabirol's poem *Keter Malkhut* [The Royal Crown]: "And He called unto nothingness and it was split, and unto being and it was urged, and to the universe and it was spread out." This line calls forth clear parallels with kabbalistic symbolism, since *nothingness* [*ayn*] , like *air*, is a symbol of the *sefira* of *keter*, whereas *being* [*yesh*] is *hokhmah* and is also the point. This claim seems plausible, but it is not necessary to assume that sources are mutually exclusive and especially in the Zohar, which tends to integrate many and varied motifs. Moreover, neither the contents nor the source of Ibn Gabirol's line is sufficiently clear; S. Pines has recently argued that Ibn Gabirol relied on Avicenna's exegesis of a Koranic *sura*, an interesting claim though not without vulnerable points on both counts.[64] We should also consider the possibility that this Orphic myth was known to all—to Gabirol, to the *Iyyun* circle writers, and to the the author of the Zohar. After all, it is not implausible that a neo-Platonic philosopher like Gabirol had access to sources preserved mainly in neo-Platonic texts, the more so as he was apparently versed in other ancient writings (see later, note 74). True, Gabirol spoke of splitting the *ayin* rather than the air, but this could be seen as a simplification of the myth, in line with a course adopted by other neo-Platonists before him regarding the Orphic and other myths. *Iyyun* circle kabbalists had indeed identified the *ayin* with the split air, and this could also have been Gabirol's view: His split *ayin* is a kind of air and, as was the case for other kabbalists, denotes plenitude rather than emptiness.[65] This parallel between air and *ayin* is already found in the *Sefer Yetsira* and Ibn Gabirol, who relied on the *Sefer Yetsira* widely, must have found inspiration for his own metaphor in the following source in *Sefer Yetsira* 2:6: "Turned nothingness into being and hewed great columns from ungraspable air."[66] Only a few lines before, Gabirol had compared the being splitting the *ayin* to light: "To draw up the films of being from nothingness as light is drawn that darteth from the eye"; in another one of Gabirol's poems ("Who is like Thee, that cleft the Heavens") a darting spark is specifically mentioned: "Cleft the Heavens, set the lands, darted a spark." On this basis, it seems reasonable to assume that the Orphic myth of the egg was the background of Gabirol's split *ayin*, and the poet-philosopher proceeded to demythologize the story. One could also suggest—though indeed reticently—a far-fetched hypothesis, arguing that the word *ayin* contains a remote allusion to the Orphic egg, as *oion* means egg in Greek (though this would require us to assume that the Greek word appears untranslated in the Arabic versions of neo-Platonic writings used by Ibn Gabirol). It must be pointed out that Gabirol's use of the word *ayn* is not obvious; this is apparently the first time in which this word occurs as a noun and even has a definite article attached to it (had this linguistic option been open to the author of the *Sefer Yetsira*, he would most certainly not have written "turned what is not into being").[67] (On this passage, see my article "Rabbi Solomon Ibn Gabirol's Use of the *Sefer Yetsira* and a Commentary on the Poem 'I Love Thee' ").[68]

Another motif in this passage from the Zohar is clearly parallel to the Orphic egg myth. We learned that in the supernal purity there is no color at all—no white, no black, no red, no yellow—but rather an emerging spark that colors the supernal world. A similar notion recurs in an Orphic text, also in relation to the egg. This passage is included in the *Pseudo-Clementines*,[69] which tells us the following about the cosmic egg: This egg contained the plenitude of life and could bestow its many elements and colors, though itself it is not more than one entity and one color. As the egg of the peacock seems to be one color but potentially contains all the colours of the peacock that will hatch from it, so this egg.[70]

This passage, as well as the whole work from the *Pseudo-Clementines* containing it, was known to the Jews of Alexandria, where it was originally composed. It has recently been confirmed[71] that this is in fact a Jewish work written in response to an anti-Semitic attack by Apion—famous for the book Josephus wrote against him, which includes several Jewish elements and quotes the Orphic myth in Apion's name.

The notion of the cosmic egg appears not only in Orphic texts but is also widespread in Alexandrian Gnostic circles—both Jewish and Christian—where the peacock parable is found in the writings of the second century Alexandrian Gnostic Basilides.[72] It is noteworthy that Basilides relies on many notions replicated in the Lurianic doctrine on the origins of emanation, such as *tsimtsum* (withdrawal) and the breaking of the vessels. Moreover, both Basilides and Luria cited the detailed parable of the *reshimu* (vestige) left on the broken vessels, resembling the residue of fragrant oil left in the bowl that had contained it. G. Scholem had already pointed to these parallels[73] that, beside the egg myth, could lend further support to my thesis about the Jewish-Alexandrian origins of the kabbalistic myth.

There are traces of a basic mythical platform shared by several Gnostic texts of early Christianity and contemporary Orphic writings—particularly from Egypt—that eventually reapppear in the Kabbala. Thus, the Lurianic myth—of the vessels breaking because they failed to contain the divine light—is paralleled in Augustinus's *Confessiones* I:3, which deals with divine facets that later Jewish mysticism called "circles the whole world," "suffers the whole world," and "fills the whole world." Augustinus wondered (probably after Solomon's prayer, Kings I, 8:27) whether heaven and earth can contain God, who fills them, or any residue will be left after the vessels are filled and what will be done with it. He immediately retracted his question, stating that it is not the vessels (*vasa*) containing Him that stabilize God but rather God who stabilizes them by filling them, and He would not spill out even if the vessels were to break (in the original, *Non enim vasa quae te plena sunt, stabilem te faciunt, quia etsi frangantur non effunderis*). Rather than as a myth, the breaking of the vessels appears here as a rejected hypothetical option, but it is possible that Augustinus knew of a Gnostic myth whose echoes resound here. As we know, Augustinus was interested in Gnosis and was a Manichean for part of his life, as he tells us in this autobiographical book. In the *Confessiones*, Augustinus became involved in a lengthy controversy with Gnosis, and this passage, where a latent Gnostic myth is cited as a hypothesis to be rejected outright, might be part of this polemic. Indeed, the myth of breaking the vessels is also found in the Gnostic work *Evangelium Veritatis*.[74] A description of the world as a vessel being filled by its father and mother (God and wisdom) appears in Philo,[75] as well as the notion that God bestowed His goodness upon the world only sparingly, so as to prevent its destruction.[76]

A further quote from the *Ra'aya Meheimana* (Zohar II:42b), describing the breaking of the vessels as an hypothetical option, is worth mentioning in this context: "And if the artisan were to break the vessels that he had prepared, the waters would return to the source, and there would be left broken vessels, dry and waterless. Thus the Cause of causes makes ten *sefirot*. . ." This description—identical to Augustinus's although drawing slightly different conclusions—served Luria as a source when he formulated his doctrine on the breaking of the vessels,[77] as R. Abraham Galante mentioned, although he refrained from mentioning Luria's name, which he apparently considered to be esoteric.[78] Kabbalists could have drawn this simile of the broken vessels as a metaphor for destroyed ancient worlds from Genesis Rabba 12:15:

> This may be compared to a king who had some thin glasses. Said the king: "If I pour hot water into them, they will burst; if cold, they will contract [and snap]." What then did the king do? He mixed hot and cold water and poured it into them, and so they remained [unbroken]. Thus said the Holy One, blessed be He: "If I create the world only with the attribute of mercy, its sins

will be great; only with the attribute of justice, the world cannot exist. Hence I will create it with the attribute of justice and with the attribute of mercy and may it stand."

It should be noted that, according to the Zohar, these worlds had been destroyed because of their failure to balance between justice and mercy, male and female.

In the Orphic passage quoted earlier from the *Pseudo-Clementines*, there is a parallel to the Lurianic myth of the breaking of the vessels in which the broken fragments are used to create the *kelippoth*, the world of evil. The Orphic myth goes on to describe the fate of the broken egg. Its various parts served to create the cosmic elements, and the lower and heavier ones (the eggshell?) to create Hades. Moreover, it is worth noting that the notion of evil as made up of fragments from destroyed worlds is not a completely original Lurianic concept but is already intimated in the Zohar (II:34b).

Basilides's notion of *tsimtsum* and the origins of emanation are not the only Gnostic simile to Lurianic Kabbala. Scholem also cited a very interesting parallel in the *Book of the Great Logos*, a work of Gnostic literature preserved through Coptic translation (in Egypt!) indicating that, prior to emanation, God moved "from Himself into Himself" (or "withdrew from Himself into Himself"). As we know,[79] Kabbala uses this formula in the same sense (in Cordovero's writings and in R. Shabtai Sheftel Horowitz's version of *Lurianic Kabbala*). Even more surprising, this very parallel is also found in the Orphic passage in the *Pseudo-Clementines* from which we quoted the reference to the peacock's cosmic egg. According to a summary of this passage, our world was created thus:

> The primeval material, made up of four elements and permeated with the life-force, was as a flowing, endless abyss, accidentally rising and creating infinite combinations incapable of begetting a living creature. And it once happened that this endless sea, from its own nature, deliberately flowed from itself into itself [*ap tou auton eis to auto* in the original] as a whirlwind, and mixed the entities so that each one's fertile part flowed onto the center.

The egg crystallized at this center and all the worlds came from it.

It is not only the expression "from itself onto itself" that is familiar to us from kabbalistic writings, but the picture as a whole. Luria held a similar view on the question of the origins of reality. An internal movement of the sealike infinite, from itself unto itself, resulted in those parts fit for creating worlds grouping onto the center, the only place suitable for Creation or, in kabbalistic parlance, ingathering the sources of evil as in the "kingdom" at the center of the Ein-Sof.[80] This movement and this concentration later resulted in the tsimtsum at a center point, within whose space all worlds have emanated. This doctrine was rejected by Hayyim Vital, Luria's chief disciple, who did not wish to reveal anything about the entities within the Ein-Sof or picture events in the higher world as mechanical acts and thus described tsimtsum as a voluntary act of God. But the alternative version has been preserved in less veiled fashion in the writings of other disciples of Luria, mainly R. Yosef Ibn Tabbul.[81] Indeed, Vital did not delete the description of the tsimtsum occurring at the center of the Ein-Sof, a meaningless statement were it not for Vital's knowledge of other facets within the realm of the Ein-Sof.[82] It thus seems that, when describing the first ontological stages, Lurianic Kabbala preserved an ancient myth partly shared by both Alexandrian Jews from the Hellenistic period and Orphic faithful. This Orphic description also has deep roots in Greek and Oriental myths and in pre-Socratic philosophical thought.

Let us now return to the hatchling from the cosmic egg, the god Phanes-Erikapaios. All Orphic sources and their Phoenician parallel versions unanimously agree on its gender. Erikapaios is per force androgynous, since it alone is to beget all the gods and carries their seed.[83] Similarly, the Zohar says the following about Attika Kaddisha and about Ze'eir Anpin:

When Attika Kaddisha, the mystery of all mysteries, sought to prepare itself, it prepared everything in the form of male and female. Once male and female had been included, they existed in no other way except as male and female. This Hokhma, which includes everything, when it emerged from, and was illuminated by, Attika Kaddishah, was illuminated in no other way except as male and female; for this Hokhma extended itself and brought forth Binah from itself, and so there existed male and female. Hokhma father, Bina mother. (Zohar III, 290a, Idra Zutta)

As is clarified in the preceding pages (Zohar III:288–289), Hokhma, which includes male and female, is simply the third head of Attika Kaddisha (we discussed these heads earlier), and it is called Attika Kaddisha in the phrase "when it emerged from, and was illuminated by, Attika Kaddisha, was illuminated in no other way except as male and female." From this third head, called Hokhma, emerge concrete, separate male and female entities, unlike the "seemingly male and female" jointly included in *Attika Kaddisha*. The real male and female are the *sefirot* of *Hokhma* and *Bina*—the beginning of *ze'eir anpin*—and they are the very heads of *Hokhma* in *Atika* after it developed. This duality of *Hokhma* appears in several places in the Zohar, such as I:15a, next to the passage discussed earlier about the Orphic egg.

Phanes-Erikapaios begot gods, people, and a whole cosmos. However, as all Orphic descriptions tell us,[84] this world did not last. All of it, including its begetter Erikapaios, was swallowed up by Zeus. Only after staying inside Zeus and acquiring a new shape could the children of this ancient world be reborn—including the famous Titans—created by Zeus, whose creative power accrued to him from the flesh of Erikapaios inside him.[85] A parallel myth dealing with the early and flawed creation of *Attika Kaddisha-arikh anpin*, appears several times in the *Idrot*, such as III:135a, *Idra Rabba*:

> Before *Attika de-Attikin* prepared His attributes, He constructed kings, inscribed kings and conjectured kings, but they could not survive, so that after a time he concealed them. This is [the meaning of] the verse "And these are the kings that reigned in the land of Edom" (Genesis 36:31). "In the land of Edom"—in the place where all the judgments exist. None [of the kings] could survive until the white head, *Attika de-Attikin* was prepared, When He was prepared, He prepared all the attributes below; He prepared all the attributes of the upper and lower worlds. Hence we learn that unless the leader of the people is prepared first, his people are not prepared; but if he is prepared, all are prepared; and if he is not prepared first, the people cannot be prepared.

Discussing the myth of "the death of the kings" far exceeds the scope of this essay. It has been widely analyzed and I myself have written on it at length, dealing with its ontological, historical and religious implications, as well as with its sources.[86] The various sources to which I direct the readers of that work—such as rabbinic statements on the Holy One, blessed be He, who creates and destroys worlds or who had attempted to create His world according to the measure of justice and then included the measure of mercy—cannot explain the presence of a myth as surprising and daring as this one. These rabbinic statements lack the dualistic and prominently mythical-theogonic element that figures highly in the Zohar (although they still merit the title of myth); they do not deal with kings and fail to mention the new creation out of the rubble of the old one. All these elements appear in the Orphic myth. Phanes-Erikapaios is like *Attika-arikh anpin*, and the gods and Titans born from him and swallowed with him resemble the kings of Edom who died because of the flaws of their creator—*Attika-arikh anpin*. The Titans' rebellious and warlike character parallels the rule of the Edomite kings. (There is hardly any difference between *Attika* and Edom, and there are kabbalists who indeed claimed they are one and the same.[87] On the other hand, after his *tikkun*, *Attika* is always described as symbolizing absolute mercy, unalloyed by justice. In this respect, his realm is similar to that of the Golden Age, characterizing many accounts of early creation in the Greek and Orphic myths. It is worth noting here that gold in the Zohar symbolizes the attribute of justice.)

Zeus, who had himself engendered the second creation, parallels *ze'er anpin*, the human figure in which kings had been constructed, inscribed, and conjectured, as the Zohar explains further in the same passage (III:135a,b). As Zeus is king over the Greek gods, thus the Zohar refers to *ze'er anpin* by the holy names of the Jewish religion, among them the Tetragramation (III:138a). Moreover, after Zeus created his world on the ruins of the previous one, Orphic writings refer to him as "beginning, middle, and end," and scholars have established that this is the source for similar expressions found in Judeo-Christian tradition.[88] However, I would favor a more moderate version of this claim and argue that the similar formulas found in the New Testament and in rabbinic literature reflect an Orphic variation of an ancient Jewish tradition already found in Deutero-Isaiah (41:4; 44:6' 48:12). It still remains very significant that this expression, as found in the Zohar, appears in the same context as in the Orphic myth. In a passage parallel to the preceding one, at the beginning of the *Idra Rabba* III:128a, a further detail is added—when the *Attika Kaddisha* was carving the kings that failed to survive, there was neither a beginning nor an end, implying that the opposite was the case in regard to the second creation of *ze'er anpin*.

True, the myth is slightly attenuated in the Zohar and suited to monotheistic purposes or, at least, to the harmony prevailing in the divine realm according to Jewish religion. Obviously, *Attika Kaddisha* neither died with his kings nor is he, Heaven forbid, swallowed by *ze'er anpin*; on the contrary, the process of *tikkun* in *ze'er anpin* begins and depends on the *tikkun* of *Attika*. However, in the Zohar as well, *Attika's* flaw parallels the kings' adversity, a point stressed in the Zohar through the political parable claiming that the disgrace of a people is contingent on the disgrace of their king. Even the story of Zeus swallowing Erikapaios might appear to be softened in the Zohar. *Ze'er anpin* attains *tikkun* only through *Attika Kaddisha*-

arikh anpin, who aids him to act and create in this world, just as Zeus' power to create and engender gods comes from the swallowed flesh of Erikapaios in his limbs. Indeed, *ze'er anpin* does not swallow the flesh of *arikh anpin*, but three brains burst from the face of *arikh*, fill the head and the body of *ze'er*, and sustain him, especially the third brain, the brain of *da'at*, which is the source of his procreative powers.[89] The sources for this notion are also found in an Orphic myth. Phanes Erikapaios is also called Metis, meaning counsel or wisdom. Metis, in Orphic and in Greek mythology in general, was swallowed by Zeus and dwelt in his head; her daughter, the goddess Athena, was thus born from Zeus' head and is also called *synesis* (wisdom) in Orphic writings. It is also said that it was precisely this intellectual element that enabled Zeus' creation.[90]

This comparison with the Orphic myth may deepen our understanding of "the death of the kings." According to the Zohar, the Edomean kings were punished with death because they were guilty of celibacy. This is a matter requiring serious consideration, and I have dealt with it before.[91] The Zohar deals with this matter elsewhere, after the statement claiming the flaws of the people are contingent on the flaws of their leader (III:135a–b). We could thus infer that this was also the flaw of *arikh anpin* (and it is not at all surprising that the Zohar does not say so explicitly). This could perhaps be related to the fact that *arikh anpin*, like Erikapaios, was androgynous, providing us with a possible interpretation of the Orphic myth—why did Zeus' creation and progeny prevail, unlike that of Erikapaios? Because Zeus begat his progeny with a female separate from him. This explanation indeed appears in several Gnostic doctrines resembling Orphism on various counts, claiming that the flaw of this creation is its unisexual source.[92] I found a parallel in *Tikkunei Zohar*, wherein the sinful man, the *Adam de-Beri'a* (man of creation)—also called *foolish son* [*Ben Kesil*]; *Sakala* is one of the common names of the parallel monster in Gnosis—was created only by the mother and without the father's aid, a notion which I believe clearly reflects Gnostic influences.[93] Indeed, Gnostic literature contains parallels to the passage on "the death of the kings" that also deal with the question of celibacy, and I have already pointed to one.[94] This myth was also shared, *mutatis mutandis*, by other Gnostic-Jewish trends and by Orphism and could have reached the Zohar from several directions; thus, in this case as well, we cannot be exactly sure of its author's sources and of the course of its development.

Finally, I will try to point to several allusions to *arikh anpin* myth in Jewish texts preceding the Zohar. " 'And Moses made haste, and bowed his head toward the earth, and worshipped' (Exodus 37:8)

What did Moses see? R. Hanina b. Gamla said: He saw *long suffering* [*erekh appayim*] The Rabbis say: He saw truth." (Sanhedrin 111a). *Arikh anpin* and truth appear as two divine hypostases, fitting the Zohar's *arikh anpin* and *ze'er anpin* exactly.[95] The figure of the angel Anafiel, known from the *Hekhalot* literature, also hints to *arikh anpin*. Neither the source nor the name of this angel are at all clear; he is described as superior to all other angels, even to Metatron Sar Hapanim, and at times compared to the *Yotser Bereshit* or *Yotser Olam*, and J. Dan has already indicated its similarities with the Gnostic Demiurge.[96] This description, and even the name of the angel, corresponds to the demiurgical role of *arikh anpin*-Erikapaios that we discussed earlier (though here he has been demoted to angel rank). In the literature of the *Iyyun* circle, the figure of Anafiel is even closer to that of the Zohar's *arikh anpin*, where he is described as a head above all limbs,[97] as he is in the Zohar (III:289b, *Idra Zuta*): "This *Attika Kaddisha*, the secret of secrets, because it is the supreme head of the upper worlds, is referred to only as a single head without a body."

Picco della Mirandola offered the first suggestion of a link between Orphism and Kabbala, 400 years before Robert Eisler. Out of his renowned 900 theses, Picco devoted 31 to the collection of Orphic hymns (though he was not concerned with the theogonies that were the subject of this study) and in most of them the hymns are interpreted through a kabbalistic perspective. Many of Picco's interpretations have remained enigmatic, and it is hard to recommend his interpretive approach, even when clear.[98] However, even today, scholars might be attracted by one element of his Renaissance spirit—his understanding that ancestral religion and the human spirit are strange and wonderful, and those searching for their mysteries will not be content with treading the "royal road" of inner tradition that, as it goes on, becomes straighter and narrower. Depth and variety accrue to the Jewish religion from places where the Torah was exiled, and we might learn about the wisdom of Kabbala even from Orpheus.

APPENDIX

After the original article went to press, S. Pines directed my attention to a paper by Nicole Zeegers and Vander Vorst, "Les Version Juives et Chretienes du fr. 245–247 d'Orphee," *L'antiquite classique* 39 (1970): 475–506. This article deals with Orphic fragments 245–247 in Kern's collection (see note 23), which include an Orphic text attributed to the second century B.C. Alexandrian Jewish philosopher Aristobolus from Phaneas. This Orphic work indeed includes many Jewish elements—among them allusions to Abraham and Moses, to the two tablets of the law, and to the ten commandments—confirming my claim regarding Jewish elements that entered Alexandrian Orphism in the second century B.C. However, the authors demonstrate that neither Jewish nor Christian elements appear in the original version of the text and that these were added later by Jewish and Christian writers. This attests to a certain linkage between Orphism and Judaism in antiquity (in the first centuries of the Christian era), even if, in light of our present argument, we could have assumed that certain Jewish elements could have been found in the Orphic texts' original version and the forgers found something to rely on.

This text is also discussed in Y. Gutman, *The Beginning of Jewish-Hellenistic Literature* [Hebrew] (Jerusalem, 1969), part I, pp. 148–170. In the chapter "Orphism: The Jewish-Orphic Poem," Gutman published a translation of two versions of the poem, discussed them at length, and preceded them with an introduction on Orphism and its Alexandrian branch. He also cited, although to reject it, Eisler's conjecture on Erikapaios. Gutman dealt only with adaptations of Orphic poetry for Jewish purposes, but also indicated that "Orphic doctrines were capable of integrating seemingly alien trends." After Gutman alluded to the closeness between these two religions, the reader should find it easier to accept the notion of influence in the opposite direction, which was the subject of this essay.

3

Sabbatean Messianism

Introduction

Sabbateanism is used by modern Israeli publicists as a derogatory name for religious groups seeking immediate political redemption. In the past, anti-Zionist religious groups also used this term to describe the Zionist movement,[1] and there were indeed some Zionists who, wishing to see Sabbateanism as a forerunner of their own movement, found this affinity congenial.[2] It is not by chance that the study of Sabbateanism was extensively developed by Zionist scholars, mainly Gershom Scholem; it is noteworthy that two of Israel's past presidents, Izhak Ben-Zvi and Zalman Shazar, are among the important scholars of Sabbateanism. They were preceded by Nahum Sokolow, who had served as president of the World Zionist Organization.[3]

The Sabbatean movement is thus considered a symbol of the yearning for political redemption. We will see later that this is not at all the picture emerging from the historical sources. Why then has this image clung to the Sabbatean movement? The answer is very simple. Given that Sabbateanism was a classic messianic movement, its political character was generally assumed. What is Jewish messianism, after all, if not the hope for political redemption? Sabbateanism seemed an adequate pejorative in the eyes of those opposed to movements aspiring for political redemption, because it was the largest, most important, and most sweeping messianic movement that arose in Jewish history. Moreover, a shameful failure is attached to it: Instead of bringing about redemption, the Messiah converted and so did many of his believers.

This image of Sabbateanism, which assumes that Jewish messianism has an exclusively earthly character, was widespread among scholars in later generations. The roots of this assumption about Jewish messianism apparently lie with certain circles in the Catholic Church, which accused millenarians of reflecting Jewish influence. This view of Jewish messianism later spread among Jewish scholars and was greatly strengthened under Zionist influence. Let

us take, for instance, Gershom Scholem's statement in the opening
paragraph of "Toward an Understanding of the Messianic Idea in
Judaism," where he adopts the contrast suggested by Christians
between their own messianism and that of the Jews, characterizing
Jewish messianism as follows:

> Judaism, in all its forms and manifestations, has always
> maintained a concept of redemption as an event which takes
> place publicly, on the stage of history and within the community.
> It is an occurrence which takes place in the visible world and
> which cannot be conceived apart from such a visible appearance.
> In contrast, Christianity conceives of redemption as an event in
> the spiritual and unseen realm, an event which is reflected in
> the soul, in the private world of each individual, and which
> effects an inner transformation which need not correspond to
> anything outside.[4]

Zionist historians of the messianic idea in Israel, such as Joseph
Klausner, Ben-Zion Dinur, Judah Even-Shemuel, Abba Hillel Silver
and Aaron Zeev Aescoly, rely on a similar notion, which has been
undermined only recently, as new studies have begun to shed light
on other forms of Jewish messianism that have lived alongside the
historical-political one. These studies do not attest to a parallel erosion
in the Zionist commitment of the new historians but rather to their
view that Zionism no longer needs to be defended or to be backed by
claims of ancestry. This allows them to delve into the sources without
ideological interference. An example of this new approach to Jewish
messianism appears in Moshe Idel's introduction to a new edition of
A. Z. Aescoly's book *Messianic Movements in Israel* and elsewhere.[5]
The time has thus come for a reevaluation of Sabbatean messianism.
Such a reevaluation may shed new light on our understanding of
Jewish messianism in general and on that of Hasidic messianism that,
as is well known, has been hotly contended in scholarly circles. New
concepts may allow for progress in this complex issue, particularly
given the increasing knowledge about the influence of Sabbateanism
on Hasidism.[6]

I. The Place of the Earthly Element
in Sabbatean Messianism

For many years, I have been dealing with original Sabbatean works,
where the writers have revealed their intimate hopes. It is becoming

clear that this vast body of literature, in all its thousands of pages, is one where the ideal of political and national redemption is hardly ever mentioned. The main concern of Sabbateanism has to be defined differently. I am not claiming that the earthly element is altogether absent in Sabbateanism, but rather that its place needs to be defined precisely and, for this purpose, two distinctions are necessary. The first relates to the separation between two periods, the initial one extending from the outbreak of the movement in May 1665 until Sabbetai Zevi's conversion to Islam in September 1666. In this period, Sabbateanism was not yet a special sect and almost all the Jews believed then that the Messiah had indeed come. The second period, extending from the conversion until the actual demise of Sabbateanism some 150 years later, is the sectarian stage of the movement.[7] A further distinction is needed between two groups: the ideological "hard core" of the movement as opposed to peripheral circles; the latter were either influenced only indirectly or did not accept the movement's separate ideology and saw in it simply the realization of traditional messianic longings. During the first period, Sabbetai Zevi's inner circle, which remained loyal to him after the conversion, belongs in the first group, whereas the peripheral circles contained the masses of Jews who "failed" in this test.

It is only for the latter that Sabbateanism was predominantly a belief in earthly and political redemption, and only they lent an ear to rumors such as the one about the army of the Ten Tribes conquering the city of Mecca. They were also those who, swept by messianic tidings, sold their property cheaply and waited for the Redeemer to bring them to the land of Israel.[8] It is therefore not surprising that when rumors about Sabbetai Zevi's conversion became public, most of them despaired of their Sabbatean faith. The rest of them abandoned the movement ten years later, after Sabbetai Zevi's death, since a political belief in the victory of the people of Israel and its religion cannot be pinned on a converted, dead Messiah. Though they were indeed the majority, it is doubtful whether they can be called Sabbateans. These were ordinary Jews upholding conventional beliefs about the coming of the Messiah; they felt the time for his arrival had come until reality proved the contrary, and their messianic beliefs had not been formed by Sabbetai Zevi, his prophet, or his other propagandists.

As for Sabbetai Zevi and his committed followers, during the first stage, elements of political redemption are also found among them. Sabbetai Zevi even had a practical plan of action that was outlined in a letter from the movement's early days written by Nathan of Gaza, perhaps the movement's first theorist, to R. Raphael Joseph, the leader of Egyptian Jewry.[9] According to this plan, Sabbetai Zevi would persuasively address the Turkish sultan, would remove the latter's crown, place it on his own head and, from then on, the sultan would be Sabbetai Zevi's slave and fulfill his wishes. Sabbetai Zevi was to use the sultan's army to fight the Gentiles (the Christians of Europe, responsible for the 1648–49 massacres), to gather in the exiles and redeem Israel. This plan (which slightly resembles Herzl's notion of "The Charter") was not as impractical as it may sound. Sabbetai Zevi's charming and charismatic personality truly impressed the sultan at their first meeting when, contrary to all predictions, the sultan did not have him killed but honored him with money, distinction, and a position. Indeed, the redemption of Israel was not part of these honors and, as is well known, the meeting with the sultan ended with Sabbetai Zevi's conversion to Islam. This project seems to have failed even before it began because a bout of depression apparently overcame Sabbetai Zevi before the meeting. As the story is told, when going to meet the sultan Sabbetai Zevi was afraid to wear a green belt, the Muslim color of distinction forbidden to Jews. His listeners were filled with despair when they understood their hopes had been dashed— only yesterday he had thought of removing the crown from the sultan's head and today he is afraid of wearing a green belt.[10] Possibly, if Sabbetai Zevi had attached greater importance to this plan, he would not have recoiled from the attempt to implement it. On the other hand, Nathan of Gaza did not relinquish this plan even after the conversion; when he was at Ancona a year later, on his way to Rome on a mystical mission on behalf of Sabbetai Zevi, he repeated it to his host, R. Mahallelel Halleluya, when the latter begged him to "comfort us with some consolation about our redemption." This time Nathan claimed that Sabbetai Zevi, by now one of the sultan's slaves, would charm the sultan with his singing (Sabbetai Zevi was very musical and had a pleasant voice) and thus accomplish his aim,[11] in a feat resembling the sirens's story in the Odyssey.

However, this plan seems to epitomize Sabbatean political thought. The Sabbateans' religious imagination almost never touches upon the earthly realm. Scholem in fact believed that Nathan of Gaza was the author of the apocalypse appended to *Zerubabel* describing the stages of redemption, but this appendix seems to have been written before Sabbateanism.[12] From the end of the seventeenth century onward we do find certain groups of kabbalists, who had shared in Sabbatean thinking, emigrating to the Holy Land. Among them are R. Jehudah the Hasid (1700), R. Abraham Rovigo (1702), R. Emanuel Hai Ricci (his last stay in the land was in 1738–1741), R. Hayyim ben Atar (1741), R. Moshe Hayyim Luzzato (1743), and their followers, but their numbers are negligible relative to a messianic movement as important as Sabbateanism. Moreover, we do not know the exact motive for these migrations, which should perhaps be sought in the climate of expectancy and in the mystical virtues of the land as they are exalted, for instance, in *Tuv Ha-Arets*. This book was published before the outbreak of Sabbateanism and comprises mainly kabbalistic propaganda about the land of Israel and the virtues of dwelling there, without a strong messianic emphasis.[13] It is against this background that we find the early Hassidic migrations immediately following this period. R. Hayyim ben Atar's move was perhaps linked to the renewal of Jewish settlement in Tiberias by R. Hayyim Abulafia, whose ideological background is as yet unclear; as for R. Abraham Rovigo, it will be noted that his teacher R. Moses Zacuto prepared himself to go although, by that time, he was no longer a Sabbatean.[14] Even those migrations motivated by definite Sabbatean causes were not necessarily related to political redemption. There is evidence of Sabbatean migrations being linked to the revelation of the mystery of Sabbetai Zevi's divinity, which could only be disclosed in the Holy Land, or to the reincarnation of Sabbetai Zevi himself. The reincarnation could occur only in the Holy Land, possibly because the land of Israel is also the best place to abrogate the *Torah di-Vri'a*, namely, the commandments.[15]

Even if the motivation of certain Sabbatean migrations were political messianism, we may ask whether it is appropriate to define Sabbatean messianism in their light. The vehemence of the controversy among Jewish scholars, which has in the past attended the study of Sabbateanism, has at times blurred balanced theoretical distinctions. Portraying somebody as believing Sabbetai Zevi is the Messiah does not necessarily exhaust the description of that individual's spiritual world. There had been yearnings for immediate redemption before the emergence of Sabbateanism and they certainly persisted after it, having even been strengthened in its wake. The general messianic outbreak in 1666 had raised the hopes and expectations of those urgently awaiting redemption. Nor is it surprising that some of them identified Sabbetai Zevi with the expected Messiah, yet these elements do not suffice to define Sabbateanism as either a sect or a spiritual movement. The sources reveal a large number of possible names for the expected Messiah and the main Sabbatean innovation is not in the addition of the name *Sabbetai*. Sabbateanism could influence the hopes for redemption in many different ways, among them also the desire to go to the Holy Land, but this is not its main feature. Against this background, it is noteworthy that, of all people, Jacob Emden, Sabbateanism's prominent opponent, expressed hopes to go to the Holy Land. Without the appropriate distinctions, it would have been possible to claim that Emden's intention too had a "Sabbatean background," because he had shaped his messianic approach according to the Sabbatean model, which he had meant to oppose and had even considered the messianic awakening of 1666 as a chance for divine goodwill which had been missed.[16] On the other hand, his adversary, the Sabbatean R. Jonathan Eybeschuetz, seems to have stated that even in messianic times the Jews should not go to their land but should find "pleasure and clemency" in the eyes of the peoples among whom they dwell.[17]

Eybeschuetz is not alone among the theoreticians of Sabbateanism in maintaining this belief. As Gershom Scholem has shown, Jacob Frank shared in this "territorialist" approach that replaces the land of Israel with the countries of European Gentiles where Jews live;[18] however, unlike Scholem, I do not see this as Frank's innovation. As we shall see later, Frank's approach continues the trend of Sabbetai Zevi and the Doenmeh sect, and this is also the case here. Further evidence in support of this approach can be found in Nathan of Gaza's statement that "for now it is better not to go to the land of Israel";[19] the dispute between Cardozo and R. Jehuda the Hasid over the mystery of divinity may also reflect opposition to the migration of R. Jehuda and his followers.[20]

It should not be concluded that expectations of political redemption as well as the identification of the earthly redeemer with Sabbetai Zevi, all of which are connected to emigration to the Holy Land, necessarily contradict the wishes of Sabbatean ideologues. However, these elements are not derived from their new ideology, the only one meriting the title *Sabbatean*. It does not seem extravagant to demand that this ideology be learned precisely from Sabbetai Zevi, the movement's leader and its Messiah, from Nathan of Gaza, his prophet and the one who, together with him, shaped the movement, and from Miguel Abraham Cardozo, who ranked third after them, as well as from all their faithful followers. Under these circumstances, when the new learning is entangled with traditional faith and particularly when the new ideology, rather than explicitly posing a challenge to the messianic tradition pretends to realize it, we are certain to find in the periphery of the new movement documents that would interpret it in light of the ancient tradition. This is the appropriate background for approaching the apocalypse written in far away Yemen during the movement's early days,[21] *Gey Hizaion* [The Valley of the Vision], as well as the apocalyptic chapters by R. Mordechai Eisenstadt.[22] It should be noted that nothing in these two documents is reminiscent of the new kabbalistic Sabbatean approach developed by Sabbetai Zevi,

Nathan of Gaza, or Cardozo. Even the book *Hemdat Yamim* [The Beloved of Days] cannot provide a guide to the Sabbatean messianic essence, though it is a kabbalistic book suffused with messianic feeling and connected to the Sabbatean movement, including statements by Nathan of Gaza.[23] *Hemdat Yamim* adheres strongly to Lurianic Kabbala and consciously serves as an important channel for its dissemination, without any traces of Sabbatean Kabbala, the mystery of Sabbatean divinity, or the figure of the Sabbatean Messiah.

In the ideological Sabbatean movement, the messianism of its leaders is concerned with political redemption only in the context of religion and faith. In their eyes, earthly redemption was merely an additional touch or a conventional saying derived from the Scriptures or, at most and only for some, a side effect of the *Supreme Emendment*.[24] Until Sabbetai's conversion, they had indeed referred to it at times, influenced by the enthusiasm and hopes of the masses in which even many Christians, such as the English millenarians, had a share. However, the failure of the conversion and Sabbetai Zevi's death did not bring their faith to an end because, a priori, they had not put a prize on historical success. The conversion only provided a possibility for delving deeper into those aspects which truly interested them and, from then on, political redemption practically disappears from their writings. I believe that these writings support my interpretation more clearly than Scholem's. Scholem had claimed the movement continued its activity even after the conversion because the Sabbateans were so profoundly sure redemption had come that their spiritual transformation was stronger than external reality.[25]

What then are the true contents of Sabbatean messianism? Generally, it may be said that it is not concerned with the redemption of the people but rather with the redemption of religion and faith, the redemption of God, and the redemption of the Messiah. However, general definitions blur rather than clarify. Sabbateanism encompasses several currents of thought; each one is different, and each one follows its own development. I shall now examine these different currents and attempt to define their specific messianic approaches.

II. Sabbetai Zevi and His Followers

We shall start at the beginning, namely, with Sabbetai Zevi himself. His own awareness of himself as the Messiah had accompanied him from his childhood years until his death, at times replaced by hard misgivings and even by heresy and despair. What was the nature of his misgivings? At whom were they directed? The redemption of the

Jewish people is never mentioned in this context. Sabbetai Zevi's utmost concern was not the fate of the people but rather a spiritual realm the people could not reach, and he was profoundly alienated from the masses of his followers. Even Nathan of Gaza failed to understand him and was at times forced to take insult and abuse or to work strenuously to restore to the Messiah his faith in himself (it is indeed possible that Sabbetai Zevi's estrangement from public concerns and his immersion in the spiritual realm added to his messianic charm in the people's eyes). Sabbetai Zevi's messianism was directed upward, to his God, which is why he was always careful to refer to himself precisely as the *Messiah of the God of Jacob*, a title he did not approach as a metaphor.[26] Sabbetai had always had misgivings about the mystery of faith or the mystery of divinity, about the special God he alone had discovered and did not fully share with anybody and therefore also addressed as "the God of my faith" or "the God of Sabbetai Zevi." Sabbetai Zevi took pains to know and define this God, especially to himself, and thus redeem both of them: himself—by releasing from the *kelippot* (the world of evil) the full stature of his soul, the soul of the Messiah—and his God. In a formulation he must have heard from Sabbetai Zevi, Nathan of Gaza defined this endeavor as follows: "And our king, his majesty, took pains about this faith until he seated the King on his throne."[27] Similarly, Sabbetai Zevi himself wrote a letter to his brothers after his conversion: "My brothers, know. . .that the True One, which only I have known for many generations and for which I have toiled, wanted me to enter Islam with all my heart." This phrase reveals how devoid of nationalism is Sabbetai Zevi's concern for his God. (I deal only briefly with this question here; I have republished elsewhere a detailed version of the letter, where Sabbetai Zevi's views are analyzed at length).[28] In his eyes, the people and the religion are nothing but a means for the worship of "the true God" and, if this God's essence is not precisely known, then God is not true, religion is an empty shell and new frameworks must be sought. True, Sabbetai Zevi intimates in the letter that God and his Messiah forsake Judaism only "until the end of days", but this is still a far cry from a message of national redemption.

Together with Sabbetai Zevi and after him, many Jews converted to Islam and remained within it as a special Sabbatean sect, the Doenmeh. Several of this sect's theoretical writings have reached us,[29] as well as a prayerbook[30] and collections of poems and praises.[31] These include many praises to Sabbetai Zevi and other heroes of the movement (Nathan of Gaza and Cardozo) as well as hints of Sabbetai Zevi's kabbalistic *tikkunim*. They express hopes for Sabbetai Zevi's revelation, but there is no mention of either the redemption of the Jews or the return of the converts to the fold of the community. At times, it even seems that redemption is simply redemption from the Jewish religion and the Jewish frameworks, namely, the *Torah di-Vri'a*. It is noteworthy in this context that R. Israel Hazzan, who was in Nathan's circle and remained Jewish, already stated in a commentary to Psalms written shortly after Sabbetai Zevi's conversion that, even when Sabbetai Zevi's kingdom is revealed, "the believers" who "entered the trial" of conversion "will keep their fez!"[32]

The Frankists adopted a similar approach. In Jacob Frank's book *The Words of the Lord*, there are numerous allusions to the reform and disintegration of religion, descriptions of the Messiah's personality, and entreaties to enter "the Holy *Da'at* of Edom," which stands for the Catholic Church, without any hint at the possibility of leaving the Church or at the political redemption of the Jewish people. Frank should thus be seen as following in the path of Sabbetai Zevi and the Doenmeh sect. Though Frank differs from his predecessors in his personality and style of leadership, his approach to messianism is essentially the same. His conversion to Christianity is even supported by the Sabbatean ideology of Sabbetai Zevi's circle: R. Israel Hazzan alludes to two Messiahs in his mentioned commentary to Psalms, "one entering the religion of Ishmael and the other the religion of Esau,"[33] and so do the Frankists who remained Jewish. In those of their writings which have reached us,[34] great admiration is expressed for the reform and the spirituality of religion as revealed through Frank, the incarnated God,[35] without any intimations of yearnings for political redemption.

III. Nathan of Gaza and His Followers

We turn now to the figure ranking second in Sabbateanism, without whom the movement would not have existed—Nathan of Gaza, the prophet and ideologue. Nathan of Gaza was one of the most profound and original thinkers in Jewish history. He combined various degrees of mystical apprehension—including that of prophecy, as he understood it—with unswerving loyalty to Sabbetai Zevi's paradoxical personality (he believed in him more than Sabbetai Zevi believed in himself), as well as astonishing creative powers in several literary genres. His kabbalistic work reaches hundreds of pages, most of them unpublished and barely researched. Even in the work of this prophet of Sabbateanism, there is hardly any room for the idea of political redemption. This notion obviously appears in Nathan's first prophecy about

Sabbetai Zevi's messianism (even if only in very general terms),[36] as well as in several epistles of consolation that he sent to his followers in the movement's early days and in the first two years following the conversion. At times, these epistles also include apocalyptic visions, beside the political plan mentioned previously. However, though some of these letters reveal deep faith and a strong style, Nathan's foremost concerns were formulated in his voluminous books that, unlike the letters, were not motivated mainly by the wishes of the recipients or by the need to apologize for the conversion.

Nathan's original writings do not reveal him as mainly preoccupied with the messianic redemption of the people but rather with the figure of the Messiah and his God. Before the conversion, Nathan's description of the Messiah was more personal and also dealt with the Messiah's role and his historical manifestations, as in the apocalypse *Mar'e shel Avraham He-Hasid* [The Vision of R. Abraham] and also, to a certain extent, in the *Derush Ha-Tanninim* [Treatise on the Dragons]. However, after Sabbetai Zevi's conversion, the development of these elements took on a more theoretical direction. In his magnum opus *Sefer Ha-Beri'a* [The Book of Creation],[37] written in 1670, Nathan delved into the problems that truly concerned him: the mystery of divinity, its boundaries, the structure of the soul, the definition of faith, and above all, the psychological disposition of Sabbetai Zevi and of Nathan himself, as well as the relations between the two of them. Indeed, the personal background of this description is not explicit and will be captured only by the initiated. The book is devoted to the construction of a detailed kabbalistic system based on a psychological symbolism formulated in general terms, but I believe evidence can be brought to show that the symbolism is based on the figures of Sabbetai Zevi and of Nathan of Gaza. (Among other things, this evidence relies on the parallels between *Sefer Ha-Beri'a* and the epistle of apology for Sabbetai Zevi's conversion.[38] Only through the perspective of the *Sefer Ha-Beri'a* can the depth of thought behind the legalistic and apologetic argumentation of the epistle be fully appreciated.) In sum, I believe the principle of this book, one of the most complicated in kabbalistic literature, is that all worlds are built on two psychological elements: the first is the primeval element, free from thought and inessential factors, modeled on Sabbetai Zevi's personality. Nathan of Gaza represents the second element, which curbs this power with the bridle of thought and turns it from a destructive into a constructive force.

As was noted, political redemption is not part of this book nor of others Nathan wrote during this period. Its place is taken up by a paradoxical description of a cosmic war between good and evil, won by the good with the assistance of a primeval element resembling evil and rooted in it. According to this literature, souls are redeemed only though their paradoxical faith and their love of the good, despite the latter's resemblance to evil implying—in my understanding—that their love for Sabbetai Zevi after his conversion demonstrates that good is at the root of their souls.

For close to a century, Nathan's books were followed by an extensive body of kabbalistic-Sabbatean literature that does not discuss political redemption. This literature is defined as Sabbatean because traces of Nathan's Kabbala can be found in it rather than because of any messianic ideology. This is how I. Tishby, for instance, rightfully identified the kabbalist Jacob Koppel from Mezhirech as a Sabbetean,[39] although Koppel never alluded to redemption or to Sabbetai Zevi and, in a similar way, I recognized as a Sabbatean work the book *Tsaddik Yesod Olam*. *Tsaddik Yesod Olam* had been attributed to Luria[40] whereas I later found it had been written by the Sabbatean prophet R. Leibele Prossnitz.[41] Yael Nadav was also able to trace as Sabbatean the pamphlet by R. Solomon Ayllion, who is also part of this school.[42] After Nathan, Sabbatean writers were no longer able to draw direct inspiration from Sabbetai Zevi's personality, because they did not know him. Instead, they developed Nathan's theories in a very extreme mythical direction, sexual to the point of pornography. Sabbatean kabbalists of this variety discuss redemption from the reins of law and morality, though without adopting this approach in their everyday lives; the opposite is rather the case, as most of these writers were also prominent rabbis and halakhists. They awaited another redemption, their own "coming out of the closet" as it were, and the transformation of Sabbateanism into the official Jewish theology. The Messiah figures prominently in their writings, but not as a historical redeemer. I have discussed extensively and in great detail[43] the theory of the Messiah in some of these writings, such as the book *Va-Avo Ha-Yom el Ha-Ayin* [I Came This Day unto the Fountain]. I have shown that the Messiah, or the Messiahs (one of the writings, *Perush Sifra De-Tsni'uta*, speaks of three Messiahs: the messianic king or the son of David, the Messiah son of Ephraim and the Messiah son of Menashe) are kabbalistic entities in the supernal world, temporarily charged with the defense and protection of the divine Sabbatean entities. At the time of redemption, these Messiahs will be revealed and released from this task. When these Messiahs represent historical figures, their main role is in fact to conceal Sabbateanism and its God.

IV. Cardozo and His Followers

The third ranking figure in the Sabbatean movement is Abraham Miguel Cardozo. His ancestors were Marranos and he returned to Judaism for theological reasons. Throughout his life he sought a precise definition of religious faith and the God that is to be worshipped. He wrote over sixty treatises (*derushim* in his terminology) dealing with the characteristics of the Jewish God. Cardozo did not see the essence of redemption as political but as redeeming religion from its mistakes because, up to his days, all Jews had "worshipped idols in purity." What reason can there be for observing the commandments if the commander is unknown? The ignorance of God is the very definition of exile, and the messianic period is defined as the era of correct knowledge. Thus, in the future, only religion will be redeemed, rather than the people or the land. Even if not explicitly stated, this is the message surfacing from writings of Cardozo, who does not deny political redemption but simply ignores it. He thus resembles Sabbetai Zevi, who placed no value except on "the God of his belief" and "took pains," as mentioned, "until he seated the King on his throne," a metaphor Cardozo applied to himself.[44] However, unlike Sabbetai Zevi, Cardozo was in competition with Nathan of Gaza as to their powers of abstraction and theological expression. Cardozo's mystery of divinity may, and perhaps must, be defined abstractly, whereas for Nathan the feeling aspects—faith and love—were more important than intellectual knowledge for the relation between the believers, God, and the Messiah.

Despite the similarity between Nathan and Cardozo's theories, the two are totally different. First, Cardozo did not create a complicated kabbalistic myth and simply dealt with theological definitions; he even explicitly proclaimed that he was acting precisely in line with the needs of the times, when saying: "And at this time we do not need the details of wisdom, since redemption depends on knowledge of its principles: who is the Holy One, blessed be He, what is the name of His holy *Shekhinah,* as it says (Psalms 91:14–16) 'Because he has set his delight upon Me, therefore will I deliver him: I will set him on high, because he has known My name...and show him My salvation.'"[45] Second, Cardozo and Nathan grant a totally different status to the Messiah. As mentioned, Nathan assigned a place to his Messiah within his theory of divinity: he built his theosophy around the personality of the Messiah and even explicitly proclaimed the Messiah's divinity. Cardozo deeply opposed this proclamation[46] and the Messiah for him is none other than he who discovers the mystery of divinity, a task he shared with Sabbetai Zevi; he felt it was his duty to elucidate the mystery of Sabbetai Zevi's divinity, a mystery Sabbetai Zevi himself had difficulty explaining. The Messiah Son of David faces this difficulty because of his character; the power to explain and the role of the expounder are thus incumbent on the Messiah Son of Joseph, namely, on Cardozo, who bestowed this title upon himself. Since this is his role, Cardozo allowed himself to write the treatise *Raza de-Meheimanuta* [The Secret of Faith] and claim that these had been Sabbetai Zevi's dying words (in an article I devoted to this issue I demonstrated and clarified this pseudoepigraphy).[47]

Occasionally, it seems that in Cardozo's eyes the status of the Messiah is even lower, and the connection between his theology and the messianic movement is not always presented as necessary. According to his own testimony, Cardozo started to compose his theological *derushim* [treatises] before the outbreak of the messianic movement,[48] and once even explicitly wrote to one of his students: "Now, on the question of the Messiah or of redemption believe what you wish. But regarding God, blessed be He, be careful lest Yom Tov Romano and others like him take you away from our faith."[49] Cardozo's long and hard disputes with Yom Tov Romano and other Sabbatean theologians on the essence of divinity and of the Messiah resemble those of the Church Fathers in the early centuries of Christianity. Other Sabbatean theologians numbered among Cardozo's adversaries, in addition to Nathan of Gaza, were R. Samuel Primo, R. Hayyim Malakh, R. Jehuda the Hasid, and others.

But Cardozo also had followers, the best known among them being R. Nehemia Hayyun. Hayyun's main work is a commentary on the mentioned *Raza de-Meheimanuta* where, in the introduction, he supports the attempt to seek and disseminate the mysteries of divinity. As I have shown,[50] Hayyun was not persecuted because of his messianic and Sabbatean views, but for the radicalism of his hope for religious renewal and for his ideology of exoterism, which breaks all bounds in its search after the mysteries of divinity. This ideology is typical of Cardozo and opposed to the approach of Sabbetai Zevi and Nathan of Gaza. Among those who followed in the trail of Hayyun and Cardozo are R. Jonathan Eybeschuetz in his book *Shem Olam* [The Everlasting Name], which is devoted to an inquiry into religion in line with the Cardozian approach (unlike the book *Va-Avo Ha-Yom el Ha-Ayin* and others from the same circle, which belong to the school of Nathan's followers described earlier), and perhaps also R. Isaac Lopez, who wrote *Sefer Kur Matzref Ha-Emunot U-Mar'e Ha-Emet* [The Crucible of Religions and Indicator of Truth].[51]

Summary

The Sabbatean messianic movement was mainly a movement of religious rather than political redemption. I do not mean a movement of redemption that is religious, given that religion also includes a theory of political redemption, but rather one attempting the redemption of religion itself. This was the aim of Sabbateanism—the redemption and renewal of religion, of faith, and of the true God. In the eyes of Sabbateans, exile is the exile of religion, and its place of exile is the fossilized tradition, which has long since forgotten its roots and its aims. In Sabbatean literature, the most common verse for describing exile is "Now for a long time Israel has been without the true God [. . .] and without Torah" (Chronicles II, 15:3) and, as Sabbetai Zevi himself excelled in commenting on this verse in the letter to his brothers mentioned earlier: "Because they do not have the true God, their Torah is not Torah." A sense that the Torah had fossilized, coupled with a hope for reform and renewal, had once resulted in a dramatic and ritual breakthrough in halakhic prohibitions, mainly those under penalty of *karet* (transgressions punishable with death by Heaven), turning them into commandments. Sabbateans had an ambivalent attitude to religion: On the one hand, they aspired to its renewal, reform, and redemption; and on the other, they wanted to destroy, punish, and relinquish religion. This was their attitude to other religions as well. Latent in this phenomenon is also the explanation of one of Sabbateanism's greatest paradoxes—a movement for the redemption of Judaism that at times leads to apostasy. Their twin aspirations to renew and undermine the tradition generated their enormous interest in other religions, out of an intimacy unparalleled in Jewish history. This intimacy had two aspects: one of anger and revenge, which brought them to convert out of a desire to destroy their newly adopted religion from within; and the other a friendly one, including attempts at religious renewal assisted by other religions. These attempts did not always end in apostasy. They also contributed to the syncretic character of the religion of those Sabbateans who remained in the Jewish fold. We have even found an instance of inverse Marranos—Sabbateans who converted to Christianity in their hearts but ostensibly lived as Jews in Christian countries.[52] All Sabbateans, those who abandoned Judaism and those who remained within it, retained a broad common denominator and even a feeling of unity and continued mutual ties[53] that would not have survived had the movement's aims been national and terrestrial. This common denominator was revolt and spiritual renewal. It is precisely from this perspective that Sabbateanism may be seen as a breakthrough toward modern times in Jewish history.

SO
too
Anderman
"Kabbalah + Subversion..."

4

Sabbetai Zevi's Religious Faith[1]

More than any other Jewish messianic movement, except for Christianity, Sabbateanism shows high interest in theological issues, and this concern shaped its messianic visage. Problems of religious faith were Sabbetai Zevi's main concern throughout his life, and he seems to have approached his discovery of the *Mystery of the Godhead* as the linchpin of his messianic activity. This mystery also determined his "religious faith" in the other meaning of this term, namely, his bond with the two religions—Judaism and Islam.

But what were the contents of Sabbetai Zevi's religious faith? I think they have remained rather vague until now because they have not been duly separated from the thought of two other Sabbatean theologians—Nathan of Gaza and Miguel Cardozo. The latter were prolific writers and their powerful theories indeed shaped Sabbatean ideology in the historical consciousness (though there are striking differences not only between them and Sabbetai Zevi, but also between themselves). As we shall see, Sabbetai Zevi's *Mystery of the Godhead* cannot, by its very nature, be fully articulated or easily communicated to others. Sabbetai Zevi's faith was vital to the emergence of Sabbateanism and was certainly the decisive influence in the thought of other Sabbatean thinkers. The latter were impelled by the faith and the strong personality of their Messiah even when failing to understand him fully but, nevertheless, the contents of Sabbetai Zevi's *Mystery of the Godhead* have been forgotten in the course of time.

Ostensibly, we do possess a theological work written by Sabbetai Zevi—the treatise *Raza de-Meheimanuta*. However, I would not recommend this as a reliable source for the purpose of understanding Sabbetai Zevi's religious faith. Although he carefully endeavored not to leave any traces, I believe that Cardozo, rather than Sabbetai Zevi, wrote this book and then attributed it to Sabbetai Zevi many years after the latter's death.[2] A comparison between this work and other of Cardozo's writings should make this clear. This comparison will indeed demonstrate that the contents of the *Raza de-Meheimanuta*, including its title, appear in Cardozo's treatise *Boker de-Avraham* [Abraham's Morning]. Cardozo wrote this work even before the time at which he later claimed Sabbetai Zevi had written the *Raza de-Meheimanuta* and many years before, according to Cardozo, Sabbetai Zevi's treatise had happened to reach him. Years later, a theological dispute arose between Cardozo and other Sabbateans, led by Samuel Primo. Cardozo was at a disavantage, because Primo had received the *Mystery of the Godhead* directly from Sabbetai Zevi whereas Cardozo had never met his Messiah; it was only then that Cardozo wrote the *Raza de-Meheimanuta*, which contains his own ideas, and attributed it to Sabbetai Zevi.

To make best use of this treatise as a reliable and effective weapon in this dispute, Cardozo added a fabrication describing how Sabbetai Zevi wrote it at the end of his life and how it reached Cardozo's hands through the offices of anonymous intermediaries, who were themselves surprised to find such close similarities between the *Raza de-Meheimanuta* and Cardozo's views. From the claim that the treatise was written at the close of Sabbetai Zevi's life, Cardozo concluded that this was the authoritative and final version of the *Mystery of the Godhead*. As further evidence, he cited the fact that, unlike the time when Sabbetai Zevi had revealed the *Mystery* to Samuel Primo, he did not swear the listeners of the *Raza de-Meheimanuta* to silence. As we shall see, this claim proves that Cardozo failed to understand the real motives behind Sabbetai Zevi's adjuration.

This forgery might explain why other Sabbateans, such as Nathan of Gaza and Samuel Primo, who were much closer than Cardozo to Sabbetai Zevi, knew nothing of the *Raza de-Meheimanuta*, his only work. Cardozo's testimony is indeed the only source for Sabbetai Zevi's authorship of this work, which was published by Cardozo's best known disciple, R. Nehemya Hayyun. There is evidence that other Sabbateans also questioned the attribution of this work to Sabbetai Zevi.

Furthermore, this forgery might be better understood when placed in the context of Cardozo's spiritual and ideological attitude toward Sabbetai Zevi. Cardozo dwelled at length on his ambivalence in the treatise *Kodesh Israel la-Adonai* that, on the one hand, reflects Cardozo's spiritual identification with Sabbetai Zevi while, on the other hand, attests to his jealousy and his reservations about him. In this treatise, Cardozo also developed a theory claiming that he himself is in the role of the Messiah Son of Joseph and, as such, he is to clarify and explain the *Mystery of the Godhead* that the Messiah Son of David—Sabbetai Zevi—could not fully articulate. Cardozo furnished kabbalistic explanations for the characteristics and the roles of the two Messiahs, according to their origins and their places in the different *sefirot*.

We may thus infer that, before Cardozo decided to write the *Raza de-Meheimanuta*, he had already been concerned with Sabbetai Zevi's lack of literary and kabbalistic productivity, and later solved the problem by writing the *Raza de-Meheimanuta* and attributing it to Sabbetai Zevi. He may even not have seen this as a forgery because, as the Messiah Son of Joseph, he is authorized to clarify the intentions of the Messiah Son of David—Sabbetai Zevi—even if these intentions are not clear to the Messiah Son of David himself. A similar concern appears in another description by Cardozo, claiming he had stopped believing in Sabbetai Zevi's messianic powers after hearing the Mystery of the Godhead as known to Samuel Primo; he was only relieved when, after finding the *Raza de-Meheimanuta*, he discovered that Sabbetai Zevi completely agreed with him. It should be noted that, besides the discovery of the *Mystery of the Godhead*, Cardozo seems to have been totally uninterested in any other aspect of the messianic role.

The fact that the *Raza de-Meheimanuta* has proven to be a forgery casts doubts on all other statements by Sabbetai Zevi that have reached us via Cardozo. Sabbatean scholars may have exagerated the value of statements such as those found in Cardozo's treatise *Raza de-Razin*, where Sabbetai Zevi is quoted as having said that Luria "built a perfectly beautiful carriage, but did not say who rides it." In another statement, Cardozo quotes R. Azariah Levy as having heard Sabbetai Zevi say more than a hundred times that "the Holy One, blessed be He, the God of Israel, was a Second Cause clothed in the *sefira* of *tiferet*."[3]

The only unimpeachable testimony by Cardozo about Sabbetai Zevi, which has also been confirmed by many other sources, is a negative one; namely, that Sabbetai Zevi failed to specify his kabbalistic views and that he swore to secrecy all those followers to whom he did reveal the *Mystery of the Godhead*. However, Sabbetai Zevi did not act in this way for the reasons adduced by Cardozo—his lack of kabbalistic and literary ability or his doubts about the truth of his own beliefs.

Understanding the meaning of Sabbetai Zevi's behavior requires us to delve into the essence of his *Mystery of the Godhead*. Rather than limited ability, his conscious opposition to the technical and impersonal style adopted by Lurianic Kabbala—in which an advanced, multifaceted machine had replaced the personal God—guided Sabbetai Zevi. (By the way, merely understanding Sabbetai Zevi's opposition on this count would suffice to eliminate him as the possible author of the *Raza de-Meheimanuta.*) His main challenge against Lurianic Kabbala is in posing the very question that no kabbalist had ever raised before—who, then, is the God of Israel. Sabbetai Zevi did not refrain from answering this question, but his answer could not be exhausted through technical kabbalistic terminology or through human language altogether. The God known to Sabbetai Zevi was personal, more easily found in his soul than in his mind. I believe that Sabbetai Zevi expressed the personal nature of this God in the name *true God* and stressed his personal attachment in names like *the God of Sabbetai Zevi* or *the God of Sabbetai Zevi's faith.* Sabbetai Zevi himself clearly formulated this link between his soul—both in its present form and in its previous incarnations—and the God of his faith, in the opening of a letter sent to his two brothers: "The true One that only I have known for generations and for whom I have so strenuously toiled."[4] Replacing the Lurianic machine with a personal God led Sabbetai Zevi to abandon Lurianic devotional prayer and pray "as someone who prays to His King," as attested by his fellow student R. Moses Pinheiro.

Sabbetai Zevi obviously attempted to articulate his faith and used kabbalistic terminology for this purpose, though he resorted to the personal Kabbala of the Zohar rather than to the mechanistic Lurianic one. We do not know Sabbetai Zevi's detailed formulations because he guarded their secret very carefully; however, it is known from many sources that his God became manifest, in one way or another, in the *sefira* of *tiferet.* This use of *tiferet* for "the God of Israel" is not new and appears frequently as a kabbalistic notion, but the personal approach to divinity symbolized through this *sefira* is his own.

This personal approach could not be communicated—it is not words that are vital, but the direct relation between the bearer and the receiver of the message. For this reason, Sabbetai Zevi did not write a book explaining his view (such as the *Raza de-Meheimanuta*) and also swore to secrecy those to whom he had revealed the *Mystery of the Godhead* lest they reveal it to others, as such a revelation necessarily entails further distortion.

Nathan of Gaza was indeed guilty of such a distortion though, unlike Cardozo, Nathan cannot be accused of deliberate forgery. However, because he was committed to Luria's mechanistic Kabbala, Nathan relied on it for interpreting Sabbetai Zevi's mystery and thus highly distorted its original intention. Indeed, Sabbetai Zevi strongly admonished him for "betraying a great and awesome ban"; namely, for reneguing on his oath and revealing to others the *Mystery of the Godhead*—"and stole and fed others after him."[5] At the same time, he ordered Nathan to appear in front of him and hear anew the *Mystery of the Godhead* from his own lips. This event is also mentioned in a letter by Hayyim Malakh, who explicitly states that Sabbetai Zevi accused Nathan of distorting his *Mystery of the Godhead.*[6]

The personal knowledge of God entails the possibility of antinomianism. Whoever knows God through his own soul can receive knowledge of positive and negative commandments directly from Him, dispense with the mediation of halakhic authorities who lack this direct attachment, and be above any halakhic establishment. Indeed, his private and direct acceptance of the commandments might explain Sabbetai Zevi's "strange acts" and, most important, his apostasy.

For Sabbetai Zevi, his apostasy was indeed linked to the revelation of his *Mystery of the Godhead*—before demanding from any of his adherents to follow his lead and convert, he would reveal the *Mystery.* Once a disciple heard the *Mystery of the Godhead* from Sabbetai Zevi but refused to convert, and Sabbetai Zevi chided him with the verse "why did you steal my God."[7] It appears that when Sabbetai Zevi admonished Nathan of Gaza in similar words, this rebuke was also related to Nathan's unwillingness to convert.[8]

In a note sent to his brother Elijah immediately after his conversion, Sabbetai Zevi claimed that it reflected God's arbitrary will and he himself was simply clay in the potter's hands and could not understand its meaning,[9] a view confirmed by Elijah Mujajun's testimony.[10] When Sabbetai Zevi later realized why God had wanted him to convert, he wrote another letter to his brothers and added the explanation he had been unable to provide in the first note. The letter opens with the sentence (quoted earlier) expressing God's personal character and His wish for Sabbetai Zevi's apostasy, a wish that, here as well, precedes all explanations: "The true One that only I have known for generations and for whom I have so strenuously toiled wanted me to enter the religion of Islam with all my heart." In later passages, Sabbetai Zevi suggested grounds for God's wish, though his reasons are far removed from the reknowned Sabbatean explanations for the apostasy, which are based on the Kabbala of Nathan of Gaza and develop Lurianic mechanistic theories. Sabbetai Zevi himself did not even hint at the need to descend into the *kelippot* to liberate the fallen sparks. It was Nathan of Gaza who offered this explanation of Sabbetai Zevi's apostasy and not Sabbetai Zevi himself.

According to Sabbetai Zevi, the Messiah's apostasy was a form of punishment to Israel for having failed to recognize the true God—Sabbetai Zevi's personal God. A kind of *lex talionis* is at work, as Moses says in his song: "They have stirred Me to jealousy with what is no god . . . so I will stir them to jealousy with those who are no people"

(Deuteronomy 32:21), as Moses destroyed the tablets when he saw Israel worshipping the golden calf.[11] It is not simply a coincidence that Sabbetai Zevi chose to compare himself with Moses because he, as a Redeemer, resembles Moses: as Moses was "his servant, loyal to the house" of God, namely, personally attached to Him, so is Sabbetai Zevi. The same personal attachment that conferred on Moses the authority to hand down God's Torah to the people of Israel enabled Sabbetai Zevi to revoke the Torah, in line with the wishes of the God of his faith. As we mentioned, those linked to the personal God are above the halakhic establishment. In his words, "The words of our sages, of blessed memory, are not realized until the loyal servant of the true God agrees with them." Moreover, what is the point of abiding by the Torah when God is not known? It is like a body without a soul!

In this letter, Sabbetai Zevi also accounted for the choice of Islam for his apostasy, as a form of punishment to Israel. He drew his argument from a Moslem principle of faith—the abolition of the Torah—but changed its meaning. The Moslems believed that the abolition of the Torah is final and the Koran, which ranks higher, will forever take its place. However, for Sabbetai Zevi, apostasy is only a temporary punishment (in his words, "until the last age"), and after being duly chastised, the Torah will return to its initial standing and the people of Israel, which were exchanged for Ishmael, will regain their status as first born.

Contrary to the Moslem view, the replacement of the Torah with the Koran is not to Islam's credit. Using Islam to chastise Israel attests to the measure of *din* [harsh judgement] and to the arbitrariness of this religion, based merely on blind tradition. The true God chose it to express his arbitrary will, as a punishment to Israel. Sabbetai Zevi expressed this idea in the same letter, in an Arab proverb: *"Din Islam Haq Haq."* I believe that Sabbetai Zevi thought of Islam as the law of the true God (*Haq* in Arabic means "truth"—the name of God for the mystical *sufis*). This law is the arbitrary punishment decreed by the true God, as it appeared further on, when Sabbetai Zevi expounded the phrase *Haq haq* in line with God's words as quoted by the rabbis: "I have ruled an ordinance, edicted a decree, and you are forbidden to question it."[12] (Incidentally, using the *Haq haq* quote as his point of departure, Nathan of Gaza developed a long and complicated kabbalistic treatise in his *Raza de-Malka Meshiha*, far removed from the original literal sense of the words. This is a prominent example of the difference between the two men that I pointed out earlier).

At a later stage Sabbetai Zevi abandoned this explanation for his apostasy and claimed that, from then on, "wearing a fez is no longer a punishment required for *tikkun* but a great mystery."[13] As it was not revealed, I do not know what this mystery is, but several testimonies claim that new revelations came to Sabbetai Zevi during this period. I believe that it was then that Sabbetai Zevi begun to refer to Islam as "the Torah of *hesed*" [grace] (though, in Sabbetai Zevi's terminology, this is not a positive term either) and to exclude it from the realm of *din* (in a play of words on this term, which in Arabic means "religion"), often mentioned in regard to Islam in the letter cited previously. It was perhaps then that Sabbetai Zevi ceased signing his letters with the name *Me'ammet*, which closely resembles the Hebrew word *verifier*, and returned to the correct spelling of his Moslem name *Muhammad*.

Whatever the nature of Sabbetai Zevi's new revelations, they are not the central issue. As we saw, at the time of his apostasy Sabbetai Zevi did not yet understand its meaning and, having understood it, changed his mind about it soon after. The apostasy does not depend on its explanations. The main and strongest religious reason was simply that the God of Sabbetai Zevi's personal faith wished it, and Sabbetai Zevi understood this wish without mediators.

5

Ha-Tikkun Ha-Kelali of R. Nahman of Bratslav and Its Sabbatean Links

I. The Bratslav Approach to Redemption

In Bratslav literature, *ha-tikkun ha-kelali* refers to a specific ritual that will be discussed extensively in this essay. I shall first consider the approach of Bratslav Hasidism to *tikkun* in the broader context of messianic *tikkun* as embodying the notion of universal repair; that is, Bratslav's view of redemption. Bratslav indeed differs from all other Hasidic movements in its remarkable messianic leanings.[1] R. Nahman of Bratslav, the founder and ideologue of this branch of Hasidism, is a messianic figure par excellence and his personality is indeed the main content of its ideology. The messianism of Bratslav contrasts sharply with Judaism's traditional messianic views, and R. Nahman indeed was—as he put it—a total *hiddush* [innovation] in this domain as well.[2] Therefore, the study of this particular dimension of R. Nahman will help to clarify a further aspect of the Jewish messianic ideal. I do not intend to review the various stages of R. Nahman's messianic activity, as this task has already been accomplished;[3] my aim is to trace the particular spiritual contours of Bratslav messianism.

R. Nahman was indeed a messianic figure, though this does not necessarily imply that either he or his followers believed him to be the Messiah or the final redeemer. R. Nahman might have been a pretender to this crown at various times[4] but, in most of his writings, he did draw a distinction between himself and the Messiah,[5] and at times claimed that the Messiah would be one of his descendants.[6] Nonetheless, it is clear that R. Nahman certainly saw himself as one of the phases of the Messiah,[7] and even as incarnating particular figures in kabbalistic messianism—Moses,[8] R. Simeon b. Yohai,[9] and R. Israel Baal Shem Tov. However, R. Nahman believed that he had attained a higher spiritual rung than these men during their own lifetimes[10] and that it was incumbent on him to fulfill their messianic mission.

R. Nahman's messianism entails an act of *tikkun,* and this is indeed the general meaning of "*ha-tikkun ha-kelali.*" This name aptly

115

describes R. Nahman's approach in general, since he perceived his mission as the *tikkun* of man (first and foremost himself) and the *tikkun* of his community, as well as that of the whole Jewish people from all their sins: both their worldly sins, which were first and foremost sexual, and the numerous doctrinal sins of his generation, that had ravaged traditional Jewish structures ("the Enlightenment!"). But, above all, he was concerned with the *tikkun* of the original sin that, in my view, was for him the source of all his generation's ills—Sabbateanism. Sabbateanism indeed marks a decisive turning point in Jewish history. Its zenith was also that of Jewish unity, the culmination of the kabbalistic-messianic direction that had left its imprint on the previous century. The crisis of Sabbateanism generated continued fragmentation, left an indelible impression on all Jewish factions—both those for and against the movement—and made room for new approaches that shook Jewish faith.

The Sabbatean movement was already waning in R. Nahman's time, but the splintering and the apostasy that came in its wake had not receded—quite the contrary. There was no longer any hope of restoring Jewish faith through conventional means. A totally new approach was required for this purpose, and R. Nahman intended to accomplish this task.

To what extent was R. Nahman aware of the depth of the crisis and the scope of change that this *tikkun* would require? R. Nahman defined his generation as one that "had fallen from all seventy faces of the Torah" and must hence be awakened by tales "from former years," which were at a higher spiritual rung than the Torah.[11] It must be emphasized that the Hasidim who were the potential audience for these tales closely resembled previous generations in appearance and attire—they were not *maskilim*; still, in R. Nahman's eyes, even they had fallen "from all seventy faces of the Torah" and could be roused only through untried, exceptional means.

This statement clearly shows that R. Nahman was indeed deeply aware of the scope of the religious crisis afflicting his time, a crisis that engulfed even the faithful. Although the *tikkun* he offered was the complete antithesis to "religious reform," it was nonetheless a striking innovation, the like of which "the world had never seen before."[12]

This innovation entails restoring the personal tie with the *tsaddik* and establishing it as the supreme religious value (see note 52). No such value had been known in classical Judaism, and it calls forth associations with the personal devotion of Christians to their Messiah. Indeed, the Jewish religion (or, for that matter, any other) is inconceivable without leaders and teachers to be followed and obeyed, but these leaders had always derived their authority from the Torah rather than from their own unique personality. Not so R. Nahman. The main innovation of Bratslav Hasidism is the elevation of the personal tie with the *tsaddik*— R. Nahman—to the rank of the highest religious value; it is his personality that ennobles his doctrines, however strange they might be. R. Nahman was thus able to claim that naive faith was the cardinal religious expression, a notion otherwise unacceptable to his contemporaries. In this context, naive faith is, first and foremost, faith in the *tsaddik,* the only one able to mediate Jewish faith.

Indeed, this innovation was not born ex nihilo. From its inception, the Hasidic movement as a whole had stressed the religious importance of the personal tie with the *tsaddik,* and the conceptual roots of this idea can be traced back to early kabbalistic literature[13] and particularly to Sabbateanism (see Section II). This idea took hold of R. Nahman, who had grown up in the heartland of Hasidism. However, under the influence of his forceful and profound personality, as well as of his exceptionally illustrious ancestry,[14] Bratslav Hasidim developed this notion ad absurdum and so, paradoxically, have remained without a *tsaddik* since R. Nahman's death. Bratslav has been a leaderless community for close to 170 years, not because of their failure to appreciate the importance of leadership but quite the contrary—because they cannot conceive of a higher religious principle, their leader has become a unique and irreplaceable figure. The absence of a leader has earned them the nickname of "the dead hasidim," *di toite hasidim,* a term that excels in conveying the absurdity of their condition.

Cleaving to a *tsaddik* does not eradicate spiritual problems, but it does shift the concern with these questions from the public realm to that of the individual *tsaddik.* All that is required from the hasidim is simple piety and identification with the *tsaddik*'s destiny, which mitigates the *tsaddik*'s terrifying loneliness and alleviates his spiritual burden.[15] The *tsaddik* is indeed involved in a hard and cruel strife and Bratslav texts speak mainly of R. Nahman's inner struggle, but this struggle has now assumed cosmic significance. R. Nahman's victory over his evil inclination and his doubts reflects the triumph and the rise of the community that depends on him, as well as that of the people of Israel and even of the whole world.[16] This victory thus takes on the meaning of a messianic *tikkun.*

It is R. Nahman's personality as such that resolves religious doubt in his community. As R. Nahman himself once said, in typical Bratslav syntax: *"Un 'da ma shetashiv lapikoros' bin ich"* [I am a 'know what to answer the heretic' (Avot 2:14)][17] and also: "I am the river that cleanses all stains."[18] Intellectual contemplation is thus replaced by personal adherence to the *tsaddik,* who "is himself the Torah" (see p. 130) and is himself good counsel.[19]

In this light, it is easier to appreciate the cardinal importance of the biographical material on R. Nahman within the literary corpus of Bratslav Hasidism (such as the book *Hayyei Moharan*). All of R. Nahman's actions are endowed with tremendous significance. Moreover, the philosophical teachings in *Likkutei Moharan* cannot be understood—as is also claimed by Bratslav Hasidim—without knowledge of the circumstances in which they were delivered because, rather than the doctrinal contents, the man who uttered them and his particular situation at the time are central.

The Hasidim are to be content with naive faith in their rabbi, who is Judaism incarnate, as well as with a simple and overwhelming joy. Concern over apostasy and the study of heretic books are allowed only to the rabbi,[20] and the suffering and despair usually attached to such an inquiry burden only him.[21] Indeed, in what might be a paradoxical dialectic, naive piety and perfect joy also characterize R. Nahman's devotion; were it not so, his Hasidim, who have embraced simplicity, could not have stayed with him. However, there is a vast difference between R. Nahman's "simplicity" and "naivete," which he attained after delving deeply into the ways of human reason (see p. 000) and the pristine innocence of his followers. Neither does the Hasidim's spontaneous elation resemble R. Nahman's paradoxical joy, which transcends his despair and is expressed in his anguished cry: "*Gevalt,* do not despair, there is no despair in the world at all!" [*"Gevalt, zeit eich nit meyaesh, kein yeush is gor nit far handen"*].[22]

This cry, which appears in *Likkutei Moharan* II:78 and in the pertinent biographical literature,[23] might well serve to illustrate my point, as it is wholly based on R. Nahman's situation at the time.[24] This teaching was delivered on *Shabbat Nahamu* of the year 1811, two months before his death. R. Nahman was then at his lowest ebb, both physically and spiritually—extremely ill, far away from Bratslav, in the city of Uman, and preparing for his death. He was living in the home of a skeptic, keeping company with the town's *maskilim* and in turmoil about their views.[25] It was at this time that the Hasidim came to hear their master's teachings. R. Nahman did not feel up to the task and begged them to leave him—he could not teach because he did not know. We are told in *Yemey Moharnat* how this teaching proceeded:

> this teaching was indeed revealed out of nothing because, at first, he truly did not know at all . . . and he had honestly said about

himself that his not knowing is a miraculous innovation, etc.[26] He then spoke at length of how he knew nothing at all and began a wondrous conversation until, in the course of it, he himself discovered this teaching, since he sustains himself in his simplicity, as he did on his journey to the Holy Land, and then attained great joy. . .

(I deal with the messianic meaning of joy in note 128 ff.) Thus, through the contemplation of his "no knowledge," in his sorrow and simplicity, R. Nahman eventually reached the stage of "no knowledge." This is a wonderful innovation—a "no-knowledge" that is above all knowledge, a wonderful joy, minutely described, that surges from deep despondence. At first he contemplated his state of "simplicity" and justified it as deriving from human physical needs, and then explained it as required to sustain the simple (literally simple!) people (his Hasidim), following the fundamental Hasidic principle that the *tsaddik* must descend to the rung of evil men to uplift them.[27] R. Nahman nevertheless asked: What will sustain the *tsaddik* during his descent, away from the Torah, which is the source of life? He then explained that the simplicity of the *tsaddik* conforms to the highest aspect of the Torah, an aspect revealed during Creation, before the Torah was handed down and translated into the language of the commandments.[28] R. Nahman attained this supreme Torah during his journey to the Holy Land, when found in a state of *"katnut"*;[29] his memories of this journey and the supreme importance of *"katnut"* at that time, sustained R. Nahman during his present state, when delivering this teaching at Uman. In this manner, R. Nahman was able to justify staying at the home of an heretic *maskil* as a campaign to conquer a part of exile and turning it, as it were, into an aspect of the land of Israel.[30]

Linking the *tsaddik*'s and the Torah's highest merits to the land of Israel is also evidence of the messianic character underscoring R. Nahman's doctrine; the essence of this link, yet to be elucidated, should help clarify the meaning of Bratslav messianism. I have come across two contrary approaches, both mistaken, on the place of the land of Israel in R. Nahman's teachings. One builds on sources such as the preceding one, implying that a phase of the land of Israel is possible in Exile, and relies on R. Nahman's famous saying: "My only place is the land of Israel. Wherever I go, I am only going to the Holy Land, and it is just for the time being that I am a shepherd in Bratslav and the like" (*Hayyei Moharan,* His Trip to Navritch 6) In this view, R. Nahman approaches the land of Israel allegorically rather than literally. Against this view, others lean on R. Nahman's opposite answer when questioned on the meaning of his praises for the land of Israel: "He scolded me and said, I mean literally this land of Israel, with these houses and these abodes";[31] they thus rely on R. Nahman's voyage to the Holy Land to turn him into the spiritual father of Zionism.

Neither one seems right. The land of Israel is not just an allegory. Although relating to a spiritual dimension, this aspect is connected precisely to the concrete land, and it is only through it or by yearning for it that this phase can also be fulfilled in exile. "The land of Israel aspect" is also a spiritual ideal, relating not only to individuals but to the collective too, and it is through this aspect that Jews will conquer the land from the Gentiles ruling it. However, it is not a form of Zionism. The notion of building and settling the land is far from R. Nahman; his concern is with the spiritual merit of the land that, for him, is related to the reign of miracles, faith, and prayer as, in fact, they came to the fore in the very situation of the land of Israel in his times—desolate and destroyed, its inhabitants sustained by the miracle of alms distribution from their brethren in exile.[32] The merit of the land of Israel is also linked to the merit of the *tsaddik*. In this context, it is worth noting that Bratslav Hasidim from Jerusalem and Bene-Berak yearn to pray at R. Nahman's grave in Uman in the Soviet Union because, as it were, the *tsaddik*'s grave is the land of Israel.[33]

What is the spiritual merit of the land of Israel? It seems that R. Nahman's most comprehensive statement on this question[34] is found in *Likkutei Moharan* I:20 that, more than his other teachings, includes a detailed messianic program,[35] as follows:[36] "Whosoever wishes to be a Jew, namely, to climb the rungs, can only do so through the land of Israel." The main aim of a Jew, as well as that of the land of Israel, is to climb from rung to rung, but not in the sense of attaining progress through study, or moving along mental stages, or even implying that each rung builds on the previous one, as is usually assumed by mystics and neo-Platonists. The stages alluded to by R. Nahman are those he thinks of in the here and now, totally obliterating the merits of all the previous ones; R. Nahman reached such a stage on his journey to the Holy Land. It is for this reason that this virtue was described at length in "An Account of R. Nahman's Journey to the Holy Land." I cite briefly:

> He would forever long for God. . .as if he had never known the taste of divine worship and had never begun at all. . .and he never rested and was never at peace, even in his best days, when he had already attained the highest, mightiest and most terrifying rung. . . .And immediately after his attainment he

would be slightly joyful. . .and would then begin again and forget the past altogether, as if he had never begun, and would then return once more, as if he had just started to penetrate the holiness of Israel. At times, we would hear from his holy mouth that he said clearly, in a language of yearning and longings: How does one become a Jew? And he said this truly and innocently, as if he had not begun at all; this happened several times, and he would always climb from rung to rung. . . (*Shivhei Ha-Ran* 33–34)

Then, "but about himself he would say that, if he knew that he is now at the same step and rung as last year, he would not want himself at all" (*Shivhei Ha-Ran*, 34). The virtue of "I do not know" is greatly extolled in this context, as serving to distinguish between various levels of knowledge, and his favorite aphorism is also cited: "The end of knowledge is [the understanding] that we do not know."[37]

R. Nahman's highly original outlook on the preferred approach to learning and on the virtues of forgetfulness are also derived from this ideal.[38] It is in this light that we must look at the following statement, surely one of the most ironic critiques ever leveled against philosophy:

On the paradox of knowledge [God's prescience] and free will. . .our blessed rabbi said he already had the correct answer to this question and the answer was, as usual, completely clear, for it was never his way to say anything that left any grounds for doubt.[39] He had already written it up but lost the paper where he had written it, and now he has forgotten it. (*Hayyei Moharan, Sihot Moharan,* Avoidance of Inquiry 10)

It is worth mentioning in this context that the contradiction between God's prescience and human free choice ("the question of knowledge and free will") was considered unsolvable by philosophers. Maimonides (*Eight Chapters,* Ch. 8) explains why this question cannot be answered—there is an essential difference between divine knowledge and human knowledge and, in principle, human limitations preclude the possibility of ever grasping the essence of divine knowledge. R. Nahman reached the answer after attaining the rung he had acquired in the Holy Land, but forgot it after attaining a new one (and then, unfortunately, even lost the paper). Lo and behold, that is the difference between the spiritual aspect of the land of Israel and the optimal attainment of philosophy!

A closely related question is "the righteous suffer and the wicked prosper." The Talmud tells us that Moses was troubled by this question but R. Nahman claimed that, despite Moses' attainment in apprehending everything the human mind is capable of, the answer to this question eluded him.[40] For his part, R. Nahman was able to deal with this problem when at the *katnut* stage he had attained while in the land of Israel. Thus, the *katnut* and the madness that had characterized R. Nahman's behavior in the Holy Land rank higher than Moses' understanding and are beyond human reasoning:

> Truly, reason ought to be cast aside and all cleverness discarded—God must be worshipped in simplicity. . . .For the sake of God's worship, one ought to act and do things that seem like madness, as in "be thou ravished always with her love" (Proverbs 5:19), so that for God's love one needs to do things that appear as madness in order to follow His commandments and do His will. One must roll in mud and mire for His worship and His commandments. . . .Anything where God's will is manifest and pleases his Father in heaven is as a commandment, and he must roll in all sorts of mire and mud to do His will and please God and then, when his love for God is so strong that he throws himself into mire and mud for His worship and His pleasure, this is good for the intellect, because he then reaches even beyond the intellect and attains that which even Moses did not grasp in his lifetime—why "the righteous suffer and the wicked prosper" [Berakhot 7a] which appears to be, God forbid, a distortion of justice, and even Moses failed to understand it while he was alive. . . .But, since his love for God is so strong that he throws himself in mud and mire for His worship and binds himself as a slave for His love, he can grasp what even Moses in his lifetime could not attain with his intellect, namely, the righteous suffer and the wicked prosper. There is a difference between searching in the King's archives as a son [Zohar III:111b] and searching as a slave—a slave simply does what he is told, is forbidden to inquire after the reasons for his toiling and does only his duty. But then there is a son who so loves His father that, because of his love, labors like a slave, does what slaves do, jumps into the trenches and fortifications and rolls in mud and mire to please His father, all of which not even a slave would do. And when His father sees that his love is so strong that he is willing to reduce himself to abject slavery for the sake of His love, then He reveals to him that which was not even given to the son. Because when the son is searching in the

King's archives some places are forbidden to him, meaning that there are attainments even the son is incapable of. But there is a son who casts away cleverness and binds himself into slavery, and His father takes pity on him and reveals to him that which was not even revealed to the son, namely, the righteous suffer and the wicked prosper, which even Moses failed to understand in his lifetime. Because "and I will spare them, as a man spares his own son who serves him" (Malachi 3:17) means to serve him literally—he yokes himself into slavery, casts away his cleverness and acts like a slave. And this is his son who serves him, and because of that—"I will spare them," because God takes pity on him when He sees that his love is so strong, and He shows and reveals to him "the righteous suffer and the wicked prosper." This is "then you shall return, and see the difference between the righteous and the wicked" (Malachi 3:17), meaning that for the sake of this he attains understanding of "the righteous suffer and the wicked prosper." (*Likkutei Moharan* II:5, 16)

The "son searching in his father's archives" usually refers to the mystic at the highest level Judaism has ever known, beginning with the *tannaim* (including such charismatic types as Honi Ha-Meagel, R. Hanina ben Dosa, and even Jesus, who had all been called *sons*) and up to the Zohar. Moses had always symbolized the pinnacle of human mysticism, both for the philosophers, such as Maimonides, as well as for the kabbalists, mainly in the Zohar. R. Nahman introduced a new rank, most certainly his own, higher than that of the "son" and of Moses in his lifetime.[41] The expression "in his lifetime" might not only hint to material obstacles that had prevented Moses from reaching higher attainments (see Maimonides, *Eight Chapters,* Ch. 7) but also to the Moses of the Exodus as against the Moses incarnated in R. Nahman. To the ranks of "slave" and "son" known to us from Jewish mysticism, R. Nahman added that of a "slave" who is above the "son." It seems that the usual rank of slave, lower than that of son, is reserved for R. Nahman's followers who worship "in simple simplicity," whereas the slave who ranks above the son is the *tsaddik*—R. Nahman. The "slave" facet is the link between the *tsaddik* and his Hasidim; for a similar discussion on the two levels of simplicity, see p. 119.

By pointing to himself as the slave above the son, R. Nahman meant to emphasize his unique position above all other Hasidic *tsaddikim*, who had tended to describe themselves as sons ruling in the archives of their Father in Heaven.[42] Supplying further evidence for this claim, R. Nahman quotes a miracle fable exalting his own rank of slave above the son. In this fable, the slave above the son, who appears as the wise son ranking above the foolish son of the King of Kings, is described in terms that, were they not found in *Sihot Ha-Ran,* "could not have been uttered." In this case, he explicitly states that he intends his words against the Hasidic *tsaddikim:*[43]

> When speaking of the famous miracle-workers, he told the story of a king who had two sons, one wise and the other foolish. The king put the fool in charge of all the treasures and gave no position to the wise son, who always sat beside him. The people could not understand how the unwise son has such authority, and all come to him to bring or take away from the treasures, while the wise son has no position at all. The king answered: What is the merit in the taking of ready treasures and disbursing them to the world? My wise son sits beside me and uses his mind. He brings up new ideas I would not have thought of and, through his advice, I conquer lands I would not have known of, from whence come my treasures. But the one in charge takes ready-made treasures and disburses them to the world. The rank of the wise is certainly higher and more exalted than that of the one in charge and, though it might seem he lacks a position, all the treasures come through him.

His intention in this passage is clear. The foolish son in charge of the treasures stands for the miracle-working Hasidic *tsaddikim,* who often described themselves as the channel linking God to His people and as sons searching in their father's archives. The same image is used in the last passage to describe the foolish son and in the previous one to denote the son who is not a slave, proving that both passages share the same referent—Hasidic *tsaddikim.* R. Nahman neither denies the pretensions of the *tsaddikim* nor does he differ from them in his approach to their merits—he simply places himself above them. Indeed, he has no position[44] nor does he work miracles (his very personality, as mentioned, is a miracle and a novelty) and he does not disburse the king's treasures [= miracle working]. But he advises the Holy One, blessed be He,[45] and his counsel has brought Him all the treasures. This notion is much more far-fetched than the one in the previous passage, where God is said to have revealed hidden knowledge to the son-slave ranking above the son, but without claiming that the son-slave is the source of this knowledge. However, this notion fits R. Nahman's independent, spontaneous spirit, unsatisfied with disbursing what exists and wishing to bring novel, unprecedented ideas. This is particularly pronounced in his free exegetical approach, which surpasses anything known to me from any other source.

We may thus conclude that R. Nahman's virtue resides in the spiritual merit of the land of Israel and, from the passage in *Likkutei Moharan* II:5 (cited earlier, p. 122), we also learn that R. Nahman ranks even higher than Moses in this regard. It is thus clear why Moses did not deserve to enter the Holy Land whereas R. Nahman earned this privilege because of his own superior merit, embodied in the slave's virtues of simplicity and *katnut*. This conclusion emerges from R. Nahman's statements in the two teachings discussed previously concerning the land of Israel. In *Likkutei Moharan* I:20, which was singled out as R. Nahman's most messianic teaching, he discussed the meaning of Moses' sin—smiting the rock—for which he was condemned not to enter the land. The essence of his sin was addressing God with a mighty hand, that is, relying on his own merits rather than on pleading and humility. It would then appear that relying on rights implies relying on "reason"—the belief that "the righteous prosper and the wicked suffer" is "cerebral work" or intellectual activity, whereas pleading is the path of those who are above reason, which is R. Nahman's way with Heaven. Nonetheless, R. Nahman counsels a mighty hand against the wicked of his own generation, and he himself seems to have followed this course, showing little concern in his own behavior for the finer points of justice; see notes 132 ff.

The teaching in *Likkutei Moharan* II, concerning the simplicity of the *tsaddik* that sustains his soul during the journey to the Holy Land and reflecting R. Nahman's low spirits at the end of his life, touches on this issue; see the extended discussion, p. 119. This teaching was delivered on *Shabbat Nahamu*, when the pertinent biblical reading, *Va-Ethannan*, opens with Moses' prayer to be allowed to enter the land: "And I besought God at that time, saying. . ." (Deuteronomy 3:23). R. Nahman, who speaks of this prayer in this teaching, did not explain why Moses' request was rejected. But according to the outline he had prepared (see note 24), it seems he had originally intended to discuss this point as well. These are the headings in the outline:

"And I besought," free gift, free, wantonness, the flaw of knowledge, Moses knowledge, chastity, stand here by me, creation is a free gift, the world is built by love, creation before the giving of the Torah, it is time to act for the Lord, namely, to make a world, they have made void thy Torah, cancelling the Torah, "at that time" saying in ten utterances, "that," concealment, He has declared to his people the power of his works.

This outline enables us to reconstruct the beginning of the original teaching, which was omitted from the final version, as follows: Moses asked for a free gift to enter the land,[46] but "free" is related to wantonness,[47] the potential cause of Moses' flaw, whose virtue is knowledge. Knowledge is bound to be blemished by the sexual sin,[48] and knowledge is probably linked to Moses because of his intellectual approach, as mentioned. The danger of sexual sin is what prevented Moses from entering the land of Israel and forced him into abstinence from sex, as hinted by the verse "But as for thee, stand here by me"[49] (Deuteronomy 5:28). The other headings are explained in the final teaching.

R. Nahman did enter the land and is thus superior to Moses because of his nonintellectual approach—his "land of Israel aspect." The *tikkun* of the people, a task at which Moses had failed, can now be attempted through R. Nahman's method. Furthermore, this reconstruction of the original teaching reveals that, due to his intellectual approach, even Moses was threatened with wantonness and was therefore forbidden to enter the land. R. Nahman's approach hence immunizes against the sexual flaw and amends it and might thus bring about redemption and carry its followers to the land of Israel. A clear link is thus postulated between the land of Israel and sexual chastity or, in kabbalistic terms, *shemirat ha-berit*. R. Nathan of Bratslav, as he signed his letters, was R. Nahman's chief disciple and drew similar conclusions from this outline, though without indicating that R. Nahman's was superior to Moses. The following statement appears in his *Likkutei Halakhot, Yore De'a,* Laws of Circumcision 3 (a section wholly based on teaching 58):[50]

> And all this depends precisely on sexual chastity, because the *tsaddik* is one who is chaste. Wantonness is the most shameful instinct, and a *tsaddik*—who is pure, subdues his instinct and withstands temptation— overpowers corruption and defeats all the world's evil....Our rabbi hints to this at the end of the outline to this teaching, written in his holy handwriting....It is only through sexual chastity that we shall go and inherit the land of Israel, as it is said "The righteous shall inherit the land" (Psalms 37:29) and as it is written "...didst make a covenant with him to give the land of the Canaanite..." (Nehemia 9:8).

(Indeed, the conquest of the sexual instict was an important part of the joy engulfing R. Nahman and his Hasidim when delivering this teaching; see note 128.)

Moreover, elsewhere in his book, R. Nathan was even more explicit regarding R. Nahman's intentions than what appears from *Likkutei Moharan*. He discussed extensively how the *tsaddik ha-dor* [the *tsaddik* of the generation] was assigned the task of conquering the land of Israel from the seven nations by remaining sexually chaste despite the many temptations (this conquest is a kind of circumcision). Indeed, all of R. Nahman's teachings strongly emphasize the supreme importance of sexual purity—for all men, and particularly for R. Nahman himself. The difficult sexual challenges faced by R. Nahman are often intimated in Bratslav literature,[51] and his victory over them is prominently described.[52]

In R. Nahman's view, which slightly resembles Freud's, the sexual sin includes all sins.[53] Therefore, amending this sin is *ha-tikkun ha-kelali*, the *tikkun* of all human sins and of the whole of Israel, as discussed in Section III.

The sexual *tikkun* of the *tsaddik ha-dor* paves the way for a similar *tikkun* among his Hasidim who, because of their naive faith in their rabbi and their personal link with him,[54] are spared the difficult trials experienced by him. The rabbi can thereby accomplish his role as a "*tsaddik*" and as the embodiment of the kabbalistic *sefira* of *yesod*, termed *tsaddik yesod olam* [the righteous is the foundation of the world], whose main symbol is the male sexual organ.[55] Its representative is destined to a messianic role in ancient kabbalistic tradition.[56] It hence becomes clear why the controversy about the *tsaddik*, who protects his generation from sexual sin, generates adulterous passion.[57] The struggle for sexual purity becomes the messianic activity par excellence, and the Messiah's main worldly concern is to guard from sexual sinfulness; all his Hasidim share in this war, perfecting the Messiah's stature through their own chastity.[58]

Whence the danger of a sexual flaw threatening Moses? The danger stems from his characteristic intellectual mode of worship. This answer is already intimated in the outline (see note 48) and proven according to the teachings cited earlier, explaining Moses' sin. Intellectual devotion, in addition to its lurking danger of heresy and the insoluble questions it poses—such as "the righteous suffer and the wicked prosper" that concerned Moses—entails a danger of lewdness. This link is sometimes explained anatomically, by pointing to the brain as a common source for both thought and semen (see note 53). However, it also relies on a profound understanding of the dominant role of sexuality in human life, even over the intellectual element. It is on these grounds that R. Nahman concluded that listening to heresy may lead to wantonness.[59] Hence, R. Nahman is a "know what to answer the heretic" (note 17) because of his victory over sexual temptation, and this victory enables him to restore the traditional Torah to its supreme rank. It is worth noting in this context that this link between the messianic figure of *tsaddik yesod olam* and sexual chastity, on the one hand, and the revelation of the Torah's mysteries, on the other, had already characterized in the Zohar the figure of R. Simeon b. Yohai, R. Nahman's archetype.[60]

Consequently, through his "land of Israel aspect," R. Nahman himself entails a *tikkun* of the various worldly evils. This point will be further clarified in the discussion on the *tikkun* of Sabbateanism and *ha-tikkun ha-kelali.*

II. R. Nahman's Views on Sabbateanism

For R. Nahman, the Sabbatean heresy was the root and the symbol of all worldly evil, and he believed that he had come into the world to repair it. This is a view that often recurs in Bratslav literature, and I shall relate to some of these references in the course of the following discussion.[61] Sabbateanism is a twofold wrong, compounding doctrinal heresies and practical transgressions and, worst among them, the one transgression encompassing all others—sexual licentiousness.[62]

Both these wrongs shall be amended through the true *tsaddik*— R. Nahman. *Tikkun* will be attained through his own personal experience of contending with and overcoming his heretic impulses and evil inclination and, most important, through his congregation's faith in him, as R. Nahman's personal *tikkun* carries national—and even cosmic—connotations. Thus did R. Nahman intend to restore the organic wholeness of the Jewish people and their belief in Torah— particularly in the Oral Law as it had been preserved by the sages and so gravely eroded by Sabbateanism—because the *tsaddik ha-dor* symbolizes both this wholeness and the Torah. If the *tsaddik* is the Torah, then an affront against the Torah is an affront against him though, on the other hand, this identification between them enables the *tsaddik* to amend offenses against the Torah.

The Sabbatean-Frankist heresy caused unprecedented harm to the people and to the Torah. R. Nahman pointed out that it was precisely the Frankists' eminence, as well as their broad knowledge, that made them particularly destructive.[63] The Frankists' transgression is seen as rooted in the cosmic-historical circumstances prevailing at the time as well as in their own sin that, in my view, was sexual. It was the Frankist sin that caused the death of the *tsaddik ha-dor*, R. Israel Baal Shem Tov, who died soon after the Frankist apostasy. The

Frankists were able to cause the Besht's death only because of his relatively low spiritual rung. A higher-ranking *tsaddik*, by whom R. Nahman obviously intended himself, shall repair and temper the Sabbatean teachings and turn them again into Torah. Because this teaching is extremely important to our discussion, I quote it almost in its entirety:

Know that, sometimes,[64] harsh *gevurot* [judgments][65] are issued, may God save us from them, and they befall the best and the greatest, due to their vast knowledge.[66] [It is made clear later that this reference is to the Sabbateans.] After they are issued, harsh *gevurot* enter, God forbid, the minds of the great, and come forth from their mouths[67] as words. Words are as harsh *gevurot* and ways must be sought to temper them, but we may lack the power to do this or it may be impossible to modify these words, since they have already caused a flaw or a sin—even the greatest *tsaddikim* at times err and cause harm, for there is not a righteous man upon earth, etc. [Ecclesiastes 7:20, and the verse continues: that does good and sins not. The minimization of the Sabbatean sin in this description is worth noting.] When these harsh *gevurot* cannot be tempered, bad words are then uttered about the people, or about certain individuals, or about the *tsaddik ha-dor* [who encompasses the whole people]. When, God forbid, these words befall the *tsaddik ha-dor*, he must seek to temper them by dealing leniently with their accusations and showing mercy, or by accepting with love the suffering caused by these words. However, if the *tsaddik ha-dor*, God forbid, has no power to temper them, these *gevurot* might cause him to fall far below his rung—he may indeed die through them but, after his death, his soul shall mitigate the harsh *gevurot*.[68] This is how the Besht died, because he had said he would die by the deeds of the Sabbetai Zevi, may his name be blotted out,[69] that had led astray several of the learned scholars of his generation who, as is well known,[70] abandoned the fold[71] and spoke evil of the Oral Law,[72] and this is because harsh *gevurot* befell them without being tempered, as we have said. They therefore spoke evil of the people,[73] and their words harmed the *tsaddik ha-dor* in their times—the Besht—who then died because of them. We are told that the Besht, of blessed memory, had said that the act of the Sabbetai Zevi, may his name be blotted out, had caused two holes to pierce his heart, which then brought about his death.[74] The Oral Law and the *tsaddik ha-dor* are one and the same—as it is said, the *Shekhinah* rests between two *tsaddikim*. The Oral

Law depends mainly on the *tsaddik ha-dor*,[75] who is the Oral Law, as it is said elsewhere.[76] The scholar is himself the Torah, as the sages tell us, "How dull-witted are those other people. . .",[77] but when the *tsaddik* tempers their words [of the heretics] he turns them again into Torah, as it is said elsewhere.[78] He then makes them into *torat hesed*, that is, teaching them to others, as the sages had commented[79] on the verse[80] "and on her tongue is a *torat hesed*" [a Torah of loving kindness], claiming it means one who learns in order to teach. When one turns their words [the heretics' words!] into Torah, these words can then be taught to others, making one as a *torat hesed* who had tempered their words.

Several points merit attention in this teaching:

1. The description of the Sabbateans as "the best and the greatest," who have erred "due to their vast knowledge" and have sinned as any other *tsaddik* would have; even Moses could be drawn into lascivious passion because of his overintellectualism, (see note 48).
2. The extent of their harm.
3. The urgency of their *tikkun*.
4. The relative inadequacy of the Besht, who had failed in the *tikkun* of the Sabbateans during his lifetime (in R. Nahman's terms: "if the *tsaddik ha-dor*, God forbid, has no power to temper them"). We are reminded in this context of Moses' flaw, for which he was condemned not to enter the land, and it will become clear later that both the Besht and Moses are blemished by a sexual flaw—the inavailability of *ha-tikkun ha-kelali*. On the other hand, R. Nahman's superior virtue will amend the Sabbateans by means of *ha-tikkun ha-kelali* and even accomplish the Besht's mission; see note 61.
5. The specific *tikkun* suggested by R. Nahman, which I will now consider.

First, R. Nahman stated that the essence of this *tikkun* is that the *tsaddik* "deals leniently with their accusations" or, in other words, the *tsaddik* finds merit in the heretics' imputations. R. Nahman indeed adopted this rule and often justified his oponents in his writings, both the Hasidim—led by Arye Leib, "the Old Man of Shpola"—and Hasidism's foes—the *maskilim* and the learned *mitnaggedim*. In a dialectic, paradoxical fashion, R. Nahman often showed the antagonism of his adversaries to be highly valuable.[81]

R. Nahman may indeed have had no difficulty behaving in this manner toward his heretic contemporaries, who were not Sabbateans and directed their attacks against him personally, though, in my view, R. Nahman thought of their heresy as an outgrowth of the Sabbatean crisis and believed that the *tikkun* of Sabbateanism would be a general *tikkun*, or *ha-tikkun ha-kelali*. However, the Besht could hardly have adopted this course, despite R. Nahman's apparent expectations to the contrary. The Frankists had not targeted the Besht personally—they had maligned the people and the Torah that, according to R. Nahman, were incarnate in the Besht.[82] It is even harder "to temper the *gevurot*" of the Frankists when we remember that they were apostates, responsible for slanderous blood libels and the burning of the Talmud. The gravity of these acts only highlights the paradox entailed by R. Nahman's *tikkun*. His lenient view of the *tsaddik*'s opponents resembles the notion of the Messiah bringing redemption through his suffering, which is often found in R. Nahman's writings and apparently originates in Sabbateanism rather than in Christianity.[83]

However, R. Nahman went even further: He claimed that *tikkun* requires the *tsaddik* to "turn [the heretics' words] again into Torah." After they have been rehabilitated as Torah, the *tsaddik* should teach these modified doctrines, originally Sabbatean, to others and, for R. Nahman, this is *torat hesed*.[84] It is worth noting that, through his very choice of the term *torat hesed*, R. Nahman was acting in line with his own requirement because, in this meaning,[85] *torat hesed* is a Sabbatean term. The Sabbateans used the term *torat hesed* to refer to Islam, which Sabbetai Zevi is supposed to have embraced in order to temper the evil of the Gentile nations.[86] This is also the meaning of *torat hesed* in the Bratslav context though, in this case, the evil in question is Sabbateanism. Elsewhere, the concept of *torat hesed* is used in relation to the Gentile nations together with the wicked from among the children of Israel:[87]

> It is impossible to raise His glory except through *torat hesed*. The sages said of *torat hesed* that this is the one who studies Torah in order to teach it, for this is the essence of His glory, as it is said in the Zohar:[88] "When the other nations come and recognize the Holy One, then the name of God ascends and is glorified above and below.". . . It is impossible for the wicked of Israel and for the converts from the nations to awaken to repentance except through the Torah, as it is said:[89] "Your wellsprings shall spread outward," implying literally outward.[90]

Indeed, according to another teaching,[91] the *tikkun* of Sabbateanism is also the *tikkun* of the Gentile nations. This teaching speaks of the *tsaddik* as compounded of two Messiahs—the Messiah Son of David and the Messiah Son of Joseph—who shall amend the nations of Ishmael and Esau that, like clouds, cover the *tsaddik*'s eyes and dim his wisdom. (R. Nahman relied on the verse "Your wellsprings shall spread outward" in reference to the Messiahs who amend the nations of the world, see note 90.) Weiss had already assumed that the reference to the *tikkun* of these two nations—Ishmael and Esau— was intended mainly as the *tikkun* of the two Sabbatean Messiahs who had converted—Sabbetai Zevi to Islam and Jacob Frank to Esau's religion (Christianity)—but that self-censorship had prevented such an explicit formulation. If this is the case, then it applies here as well—R. Nahman did not merely formulate a theory about the *tikkun* of Sabbateanism but actually implemented this *tikkun* by relying on Sabbatean doctrine and seizing it as his own because, in my view, this theory itself was inspired by the kabbalist and Sabbatean Messiah Miguel Cardozo.[92]

The theory that the *tikkun* of Sabbateanism might be attained by appropriating their views and approximating them was not new: the need for descending into evil in order to uplift wrongdoers was one of Hasidism's fundamental concepts.[93] A well-known tradition claims that the Besht had attempted the *tikkun* of Sabbetai Zevi until he himself was almost tempted into Sabbateanism and conversion to Christianity.[94] But R. Nahman went so far as to be taken for a true Sabbatean and, indeed, several indications suggest that the misgivings on this matter were a crucial factor in the controversy about him.[95]

R. Nahman himself admitted that his views could arouse suspicions of Sabbateanism and, when carefully examined, his statements indeed attest to his deep links with this movement (in line with the doctrine of *tikkun* through affinity). More specifically, I am referring to R. Nahman's stand on the controversy that had broken out about fifty years previously between R. Jacob Emden and R. Jonathan Eybeschuetz. R. Jonathan had been justifiably suspected[96] of Sabbatean leanings and writing Sabbatean amulets, and R. Nahman took his side in this dispute:[97]

> On the well-known past dispute over R. Jonathan, of blessed memory. R. Nahman had a book where the amulets given out by R. Jonathan were written and it said in them *avdo meviho*, while his opponents claimed that he had meant *avdo meshiho* [his servant, the Messiah]. R. Nahman discussed this with us and said that from this there was no proof. He then added that, if he himself were to write amulets and his opponents were to

find them, they would also say, etc. [in other words, he himself, R. Nahman, would also be accused of Sabbateanism] especially the name *avdo*. Because the whole Torah is names. On the use of these names as invocations, or for petition or prayer, he said that the name arouses the angel appropriate to the matter and the angel is then given a name, since the angel has no name and he is given one according to his mission. Hence, it is appropriate to write in the invocation of names *avdo meviho*, because this is an acronym of the verse: *Ve-Noah Matsa Hen be-Einei Adonai* ["And Noah found favor in the eyes of the Lord"] (Genesis 6:8).

R. Nahman must have seen R. Jonathan's amulets and their heretic exegeses in R. Jacob Emden's book *Sefat Emet*.[98] Indeed, almost every amulet mentioned in this book contains the formula *avdo meshiho*, or simply *meshiho*, by transposing the letters of *meviho*.[99] However, it was not the names *meviho* or *meshiho* that evoked the controversy around Eybeschuetz but the name Sabbetai Zevi, which appears consistently after the words *avdo meshiho* or other similar titles and could not possibly have been overlooked by R. Nahman when studying the book. Had he wished to justify R. Jonathan and acquit him of the suspicion of Sabbateanism, he should have dealt with the very name of Sabbetai Zevi or its various transpositions in the amulets. Hence, it seems to me that R. Nahman had intended to interpret the name Sabbetai Zevi as he had the name *meviho*, but this must have appeared too daring an act, and he therefore refrained from it (though perhaps he did suggest this interpretation and it was later censored in the printed version of the book). How does R. Nahman justify the use of such a formula, to the point of claiming that, were he to write amulets, he himself would have used it? He claimed that God's mission is accomplished through every name and that Sabbetai Zevi's name also qualifies for this task. This claim certainly seems to intimate that God had made some positive use of Sabbetai Zevi, as suggested by the content of the verse making up the acronym *meviho*—"And Noah found favor in the eyes of the Lord." Like Noah, Sabbetai Zevi may have been useful in his own time, as Rashi comments on the following biblical verse, relying on a rabbinical exegesis. It is noteworthy that Noah's figure played a significant role in Sabbatean literature as an archetype of the Messiah—Sabbetai Zevi.[100]

In my view, this affinity with Sabbateanism—even if only intended for its *tikkun*—posed no problems to R. Nahman, who felt that his situation slightly resembled that of a Sabbatean Messiah.

His aim, as theirs, was also messianic, and he not only wished for the *tikkun* of their sin but also for success where they had failed. Moreover, as is well known, there was a certain historical-terminological-ideological continuity between Sabbateanism and Hasidism. This continuity might shed light on some of the parallels between the Sabbatean messiahs and R. Nahman, who epitomized the Hasidic *tsaddik*.

Indeed, as his approach to *tikkun* would have it, we found that many elements in R. Nahman's doctrine were developed from Sabbatean sources.[101] After all, as R. Nahman had already said: "The Blessed King is even found in heresy."[102] However, the critical parallel is in R. Nahman's personality as a leader, which is very close to that of Sabbatean messiahs, whose doctrines also hinge on their own fate and their personal experiences. Thus, Sabbatean literature includes many descriptions of the torments suffered by Sabbetai Zevi when lured by heresy and by his evil inclination and of the profound cosmic meaning of his victory over these temptations.[103] Like R. Nahman, the Sabbatean Messiah had proffered as the supreme religious value the naive faith of his followers in his leadership—despite the contradictions of his personality—and had favored it over the study of Torah.[104] Sabbetai Zevi too wavered between bouts of illumination and depression, which he attempted to overcome by delving into its meaning, see note 26. He too would forget his previous attainments, see note 38; and he too was perceived as the incarnation of the Torah, see note 76. However, in many ways, R. Nahman seems in fact closer to Jacob Frank, see note 101, whose leadership was also marked by deep sexuality.[105] Both R. Nahman and Jacob Frank were despotic leaders who never hesitated to pour insult and abuse upon their followers and despised them for their ignoble station.[106] Last but not least, both saw it fit to describe themselves as ignoramuses and to boast about it, by referring to themselves in Yiddish as *prostik* or "the big *prostak*."[107]

The preceding two sections presented the theoretical background of the practical-ritual activity intended by R. Nahman for the *tikkun* of Sabbateanism—*ha-tikkun ha-kelali*.

III. *Ha-Tikkun Ha-Kelali*

Ha-tikkun ha-kelali is a ritual instituted by R. Nahman to repair the sexual sin of improper seminal emission. This ritual includes immersion in a ritual bath and the reading of ten Psalms selected by R. Nahman.[108]

First and foremost, the very name *ha-tikkun ha-kelali* endorses the view that, because the sexual sin includes all sins pertaining to all limbs (see note 53) its *tikkun* ensures that of all others. *Ha-tikkun ha-kelali* hence entails the *tikkun* of "all organs and arteries."[109] In the Zohar, and in the Kabbala as a whole, the sin of improper seminal emission is regarded as extremely grave, due to its critical consequences in the demonic realm (engendering demons and evil spirits) as well as in the cosmic domain (enhancing the *sitra ahra* [the realm of evil] at the expense of the *Shekhina*, entailing national implications). The *tikkun* of this sin is considered exceedingly difficult, and the Zohar even doubts whether penitence for it is at all possible, or helpful.[110] Sexual chastity and the *sefira* of *yesod* are regarded in the Zohar as a shield protecting man from all evil.[111] In stressing that this was a grievous offence whose amemdment was crucial, R. Nahman thus endorsed the classic kabbalistic approach rather than the Hasidic view.[112] In this light, it is understandable why R. Nahman and his followers saw his discovery of this easily manageable *tikkun* as such a meaningful achievement. It is on these grounds that they so strongly emphasized R. Nahman's role as the one who had instituted this *tikkun*[113] as well as the importance of disseminating it. These issues are dealt with at length in *Sihot ha-Ran* 141, and I quote briefly:

> He also said then that the issue of which ten psalms are to be recited must be revealed to all and, although it might seem easy to recite ten Psalms, it will in fact be very difficult to put this into practice. He has indeed been proven true: because of all the controversies, most people are very far from observing this *tikkun*. He, of blessed memory, had already predicted this, but we have done our duty and have announced this *tikkun* to all who wish to follow it, and let each one do as he sees fit—some will listen and some will not, but we have saved our own souls.

Bratslav Hasidim have indeed persisted in this effort and *ha-tikkun ha-kelali*, including the ten Psalms, has by now appeared in dozens of editions.[114] But the question is whether the significance of *ha-tikkun ha-kelali* and the importance of its diffusion are thereby exhausted. Is there no deeper, esoteric layer to it? Indeed there is. Weiss[115] had already sensed that R. Nahman's instruction to reveal the issue of the ten Psalms contradicts the "*panzer* story." This story is also linked to *ha-tikkun ha-kelali* but, as is made clear by another Bratslav source,[116] it is private and esoteric. Weiss merely pointed to the esoteric dimension of "the *panzer* story" without attempting to consider its meaning, as I intend to do in the following.

I shall argue that the esoteric meaning of *ha-tikkun ha-kelali* is messianic, as are most esoteric hints in Bratslav literature, Even the name, *ha-tikkun ha-kelali* suggests perhaps not only the repair of the whole individual and his sins, but the repair of the whole nation and, chiefly, the amemdment of the nation's archetypal sin—Sabbateanism.

Having clarified R. Nahman's attitude to Sabbateanism, will not surprise the reader that, though meant to repair the sin of Sabbateanism and to succeed where the Sabbateans had failed, this *"tikkun"* has deep Sabbatean roots, which R. Nahman developed further. For instance, I shall try to show that the *panzer* story which, as mentioned, conveys the esoteric content of *ha-tikkun ha-kelali*, is part of the war against Sabbateanism but is also drawn from the terminology the Sabbateans used to describe the messianic *tikkun* they themselves attempted in 1666. Given the close links between redemption and sexual purity assumed by Bratslav's theory of redemption, the messianic overtones of *ha-tikkun ha-kelali*, even though originally intended as the individual *tikkun* of a sexual sin, might seem more understandable. Moreover, given the meaning of *tikkun* for the *tsaddik ha-dor*, it is no wonder that *ha-tikkun ha-kelali* is chiefly aimed, as I show later, at the *tikkun* of R, Nahman himself, thus highlighting its messianic connotations even further, as R. Nahman's personal *tikkun* is that of the whole people.

It can indeed be shown that he had originally intended *ha-tikkun ha-kelali* for himself. R. Nahman had sternly warned that the first rule of *ha-tikkun ha-kelali*, to be strictly observed, is immersion in a ritual bath.[117] This rule might help clarify his comment elsewhere: "He said the ritual bath is never harmful, and any doctor who says it is is no doctor at all."[118] A tone of personal defiance can clearly be discerned in this teaching, which appears toward the end of the book and was obviously uttered during R. Nahman's last days, when he was ill with tuberculosis and consulting with doctors in Uman.[119] Doctors probably advised against his immersion in a cold ritual bath, an order he must have found unacceptable due to his adherence to this ritual. This approach to *ha-tikkun ha-kelali* as the personal *tikkun* of R. Nahman—and through him, of others—might also be apparent in R. Nahman's promise to intercede in favor of those reciting the ten Psalms on his grave (*Sihot ha-Ran* 141), a practice that was also supposed to benefit R. Nahman's soul (see note 151). It is perhaps worth remembering in this context that the *tsaddik*'s grave is "a facet of the land of Israel" and a means toward redemption, even after his death.

It was R. Nahman's personal *tikkun* that paved the way for the *tikkun* of the people, turning *ha-tikkun ha-kelali* into a relatively easy ritual. The messianic significance of *tikkun* for the whole people and the very possibility of *tikkun* are thus behind the unprecedented efforts invested in disseminating *ha-tikkun ha-kelali*. An option for bringing about *tikkun* had emerged, quite unlike anything ever known or, in R. Nahman's words (ibid.), "This has not been revealed since Creation."

A close reading of the theoretical explanations advanced for *ha-tikkun ha-kelali* will disclose its messianic concerns. Through *ha-tikkun ha-kelali*, the people of Israel will overcome cosmic evil and redeem the *Shekhina* (the "Princess") from its exile. The redemption of the *Shekhina* in the Kabbala means, first and foremost, the redemption of Israel, its symbol. *Ha-tikkun ha-kelali* is hence seen elsewhere[120] as purifying the *Shekhina* from its menstrual blood and curing the epileptic disease afflicting it. These circumstances might shed light on R. Nahman's reasons for choosing these particular ten psalms. As he himself attests, he chose them because they represent the ten varieties of song mentioned in the Book of Psalms.[121] *Sefer Tikkunei Ha-Zohar*[122] interpreted these ten varieties in a messianic context, as the ten knocks with which God (or perhaps the Messiah) awaken the *Shekhina* asleep in Exile, in an exegesis of Song of Songs 5:2: "I sleep but my heart wakes: hark, my beloved is knocking. . ." This certainly points to the messianic connotations of *ha-tikkun ha-kelali*, chiefly because of its association with the first of R. Nahman's tales in *Sippurei Ma'asiyyot*, "The Loss of the Princess," which all agree is concerned with a messianic theme—redeeming the *Shekhina* from its exile. This tale resembles the legend of Sleeping Beauty though somewhat in reverse, in that the sleeper is the one who seeks and redeems the kings' daughter. An even more explicit parallel is found at the end of the tale of "The Seven Beggars," where the handless pauper boasts of his ability to heal the "princess" [the *Shekhina*],[123] who had been injured by ten arrows smeared with ten kinds of poison. He then boasts further: "I can remove the ten different arrows from the princess. I know all the ten kinds of *defikin* [pulse] and can heal the princess with the ten varieties of song."

This is an obvious reference to *ha-tikkun ha-kelali* that, as was mentioned, comprises the ten varieties of song interpreted in the *Sefer Tikkunei Ha-Zohar* as the ten pulses [*defikin*] that will heal the *Shekhina*. The healing pauper is obviously no other than R. Nahman himself, whose various facets are embodied in the figures of the seven beggars as well as in all the other tales.[124] Hence, *ha-tikkun ha-kelali* is R. Nahman's way of bringing redemption to the *Shekhina* and to Israel. Further evidence comes from R. Nathan's explicit testimony regarding R. Nahman's belief that, through the ten varieties of song (in a clear reference to the ten psalms making up *ha-tikkun ha-kelali*), it will be possible to eliminate all obstructions and go to the land of Israel.[125]

The ten varieties of song intimated in the ten psalms of *ha-tikkun ha-kelali* not only redeem the *Shekhina* positively and directly but also indirectly; namely, by defeating the opposing forces of evil that confine it and harm it. In the tale of "The Seven Beggars," these ten are obviously suggested by the ten poisoned arrows wounding the princess—the *Shekhina*—and causing her illness. R. Nathan[126] interpreted these arrows as symbols of drops from an improper seminal emission. This interpretation fits well with the claim that, when discussing the healing of the princess, R. Nahman had intended *ha-tikkun ha-kelali*, which is also concerned with repairing the misdeed of improper seminal emission. This is further evidence of the cosmic and national flaw caused by the sexual sin and of the messianic character of *ha-tikkun ha-kelali*.

There is an alternative explanation for the ten varieties of song that correspond to the ten psalms prescribed by R. Nahman. In his theoretical background to *ha-tikkun ha-kelali*, R. Nahman claims that these ten varieties of song correspond to ten parallel types of song found in the *kelippa*, the cosmic evil force according to Kabbalah.[127] R. Nahman discussed only three of these evil parallels, interpreting them as hinting to the demonic spirit of Lilith in her various guises. We might infer from the three he did discuss that the remaining seven, which he did not, hint to Lilith too. In Kabbala, Lilith is not just another demon but the female aspect of the *sitra ahra* or the evil force and, consequently, the evil counterpart to the *Shekhina* ("the princess"). Lilith rises from the ruins of the *Shekhina*, and redemption will come through Lilith's downfall. Thus, for instance, R. Nahman claims that the adequate study of Talmud overpowers Lilith but that inadequate study—perhaps in the manner of the *mitnaggedim?*— enhances her strength, because the numerological equivalent of "Talmud" is "Lilith" (*Likkutei Moharan* I:214).

Lilith is linked to two domains, sadness and sexual temptation; when mating with men at night, Lilith causes their improper seminal emissions (this is a widespread notion in kabbalistic literature). Consequently, the ten psalms of *ha-tikkun ha-kelali*, comprising the ten holy varieties of song, have been instituted against her. These songs will evoke the simple joy that surges from despair and overcomes it which, as mentioned, signifies redemption in Bratslav doctrine. Joy is expressed in song, dance, and hand clapping, often identified in Bratslav literature with the hearbeat and with life and at times called *defikin* [pulses] (apparently the same ones mentioned in the excerpt from the tale of "The Seven Beggars" quoted earlier).

Bratslav Hasidism thus shares in the dominant Hassidic tradition that places high value on joy, song, and dance, though a further dimension seems to have been added—the dialectic meaning of joy emerging from despair and capable of defeating Lilith, the root of all despondence. Hence, in Bratslav Hasidism, joy is connected to redemption. In this context, it is worth noting that the end of "The Seven Beggars"—or rather its end as we know it, because it is suggested in a postscript that the end of this tale will become known only with the coming of the Messiah—deals with the healing of the princess through ten types of song. This tale begins with the words: "What do you know of joy surging from melancholy" and is wholly concerned with redemption (see note 22). This joy is what defeats Lilith (= melancholy) and heretic thoughts, and it is also related to the overpowering of the sexual instinct, as confirmed by the circumstances surrounding the messianic teaching dealing with R. Nahman's simplicity.[128] Sadness and the sexual instinct are Lilith's two aspects: "Sexual temptation results from sadness and melancholy" (*Sihot ha-Ran* 129). R. Nahman explained the three evil counterparts to the holy varieties of song as follows: the term *ashrei* [happy] in the Book of Psalms is related to sight (from the Hebrew root *shur*); its counterpart is Lilith, who entails blindness,[129] apparently intending both sexual wantonness and the heeding of heretic views, chiefly Sabbateanism.[130] On the other hand, the *maskil* of the Psalms becomes the *meshakkel* of Lilith, alluding to lewdness and improper seminal emissions, whereas the counterpart to the "Halleluja" of the Psalms are the similar-sounding "Lilith" and *yelala* [howl]. As a rule, the counterpart to Lilith's howls and sexual wantonness are the ten psalms containing the ten varieties of song, or "the height of joy, holiness, and chastity" (these ten are also parallel to the five *hasadim* [graces] and the five *gevurot* [judgments] making up the brain in Lurianic Kabbala and thereby able to repair semen, which originates in the brain).

But can these songs, which generate sadness, lewdness, and heresy and need to be repaired through *ha-tikkun ha-kelali*, be defined more exactly? In my view, these songs are a product of Sabbateanism and, by repairing them, R. Nahman sought to attain its *tikkun*. Evidence for this claim can be found in *Likkutei Moharan* I:3, concerning the *tikkun* of an evil man's song through David's song in the Book of Psalms. Weiss had already indicated[131] that this teaching deals in fact with R. Nahman's *tikkun* of the Frankist sin. Furthermore, the sin of Sabbateanism is related both to sexual transgressions (see note 62) as well as to sadness and asceticism (see notes 94 and 95). There is a similar teaching regarding the trip to Lvov, for the purpose of the Frankists' *tikkun*, see Appendix I.

Additional evidence points to further links between the *tikkun* of the Frankists' sin and *ha-tikkun ha-kelali*. As was mentioned (note 116), the esoteric meaning of *ha-tikkun ha-kelali* is embodied in the tale beginning with the words: "When going to war, one wears an armour called *panzer.*" In my view, this is a clear reference to the war against Frankism: R. Nahman had claimed that the two holes in the *Besht*'s heart that caused his death (see p. 129) were a result of the Frankist sin. Had *ha-tikkun ha-kelali*, symbolized by the armour, been known to the *Besht*, he would have worn it to protect his heart and would have succeded in his aim of "tempering" the Sabbateans' words. *Ha-tikkun ha-kelali* is hence directed against the Frankists' sin and represents R. Nahman's advantage over the *Besht*, enabling him to succeed where his ancestor had failed, namely, in tempering and repairing Sabbateanism.

The presumed link between the "armour" and the *tikkun* of the Frankist sin might serve to support a similar assumption regarding another term—*maginnei erets* [defenders of the land]. This is how R. Nahman referred to himself (*Likkutei Moharan* II:5₇), explaining that he is so called because he defeats and repairs the wicked leaders of his time, whose pride increases sexual unchastity in the world. These motifs fit well with the notion of *ha-tikkun ha-kelali* as aiming to mend the sexual sin through the *tsaddik* wearing an armour and a *magen* [shield]). *Ha-tikkun ha-kelali* thus also serves to mend those leaders opposed to R. Nahman, reflecting the notion that all controversy is in fact rooted in the original dispute with the Sabbateans (on sexual chastity and *yesod* acting as a shield, see note 111).

Whereas R. Nahman created a positive association with the term *maginnei erets* (as I believe, in connection with the *tikkun* of Sabbateanism), Arye Leib from Shpola meant it as a derogatory reference to R. Nahman implying, as will become clear, an accusation of Sabbateanism. R. Nathan linked these two meanings—R. Nahman's positive connotation and the negative one by Arye Leib.[132] Piekarz[133] had already been puzzled at this strange pejorative usage of *maginnei erets* and concluded that Arye Leib had meant to accuse R. Nahman of Frankism. According to Piekarz, the connection between this title and the sin of Frankism works as follows: The Frankists collaborated with the blood libel spread by Christian priests, accusing Jews of using Christian blood during the Passover Seder. For this purpose, they enlisted "supporting" quotes from Jewish sources, relying chiefly on the *Maginnei Erets*, a work comprising the *Shulkhan Arukh* and its two commentators, *Magen Abraham* and *Magen David*, Section 472:12, concerning the wine for the Passover Seder. The Frankists opened their attack with the words: "In the book *Maginnei Erets*" and, therefore, when Arye Leib called R. Nahman *maginnei erets*, he was hinting at this deed and intimating a spiritual connection between R. Nahman and the slandering Frankists.

Though Piekarz's brilliant hypothesis might seem far-fetched, my suggestion of a link between the title *maginnei erets* and the armour of *ha-tikkun ha-kelali*, which is the *tikkun* of Sabbateanism, might lend it credence. R. Nahman took a title hinting at his own involvement with the Frankists and transformed it into a symbol of his status as the reformer of Frankism, relying once more on his usual approach toward the *tikkun* of this sin—affinity.

Further confirmation of Piekarz's hypothesis might be suggested by another source. Rather than linking the title *maginnei erets* to the general context of Frankism, Piekarz referred to the specific charge of blood libel. It is possible that Arye Leib too had meant an explicit imputation: He was perhaps alluding to the charges that R. Nahman had brought before the state authorities against him and his followers. For Arye Leib, these charges were perhaps associated with the Frankist blood libel, which is related to the title *maginnei erets*.

Several indications suggest that R. Nahman had acted in this manner or had at least planned to do so. I am referring to the bribing of government officials in return for the punishment of his adversaries, possibly Arye Leib and his followers. This act would resemble the Frankist libel in its aims too—removing all obstructions preventing us from attaining redemption and going to the land of Israel (the wicked obstructors are described here as being the cause of sexual sin as well, and the war against them is thus *ha-tikkun ha-kelali*!). The justifications adduced for R. Nahman's false charges and his consequent wrongdoings, such as bribing the authorities, bear a strong resemblance to Sabbatean ideology: the use of Gentile laws is required to bring out the sparks of *"ha-mishpat de-kedusha"* [holy justice], which fell between the *kelippot*! It is precisely on these grounds that the Sabbateans justified all their offences—including apostasy; it is possible that the Frankists too relied on these same arguments to justify their own blood libel, and these claims could have reached R. Nahman through them. For his part, by using against his adversaries the same weapons to which the Sabbateans had resorted against theirs, R. Nahman was once more embracing the resemblance tactic to bring about the *tikkun* of Sabbateanism. Moreover, because R. Nahman related to his own conflict with his adversaries as a later manifestation of the Sabbatean controversy, his own war is to be seen as a war against Sabbateanism. When he waged war against the Sabbateans with their own weapons, R. Nahman was hence involved in a twofold struggle—the direct one and the tempering one. The use of resemblance in a positive cause elevates the Sabbatean doctrine, no matter how despicable, to the level of holiness. Obviously, this claim was totally unacceptable to Arye Leib, who saw R. Nahman as continuing the Frankist heresy.

It must be noted that we have no evidence of R. Nahman ever having brought charges against Arye Leib or any of his followers. I am merely relying on a theoretical teaching of R. Nahman, that justifies informing on other Jews and bribing the authorities for the sake of redemption, as well as on R. Nahman's statement (p. 123) that his own high rung is a form of *tikkun*, which others might see as a "distortion of justice." It seems quite inconceivable to me that anyone would develop such a theory and justify such actions merely in abstract terms, without requiring them to excuse his actual deeds. I am therefore assuming that an event of this type indeed took place. Arye Leib's use of the title *maginnei erets* lends support to this hypothesis—he indeed made his statement about a year and a half after R. Nahman's own teaching.[134]

Passages from this teaching that, in my opinion, include these views, follow:[135]

> but the land of Israel is one of three things attained through suffering [according to Berakhot 5a], caused mainly by the wicked obstructors who slander it. The wicked must first be defeated and punished by sword and death, and we shall then go to the land of Israel. The strength to punish the wicked can only be drawn from Edom [the Christian kingdoms!]. . .at times, it is not even possible for the angels [created through the *tsaddik*'s teachings] to defeat the wicked, because the angels are weak since the world is not sufficiently holy. Hence, they can only arouse the nations against the wicked slanderers of the land, as now in our exile, when we have no power of our own to punish the wicked except through their [the Gentiles'] laws "for the wicked man besets the righteous so that justice goes out perverted" (Habakuk 1:4). The wicked beset the righteous and we cannot rebuff them except through their laws, judging them by their rules and drawing on their strength to pursue the wicked. Know that at times it is caused by God [namely, it is God's will] that the wicked should beset the righteous, and the righteous cannot reject their wickedness but through their laws. And it is through the power of justice that we draw out the

mishpat de-kedusha [holy justice] that fell between the *kelippot*. It is the righteous that draw it out from the *kelippot* and justice is no longer perverted as it had been in the *kelippot* [a Sabbatean argument!]...thus, the wicked must at times be coerced through gentile justice. "And I will pay for it" [Numbers 20:19—there is an extensive exegesis of this verse and its context according to the Targum], this is their money, namely, the bribes they receive—they must be paid so that the perversion of justice might be avoided...

It is also made clear that these deeds—defeating the wicked by informing on them to the Gentiles and paying bribes—can be performed only by a perfect *tsaddik*, who acts only for the sake of Heaven rather than "for the pleasures of this world." Perhaps this was the sin of the Sabbateans, who did choose this course but failed. R. Nahman, who was a perfect *tsaddik* and all his actions were for the sake of Heaven, would succeed where they failed and thereby repair them. His perfection is linked to *ha-tikkun ha-kelali*, which he wore as an armour, enabling him to repair the sexual flaw caused by the wicked slandering the land, as he indicated in this teaching. Thus, protected by the armour of *ha-tikkun ha-kelali*, R. Nahman would repair the sin of Sabbateanism as well as all the sins and disputes that followed in its wake, paving the way toward the land of Israel and toward redemption.

Finally, I shall argue that the source of *ha-tikkun ha-kelali*, which is the *tikkun* of Sabbateanism, is itself Sabbatean and yet another instance of *tikkun* through resemblance. As is well known, the messianic fervor that accompanied Sabbetai Zevi's appearance in 1665–1666 was closely linked to a movement of repentance initiated by Nathan of Gaza, Sabbetai Zevi's prophet. This movement of repentance had general aims—returning the whole people, in the heels of the Messiah, to their Father in Heaven—but repentance was essentially a private phenomenon, touching each individual personally. Nathan of Gaza was therefore not satisfied with a public call for general repentance but also provided rituals for the *tikkun* of individual sins.[136] Beside the *tikkun* of individual offences, Nathan of Gaza, or perhaps even Sabbetai Zevi himself,[137] instituted a general *tikkun* for all transgressions and called it *tikkun kelali*, which opens as follows:[138] "Whoever wishes to attain *tikkun kelali* for all his sins..." I have found no precedent for this usage of the expression *tikkun kelali* before Nathan of Gaza.[139]

But it is not only the name *tikkun kelali* that Nathan of Gaza and R. Nahman have in common. Like R. Nahman, Nathan of Gaza also claimed in the text of his *tikkun* that the sexual sin subsumes all others, and its *tikkun* is that of all others. Moreover, this *tikkun* is also closely linked to thought and the mind, which are also repaired through sexual chastity, and Nathan hence refered to sexual chastity as *tikkun gamur* [complete *tikkun*]. Although the theoretical roots of these ideas can perhaps be traced back to kabbalistic literature,[140] before Nathan of Gaza and R. Nahman after him no one had ever brought them to this explicit conclusion, to the point of specifying a practical approach for attaining a general *tikkun*. Following is a quote from Nathan of Gaza's *tikkun kelali*:

> A man seeking his own *tikkun* must first amend his sexual sins and be severely punished, and whoever incurs a sexual transgression harms the brain too, which is the source of semen, as well as the body, because semen goes through the body and through the spine, and he therefore harms his spirit and his soul. . . .[141] But the *tikkun* of the brain and of *yesod* is a *tikkun gamur*—when man seeks his own *tikkun* he must first repair his sexual sins, as mentioned, thereby repairing other flaws affecting God,[142] and because semen stemming from *yesod* comes from the brain, the brain also requires *tikkun gamur*. These are the two aspects of *tikkun gamur*.[143]

Furthermore, even the ten psalms constituting the core ritual of *ha-tikkun ha-kelali* instituted by R. Nahman originate, in my view, in the *tikkun kelali* of Nathan of Gaza, though Nathan did not develop this aspect as fully as R. Nahman.[144]

Nathan's *tikkun kelali* implies a further connotation—not only the *tikkun* of all of man's sins, but also that of the whole people, or of all the souls of Israel as embodied in Sabbetai Zevi. The general repentance movement initiated in 1665–1666 is nothing more than a projection of Sabbetai Zevi's own penitence. These ideas are also essential to *ha-tikkun ha-kelali* instituted by R. Nahman, as I showed, namely, a similar ambivalence in the name and the *tikkun* of the whole people as dependent on the personal *tikkun* of the *tsaddik ha-dor*. I rely on the following statement, written while Sabbetai Zevi and Nathan of Gaza were still alive:

> Learn from this about *Moharan*'s [Nathan of Gaza] greatness, who returned the people of Israel to their Father in Heaven.[145] . . . And now these fools [implying those who converted to Islam following Sabbetai Zevi, of whom the author disaproves] only hurt their own souls, because they will no longer be able to draw

nearer through the *tikkun kelali* that has been ordained....And he [Sabbetai Zevi] prays to God for the whole of Israel, as he encompasses all souls, and he says: "Wash me thoroughly from my iniquity..."[146] and this is the repentance effected by *Moharan*, as we all know...because my sins [Sabbetai Zevi's] are the sins of Israel.[147]

Clearly then, R. Nahman developed his own ritual, including the name as well as the various connotations, from ideas suggested directly by Nathan of Gaza or developed in Sabbatean literature.[148] Even the armour parable, in which R. Nahman likens the esoteric meaning of *ha-tikkun ha-kelali* to a shield (see note 133) also originates with Nathan. Following is a testimony from the apogee of the movement:[149] "In his [Nathan's] last letters, dating from early *Heshvan*, it is said that he urges repentance, and those failing to wear the proper armour of repentance shall die." The *armour of repentance* is a rather unusual metaphor and, until now, I have not encountered it outside the writings of Nathan of Gaza and Nahman of Bratslav. This is an additional parallel between them, revealing that R. Nahman relied on Nathan's writings for this metaphor as well. Moreover, it appears that both connect this parable to the wearing of the *tallit katan* [a ritual fringed garment], which was also part of *ha-tikkun ha-kelali* ritual.[150]

My assumption that R. Nahman relied on Sabbatean sources is further corroborated by R. Nahman himself, who claimed that others had preceded him in the development of this *tikkun* and he was merely completing their mission: "Many great *tsaddikim* have been troubled by it and have untiringly sought a *tikkun gamur* for this sin [improper seminal emmision]. Some never understood it, and others left this world as they began to comprehend it and before they could complete their task and I, with God's help, have accomplished this" (*Sihot Ha-Ran* 141).

There appears to be some awareness, among R. Nahman's contemporaries as well as among his opponents, of *ha-tikkun ha-kelali*'s Sabbatean origins. One indication might be the vehement insistence of Bratslav Hasidim on the complete novelty entailed by this *tikkun*. Accusations of Sabbateanism directed against R. Nahman were consistently censored and are not mentioned in authentic Bratslav writings, and they were at times replaced by accusations of plagiarism (see note 95). At the end of this passage (*Sihot Ha-Ran* 141), Bratslav Hasidim strive to demonstrate that all the references to *ha-tikkun ha-kelali* failing to attribute it to R. Nahman could be dated after his death and relied on him. Bratslav Hasidim insistently demanded that the *tikkun* should always be explicitly recited in R. Nahman's name "so that his lips might whisper gently in his grave,"[151] because "they [the ten psalms] are a completely new *tikkun* unknown to any creature since Creation."[152]

To some extent, the Hasidim were indeed right. It was indeed R. Nahman who chose the ten psalms to be included in *ha-tikkun ha-kelali* and he certainly was one of the most original figures ever to enrich Jewish thought. All his writings, even if revealing external influences—like *ha-tikkun ha-kelali*—bear his deep, personal stamp.

APPENDIX I: R. Nahman's Journeys
for the *tikkun* of Sabbateanism

R. Nahman's journey to Kamenets on his way to the Holy Land, as well as his journey to Lvov, seem to have some connection with his endeavors to amend the Frankist heresy. Both these cities are reknowned as the venue of public disputes between the rabbis and the Frankists, one in Kamenets in 1757 and the other in Lvov in 1759, which ended in public burnings of the Talmud at the Frankists' demand. The journey to Kamenets as well as its objects are clouded in mystery. R. Nahman claimed: "because on that night the Besht, of blessed memory, came to me, and told me where I was to go, to Kamenets" (*Hayyei Moharan*, Journey to the Holy Land 1).

It is worth noting that R. Nahman believed that the Besht had died because of his failure to amend the Frankist heresy and that this task had now devolved on him (see p. 131). It would indeed appear that R. Nahman traveled to Kamenets as an emissary of the Besht: "he left for Kamenets immediately, and his doings there are a complete mystery that no one on earth will understand until the coming of the Messiah, speedily in our days, Amen" (ibid.). This statement makes the journey even more mysterious, but also hints at a certain link with redemption. R. Nahman himself hints that the journey to Kamenets is related to the *tikkun* of the Frankists's sin: "Our Rabbi said: Whoever knows why the land of Israel was first ruled by Canaan and only then came into Israel's hands, knows why I traveled to Kamenets before going to the Holy Land" (*Shivhei Ha-Ran*, The Account of His Journey to the Holy Land 2).

We have also indicated (note 30) that the *tikkun* of heretics, who are all considered heirs of the Sabbateans, is a further aspect of the campaign to conquer the land of Israel. It was even suggested in R. Nahman's times, mainly by his opponents, that there were Sabbatean associations to this journey: "The journey to Kamenets was a great wonder, and all tried to explain it, some praised the Rabbi and others etc." (ibid. 3). This *etc.* can be construed only as part of a consistent effort, which is all-pervasive in Bratslav literature, to deflect all accusations of Sabbateanism (see note 95). J. Dan sensed that the journey to Kamenets was linked to the *tikkun* of the Frankists (*The Hasidic Tale*, p. 87), and he was preceded in this approach by Zeitlin, as cited by Piekarz, *Studies in Bratslav Hasidism*, p. 25.

As for the journey to Lvov, the evidence (*Hayyei Moharan,* Journey to Lvov 1) indicates that on the course of this journey R. Nahman delivered teaching 282 in *Likkutei Moharan* II. This teaching deals with the *tikkun* of those far-removed from God by means of songs and joy, because through song "we pick and choose the good from the bad," and defeat sadness as well as its concommitant—heresy. As we have shown (p. 139), this precisely is the essence of *ha-tikkun ha-kelali*— the *tikkun* of the sin entailed by Sabbateanism by means of ten kinds of song, through which we separate holiness from impurity and turn sadness into joy. Moreover, during his journey to Lvov (*Hayyei Moharan,* Journey to Lvov 1) R. Nahman ordered his book to be burned in order to prolong his life and this is the "burnt book," see Weiss's comments, *Studies in Bratslav Hasidism*, pp. 215–243. In *Likutei Moharan* II:32, R. Nahman claimed that the *tsaddik,* who is like a Messiah, must burn his books so that the books of the heretics, which are like the golden calves of Jeroboam, might also be lost. Weiss, ibid., pp. 244–248, dwelled extensively on this issue, claiming that this teaching hints to the book burned in Lvov a year before this teaching was delivered, and that the "books of the heretics" and "the golden calves" are no other than the Frankist heresy. All these references seem to serve as further confirmation of the anti-Frankist purpose of R. Nahman's journey to Lvov.

R. Nahman's stay in Zlatopolie was also meant for the sake of the *tikkun* of Jeroboam's golden calves (*Hayyei Moharan,* His Birthplace, Residence and Travels 11) which, in this case as well, is a metaphor for the *tikkun* of Frankism (see Weiss, pp. 23–26). We might hence infer that all his other journeys were for the sake of messianic *tikkun,* though other personal factors were also involved, such as consulting with physicians; however, in Bratslav Hasidism, even the *tsaddik*'s health could be construed as a messianic aim. This is what we are told about his journey to Navritch: "He said at the time: 'As for me, my hands are dirty with blood and afterbirth—all in order to cleanse the woman and allow her to her husband,' and this may hint to the purpose of his journey" (*Hayyei Moharan,* Journey to Navrich 4). This statement ("As for me, my hands are dirty. . .") is a quote from

King David, the first Messiah according to Berakhot 4a. Cleansing the woman to allow her to her husband clearly refers in this context to the restored bonding between God and *Keneset Israel,* the true redemption in kabbalistic terms. This resembles the messianic *Hakhnasat Kalla* [preparing brides for their wedding], which was the mission on which R. Nahman had sent his Hasidim according to *Kokhvei Or,* p. 522; see also Piekarz, *Studies in Bratslav Hasidism,* p. 67.

As for his journey to Uman, R. Nahman undertook this trip to seek *tikkun* for the souls of the victims of the Haidamack massacres of 1768 (*Hayyei Moharan,* Uman 7) as well as of those of the many *maskilim* dwelling there (ibid., 11, 24; Weiss, *Studies in Bratslav Hasidism,* pp. 61–65, and Piekarz, *Studies in Bratslav Hasidism,* pp. 21–55).

APPENDIX II: A Note on Parallels Between
————————   R. Nahman and the Sabbateans   ————————

Weiss, *Studies in Bratslav Hasidism,* p. 34, noted: "It is most likely, and even plausible (!), that further research will reveal in his teachings [R. Nahman's] strong influences from the Sabbatean-Frankist doctrine whose sin he had endeavoured to amend, influences which had clung to his thought." I have pointed to several of these influences in the course of the discussion (see notes 82, 83, 92, 95, and 100) and in the discussion on the sources of *ha-tikkun ha-kelali* (notes 136 ff., as well as p. 142).

I shall briefly remark on several other parallels, beginning with those between R. Nahman and Jacob Frank, who, I believe, had a profound influence on R. Nahman. During his youth, in the years of his *hitbodedut* (*Hayyei Moharan,* His Birthplace, Residence and Travels 4, 7), R. Nahman may have come across Frankists who had remained Jews, of whom there were many in Podolia. I rely for these comparisons on passages from *The Words of the Master* by Jacob Frank, which were preserved in Alexander Kraushar's book *Frank y frankisci polscy.* Thanks are due to Fania Scholem, who lent me her Hebrew translation of this manuscript.

In *The Words of the Master,* there are many stories essentially similar to R. Nahman's tales such as, for instance, the motif of exchanging the sons or that of separating the boy and the girl who are fated for each other that culminates in a "happy end" (*The Words of the Master* 1021; compare with "The King's Son and the Maidservant's Son" and "The Burgher and the Pauper" in R. Nahman's *Sippurei Ma'asiyyot*). The motif of the lost virgin in "The Loss of the Princess" often recurs in Frank's work, as does that of Satan as an old man (see 1016, 1288; in R. Nahman's stories, this old man is obviously identified with Arye Leib, the Old Man of Shpola, see Weiss, ibid., pp. 46 ff.). *The Words of the Master* contains an apocalyptic vision of *tikkun* after a catastrophic and bloody war, as is also the case for R. Nahman (*Likkutei Moharan* I:260).

There are also behavioral parallels between the two men: Frank used to play war games with his friends in his childhood, imitating the war raging in his time—some of the boys played Russians and others their Turkish foes. Frank thought this detail was important and related it in *The Words of the Master* (1235). During Napoleon's siege of 1799, when R. Nahman was in Istanbul on his way to the Holy Land, he became deeply absorbed in a war game, with one side (R. Nahman?) playing Napoleon, against the Turks (*Shivhei Ha-Ran*, The Account of R. Nahman's Journey to the Holy Land 12). R. Nahman was highly concerned with Napoleon, who inspired his tale about "The King's Son and the Maidservant's Son," as the maidservant's son who was raised to royalty (*Hayyei Moharan*, Conversations Relating to His Stories 2). Moreover, both R. Nahman and Jacob Frank were very fond of the poem *Akdamut* sung on the holiday of *Shavu'ot* (a stanza from this poem is quoted by Frank in *The Words of the Master* 143, and R. Nahman greatly admired it, *Sihot Ha-Ran* 251).

There is also a strikingly accurate parallel in Frank's work to R. Nahman's famous tale about the deranged prince who, in his madness, thought himself a rooster and sat under the table. The prince was finally healed by a man claiming he was also a rooster, who gradually brought him back to "normalcy" (*Kokhvei Or*, pp. 26–27). This very same story appears in *The Words of the Master* 986 and until another source, such as an Eastern European folktale, is found to be shared by both, I shall believe that R. Nahman took it from Jacob Frank. In R. Nahman's story, the healer obviously stands for the *tsaddik* who descends into evil to bring about *tikkun*, whereas Frank apparently intended the commandments he was still compelled to observe because of his "crazy" companions; compare, for instance, *The Words of the Master* 1283.

There are several instances pointing to the influence of Nathan of Gaza on R. Nahman, such as R. Nahman's speculations on the imaginary character of the "empty void" as a source of heresy. See Nathan of Gaza, *Sefer Ha-Beri'a*, Berlin Ms 3077, 9, *Likkutei Moharan* I:64 and *ha-tikkun ha-kelali*. In this context, it is important to point out that Nathan and R. Nahman shared the names of *Butsina*

Kaddisha Moharan and *Ha-Ran*. One of Nathan of Gaza's works is called *Likkutei Moharan* (Columbia Ms X893–Z 8, Vol. 1, No. 20, p. 41 and No 16572 in the Jerusalem National and University Library).

A parable found in a Sabbatean source includes a parallel to "The Loss of the Princess." See G. Scholem, ed., "Iggeret Magen Avraham me-Erets Ha-Maarav," *Kovets Al-Yad*, 2 (1936), p. 139. On the author, see my article "Miguel Abraham Cardozo—Author of the *Raza di-Meheimanuta* Attributed to Sabbetai Zevi and the Error in Attributing the *Igeret Magen Avraham* to Cardozo" [Hebrew], *Kiryat Sefer* 55 (1980). See also note 104. In the Sabbatean parable, the king sends his servant to inquire after his imprisoned betrothed, in a tale reminiscent of the song "Meliselda, the Emperor's Daughter," which Sabbetai Zevi used to sing in reference to the *Shekhina* (See G. Scholem, *Sabbetai Zevi*, pp. 800–801). Using a Gentile song for kabbalistic purposes is in itself a widespread Hasidic practice.

Notes

Introduction

1. Y. Liebes, "New Trends in Kabbala Research" [Hebrew], *Pe'amim* 50 (1992), pp. 150–170.

2. Y. Liebes, *The Sin of Elisha: The Four Who Entered Paradise and the Nature of Talmudic Mysticism* [Hebrew] (Jerusalem, 1990).

3. To appear in an anthology of papers on myth [in Hebrew].

4. To appear in *Eshel Be'er Sheva*, in a volume devoted to the problem of myth in Judaism [in Hebrew].

1. *De Natura Dei*: On the Development of the Jewish Myth

This essay was written in loving memory of my teacher and mentor, Ephraim Gottlieb, who introduced me to the mysteries of Jewish myth. Over the many years since his death I have always been aware of his influence and encouragement, though I have developed my own style and my scholarly interests may differ from his. I fully believe that, with his breadth of vision, Prof. Gottlieb would have made no attempt to restrain his students from pursuing fields of study closest to their hearts. His only condition would have been that they be honest in their scholarly work and always hold truth as a beacon before them.

Indeed, this essay is oriented in directions that differ from those pursued by Gottlieb. He clearly distinguished between Kabbala, the sole object of his scientific research, and Talmud, rabbinical literature, and Maimonides, which he studied in the synagogue and saw as the core of his religious commitment. Although in this paper I have attempted to bridge between them, this approach also serves to sharpen the differences between these sources, and some of my conclusions may therefore be fairly close to Gottlieb's. To cite only one instance: Gottlieb used to say that the kabbalists, unlike the rabbis, had no sense of humor. I would tend to agree with him in principle—except with regard to the Zohar—and, as I show, I believe this is related to the personal quality of myth in the Talmud, as against its rigid systematization in the Kabbala.

1. G. Scholem, "Kabbala and Myth," in his book *On the Kabbalah and Its Symbolism*, (New York, 1965), p. 88. Various formulations of similar statements appear in many of Scholem's writings although in some of them the historical relation between myth and its counterpart becomes more dialectical. The following anecdote illustrates this well. In Scholem's private book collection, presently housed in the National and University Library at the Hebrew University in Jerusalem, there is a copy of I. Goldziher's interesting book, *Der Mythos bei der Hebraeern und seine geschichtliche Entwicklung* (Leipzig, 1876). On the front cover of the book, the following note appears in Scholem's handwriting: *Jugendsuenden eines Grossen Gelehrten* [Youthful sins of a great scholar].

2. G. Scholem, *Explications and Implications: Writings on Jewish Heritage and Renaissance* [Hebrew: *Devarim be-Go*] (Tel-Aviv, 1976), p. 27.

3. See Y. Liebes, "The Messiah of the Zohar," in *Studies in the Zohar* (Albany, forthcoming); Y. Liebes, "The Kabbalistic Myth as Told by Orpheus," in this volume; Y. Liebes, "Jonah as the Messiah ben Joseph" [Hebrew], in J. Dan and J. Hecker, eds., *Studies in Jewish Mysticism, Philosophy and Ethical Literature Presented to Isaiah Tishby* (Jerusalem Studies in Jewish Thought, 3, Jerusalem, 1984), pp. 269–311; Y. Liebes, "Christian Influences in the *Zohar*," *Immanuel* 17 (1983–1984): 43–67; Y. Liebes, "The Angels of the Shofar and Yeshua Sar ha-Panim" [Hebrew], in J. Dan, ed., *Early Jewish Mysticism* (Jerusalem Studies in Jewish Thought, 6, Jerusalem, 1987), pp. 171–195.

I would like to comment on a quasi-kabbalistic description of emanation in early Isma'ilism, whose origin is shrouded in mystery. I am referring to the text researched and edited by S. M. Stern, *Studies in Early Isma'ilism* (Jerusalem and Leiden, 1983), pp. 3–29. The ontology, hermeneutical approach and many other details, including linguistic ones, resemble the kabbalistic approach. Thus, the first emanation's name is *kuni* which, as the text explicitly indicates, derives from the imperative *kun*, namely, "be!" with the addition of two letters (*u* and *i*) found only in the Hebrew name of God. In the Kabbala as well, the imperative *yehi* (be) points to a sacred name denoting the beginning of *atsilut* (Zohar I:16b), and we also found a name derived from the letters *k* and *n* with the addition of *h* and *a* (*Zohar Hadash, Yitro*, 41c). Though the parallel between this name (*anokhi*) and *kuni* is purely coincidental, it may illustrate a similar approach. From *kuni* emanates *qadar*, and there may be a link between this name and the *Botsina de-Kadrinuta* of the Zohar. The entities that follow afterward may be paralleled to the *Six Ends* (in Arabic *Sittatu Hududin,* which emanated from the *Kuni* when he mistakenly assumed himself to be the only god). Also, this passage mentions seven *kerubim* (in Arabic *kurubiyya*). The names of other emanating entities are similar to those of kabbalistic *sefirot.*

Symbolic references are also similar to those found in Kabbala: *kuni* is male and *qadar* female; *kuni* is the sun and *qadar* the moon. *Kuni* is also referred to by the Koranic name *Sidratu al-Muntaha,* whose description resembles the kabbalistic "Tree of Life," while those who "hold it" are praised. Furthermore, it also mentions *Ha-Avir ha-Dak* [the Subtle Ether] and the importance of the letters, from which the world was created. God's names, like in the Kabbala, serve here as his garments; there are also parallels to some well-known kabbalistic notions, like the one who "lights his candle from another candle, and does not deprive the first one" and the *Benei Aliyya* [Excellent] "who are but few," all in a text of less than ten pages. Several scholars have already noted the mutual links between Isma'iliya and Kabbala on several issues, such as the theory of the worlds, the ten sayings, the theory of the hidden righteous men and the cyclical nature of time. The more extensive research required by these questions is beyond the scope of this essay, and I will only point to the study by S. Pines, "Shi'ite Terms and Conceptions in Judah Halevi's Kuzari," *Jerusalem Studies in Arabic and Islam* 2 (1980): 165–251.

4. See, e.g., "Myth" in M. Eliade, ed., *The New Encyclopedia of Religion.*

5. See, e.g., M. Buber, "Myth in Judaism," in N. Glatzer, ed., *On Judaism* (New York, 1967), pp. 95–107. For an analysis of this question in the writings of Buber and other thinkers see M. Schwartz, *Language, Myth and Art* [Hebrew] (Jerusalem and Tel-Aviv, 1967). Franz Rosenzweig also valued myth highly. He searched for it in Judaism and failed to find it, as rationalist views were prevalent in his time; he therefore attempted to find myth in Christianity and came close to conversion. See M. Idel, "Franz Rosenzweig and the Kabbalah" in P. Mendes-Flohr, ed., *The Philosophy of Franz Rosenzweig* (Hanover and London, 1988), p. 171.

6. This myth unites the ten *sefirot blima* of the *Sefer Yetsira* with the ten talmudic and midrashic sayings through which the world was created, as well as with other traditions found in Gnostic literature. See M. Idel, "The *Sefirot* Above the *Sefirot*" [Hebrew], *Tarbiz* 51 (1982): 239–280; M. Idel, *Kabbala—New Perspectives* (New Haven, 1988), pp. 112–122. For the essence of the *sefirot* in the *Sefer Yetsira,* see Y. Liebes, *The Sin of Elisha: The Four Who Entered Paradise and the Nature of Talmudic Mysticism* [Hebrew] (Jerusalem, 1990 [first mimeo edition, 1986]), p. 117; Y. Liebes, "R. Solomon Ibn Gabirol's Use of the *Sefer Yetsira* and a Commentary on the Poem 'I Love Thee'" [Hebrew], in J. Dan, ed., *The Beginnings of Jewish Mysticism in Medieval Europe* (Jerusalem Studies in Jewish Thought, 6, 3–4, Jerusalem, 1986), pp. 92–97. On the ten sayings and their meaning see Liebes, "Christian Influences." pp. 56–57 and n. 50, and "The Messiah of the Zohar." The ten

sayings were apparently equated with the ten fingers of God; see Genesis Rabba 4:4, which equates one of the sayings with "the finger of the Holy One, blessed be He." The *midrash* on the ten plagues that befell Egypt, in the Passover Haggada, assumes that God has ten fingers; in the *Sefer Yetsira* 1,3, the ten *sefirot blima* are compared to "the ten fingers." It is worth pointing out that in the early Kabbala, the system of the ten *sefirot* and the system of the thirteen attributes of mercy competed for precedence. See J. Dan, *The Early Kabbalistic Circles* [Hebrew], compiled from his lectures by Y. Agassi, (mimeo, Jerusalem, 1976), pp. 1–20. Two comments are in place here: (a) The *Idrot* in the Zohar also reflect this complex relation between the ten and the thirteen; (b) some count only ten in the verses in Exodus 34:6–7, usually considered as the basis for the thirteen attributes of mercy (The Lord, the Lord. . .; see Rosh Hashana 17b). Thus, e.g., in the *Shoher Tov* [Midrash on Psalms] 97, 8, this claim appears in the name of "our rabbis." For the same claim in the Samaritan tradition see Zeev ben Hayyim, ed., *Tibat Marqe* (Jerusalem, 1988), p, 349, and also: "it is by ten that we know Israel, creation, redemption, mercy of the Great Name" (p. 307).

7. On the circles that authored the Zohar, see Y. Liebes, "How the Zohar Was Written" [Hebrew], in J. Dan, ed., *The Age of the Zohar* (Jerusalem Studies in Jewish Thought, 8, Jerusalem, 1989).

8. On this point, see Liebes, "The Messiah of the Zohar."

9. Ibid.

10. See G. S. Kirk, *The Nature of Greek Myths* (Aylesbury, England, 1974); P. Veyne, *Did Greeks Believe in Their Myths?* (Chicago, 1988).

11. See Liebes, *The Sin of Elisha*, pp. 142–146.

12. See H. A. Wolfson, *The Philosophy of the Church Fathers* (Cambridge, Mass., 1970).

13. See Y. Liebes, "Sabbetai Zevi's Attitude Towards His Own Conversion" [Hebrew], *Sefunot* (New Series) 2 (1983): 267–307; Y. Liebes, "The Religious Faith of Sabbetai Zevi," and "Sabbatean Messianism," both in this volume.

14. See Y. Liebes, "Miguel Abraham Cardozo—Author of the *Raza di-Meheimanuta* Attributed to Sabbetai Zevi and the Error in Attributing the *Iggeret Magen Avraham* to Cardozo" [Hebrew], *Kiryat Sefer* 55 (1980): 603–616 and the addendum in *Kiryat Sefer* 56 (1981): 373–374. Also Y. Liebes, "The Ideological Basis of the Hayyun Controversy" [Hebrew], *Proceedings of the Eighth World Congress of Jewish Studies*, Division C, 1982, pp. 129–134.

15. I. R. Molho and A. Amarillo, "Autobiographical Letters of Abraham Cardozo" [Hebrew], in *S. Z. Shazar Jubilee Volume* (Jerusalem, 1959–60), [*Sefunot* 3–4]), p. 238. It is worth noting that Cardozo formulated his beliefs here in monistic terms, blurring the dualistic element emphasized in many

of his other writings. Cardozo also used monistic formulations elsewhere; see Liebes, "Miguel Cardozo," pp. 609–610, though the one God there is called *Malka Kaddisha* and not *Ilat Kol ha-Ilot*.

16. Yosef Hayyim, *Od Yosef Hai* (Jerusalem, 1950), 30c.

17. This last passage is a modified version of a declaration intended by Jews to cancel out any heretic statement they may have made at times of religious persecutions. See Y. Liebes, "Mysticism and Reality: Towards a Portrait of the Martyr and Kabbalist R. Samson Ostropoler," in I. Twersky and B. Septimus, eds., *Jewish Thought in the Seventeenth Century* (Cambridge, Mass., 1987), pp. 246–248. See J. Katz's comment, *Tarbitz* 52 (1983): 661, and my response, on p. 663.

18. Most kabbalistic practices developed during the sixteenth century; however, it seems some of them originate in early Kabbala, like *Tikkun Leil Shavu'ot* (the practice of holding a study vigil on the eve of the Shavuot festival). See Liebes, "The Messiah of the Zohar."

19. See G. Scholem, "A New Document Toward the History of Early Kabbala" [Hebrew], *Sefer Bialik* (Tel-Aviv, 1944), pp. 141–162.

20. See M. Idel, "We Have No Tradition on This," in I. Twersky, ed., *Rabbi Moses Nahmanides (Ramban): Explorations in His Religious and Literary Virtuosity* (Cambridge, Mass., and London, 1983), pp. 51–73.

21. E. E. Urbach, "The Traditions about Merkabah Mysticism in the Tannaitic Period" [Hebrew], in E. E. Urbach, *The World of the Sages: Collected Studies* (Jerusalem, 1988), pp. 505–508. For a critique of this article and its approach see Liebes, *The Sin of Elisha*, pp. 9–10, 122–125. On the other hand, M. Idel's view on this rabbinical passage resembles mine—see note 37.

22. On the attributes, see also E. E. Urbach, *The Sages—Their Concepts and Beliefs* (Jerusalem, 1975), pp. 448–461.

23. There is indeed a kabbalistic dispute on this question, known in Kabbala as *atsmut ve-kelim* [essence and vessels]. Some kabbalists found a personal god in the *sefirot*, though this is not the typical kabbalistic approach. A prominent example of such a personal approach may be found in the passage *Petah Eliyyahu* in the introduction to the *Tikkunei Zohar*.

24. See Todros Aboulafia, *Otsar ha-Kavod* (Warsaw, 1889), ad. loc. 4:3–4, where the name Akatriel is indeed derived from the name of the first *sefira*, *keter*; this is probably the correct etymology. However, as we mentioned, Akatriel points to the lowest *sefira*, called *malkhut*, because of the link between *malkhut*, which is also referred to as *atara* [crown] and the highest *sefira*, called *keter*, [crown]. See note 107.

25. Jeremiah 32:18: "O, great and mighty God."

26. In the Jerusalem Talmud, Berakhot 7:4 (10c), Daniel's question appears as: "His sons endure the yoke, where is His might?"

27. Daniel 9:4: "O Lord the great and dreadful God."

28. In *Avot de-Rabbi Nathan*, Version A, Ch. 23: "Who is that is most mighty? One who subdues his evil impulse"; similarly, in the talmudic passage before us: "The mightiest heroism" (though in many manuscripts only "heroism"). The reference in *Avot* may already be to God. In the *Seder Eliyahu Rabba*, Ish Shalom ed. (Vilna, 1902), Ch. 1, there is a reference to God as "rich and happy with His lot." Compare: "Who is rich? He who is happy with his lot" in *Avot de-Rabbi Nathan*.

29. Jerusalem Talmud—as earlier, note 26: "Said R. Isaac b. Elazar [apparently the son of the rabbi who made the parallel statement in the Babylonian Talmud]: the prophets know that God is true and they do not flatter him."

30. Apparently according to Nehemiah 9:32.

31. Berakhot 33b.

32. See Y. Kappah, ed., *The Book of Daniel: Commentary by Saadia b. Yosef* [Hebrew] (Jerusalem, 1981), pp. 166–167 (on Daniel 9:4); see editor's note 8.

33. Compare Avot 2:5: "In a place where there are no men, strive thou to be a man."

34. Megilla 15a: "R. Eleazar b. Hanina also said: Let not the blessing of an ordinary man be lightly esteemed in thine eyes, for two men great in their generation received from ordinary men blessings which were fulfilled in them. They were, David and Daniel.... Let not the curse of an ordinary man be lightly esteemed in thine eyes, because Avimelekh cursed Sarah...and this was fulfilled in her seed."

35. Zohar I:135a, *Idra Rabba*. Even from the "emendation of the supreme countenances," which is the central myth of the Idras, the Zohar learns political conduct. According to this myth, *arikh anpin*, the superior countenance, was set first, and *ze'ir anpin*, the small countenance, was set afterward: "And from here we learn: every head of state who [acts] improperly, his people are improper and if he is proper, all are proper."

36. On this verse see note 40.

37. *Pesikta de-Rav Kahana*, Mandelbaum ed., Section 25, pp. 379–380. M. Idel (see note 6) discussed this passage and its parallel versions, including the Akatriel issue, pp. 156–166. Idel explained the theological and thus obviously mythical character of this passage and also concluded that its approach is not far from the kabbalistic one, although he placed less emphasis on the personal and flexible character of this myth.

38. This is inferred from the Hebrew *appayim* (two faces), according to the Jerusalem Talmud, Ta'anit 2:1 (65b): "R. Samuel b. Nahman said in the name of R. Johathan: It is not written *erekh af* but *erekh appayim*: God is patient with the righteous and He is patient with the wicked."

39. Zohar II:193a. See Y. Liebes, *Sections of the Zohar Lexicon* [Hebrew] (Jerusalem, 1977; offset, 1984), p. 199.

40. Leviticus Rabba 23:12: " 'Of the Rock that begot thee thou art unmindful [*teshi*]' (Deuteronomy, 32:18), as meaning you have weakened [*hitashta*] the strength of the Creator."

41. See note 6.

42. See Liebes, "Jonah as the Messiah ben Joseph," pp. 304–311.

43. See E. E. Urbach "Ascesis and Suffering in Talmudic and Midrashic Sources" [Hebrew], in Urbach, *The World of the Sages*, pp. 437–458; Urbach, *The Sages*, pp. 420–448; Abraham Joshua Heschel, *Theology of Ancient Judaism* [Hebrew] (London and New York, 1962), pp. 93–113.

44. There is an interesting parallel in Islam, to which I would like to draw attention. The statement "There is no God but Allah and Muhamad is his prophet" is an article of faith recited daily by Muslims, equivalent to the recital of the *Shema* in Judaism. However, it is also the statement made by martyrs, just as the *Shema* has been since Rabbi Akiva's death. In Arabic, this is related to a linguistic double meaning: This statement is called the *shahada*, that is, a testimony, implying a testimony of faith, but a martyr's death is also called *shahada*, namely, the death of a *shahid*, who is not only a witness but one who dies sanctifying God's name. Thus did the Greek word *martyr*, meaning witness, assume its modern meaning in Christianity, implying one whose death attests to his or her faith. See *First Encyclopedia of Islam*, s.v. *Shahada*. Similarly, the *Shema* is perceived as a testimony in several sources in rabbinical literature—see Saul Lieberman, *Tosefta Ki-Fshuta*, Shabbat, p. 263. This may be related to the tradition stating that the letter *ayin*, at the end of the word *shema*, and the letter *dalet*, at the end of the word *ehad* [One], which appear in the *Shema Israel* verse, should be capitalized because, when combined, they form the word *ed* [witness]. I found this tradition first mentioned in the commentary of the *Baal ha-Turim* to Deuteronomy 6:4 (the verse of the *Shema*): "*Ayin* and *dalet* capitalized make *ed* as it says (Isaiah 43:10): 'You are my witness,' and the Holy One, blessed be He, is also a witness to Israel, as is written (Malachi 3:5): 'And I will be a swift witness.'" A similar idea is mentioned several times in the Zohar, such as II:160b; however, in the Zohar it is always God who testifies for man. See also Moses de Leon, *Shekel ha-Kodesh* (London, 1911), pp. 100–101. It must be pointed out, however, that the Muslim *shahid* is different from either the Christian or the Jewish martyr, since he is killed fighting a holy war [*jiha'd*] against the infidels rather than as a passive victim.

45. Reuven Margaliot, ed., *Sefer Bahir* (Jerusalem, 1951), 87a, n. 194. With corrections from Munich MSS 209, it is catalogued as number 1625 in the Institute of Microfilmed Hebrew Manuscripts in the National Library in Jerusalem.

46. See, e.g., E. Gottlieb, "The Concluding Portion of R. Joseph Gikatila's She'arei Zedek" [Hebrew], in E. Gottlieb, *Studies in Kabbala Literature* (Tel Aviv, 1976), pp. 135–138. There are many, though less detailed, versions of this portion in his other writings, in which Gikatila thoroughly discusses Moses' understanding; he also deals with the attributes as opposed to God's arbitrary essence. Indeed, God's essence here is part of the sefirotic system, as the highest *sefira*, called *keter*.

47. See Liebes, "The Messiah of the Zohar."

48. See M. Idel, "The Evil Thought in the Deity" [Hebrew], *Tarbiz* 49 (1980): 356–364. I deal with this issue in the appendix to my paper "How the Zohar Was Written."

49. This is Euhemerus' account of how myths are created, named *euhemerism* after him. It is also cited by Marcus Tullius Cicero, *De Natura Deorum*, II:24. It is partly true regarding the pagan myths, more so regarding Christianity (the deification of Jesus) and can even be said to have a place in Judaism, though to a lesser extent. Myths of this sort were built around Rabbi Simeon bar Yohai, and perhaps also around "the mother of the seven sons"; see *The Fourth Book of Maccabeans*, as I showed in "How the Zohar Was Written," n. 297.

50. Some tend to ascribe the Exile and all the sufferings afflicting Israel to the sin of Joseph's sale by his brothers; there is an interesting link between this matter, the Christian notion of original sin, and the sin of Jesus' crucifixion. I intend to deal with these issues in a study on the author of *Livnat ha-Sapir*, who is particularly concerned with this matter.

51. See *Sha'ar ha-Kavvanot* (Jerusalem, 1902) on *Nefilat Appaim*, 5:48c. Compare to the reading of the *Shema*, ibid., pp. 23–24 ff..

52. See J. Angelet, *Livnat ha-Sapir* (Jerusalem, 1913), 4b. In H. N. Bialik's poem *"Hetsits va-Met,"* this gate is called *Shaar ha-Blima* [the gate of nothingness].

53. M. Cordovero, *Shi'ur Koma* (Warsaw, 1883; offset, Jerusalem, 1966), 65d. Indeed, I could not find an earlier source that explains Edom as derived from *demama* [silence], as I could not find a source for the saying on the gate of silence that appears in *Livnat ha-Sapir*—see the previous note—and we cannot be sure that these two motifs were created together.

54. *Daat Edom* is conversion to Christianity and *Masa Duma* [the burden of Duma] refers to the curtain of silence that is to surround this issue and all its implications; see G. Scholem, "Redemption Through Sin," in G.

Scholem, *The Messianic Idea in Israel* (New York, 1971), p. 132. Scholem does not cite references for this term. The verse from Isaiah 21:11, clearly related to Edom, serves as background: "The burden of Duma, One calls to me out of Se'ir." The Zohar (III:22a) expounds it as derived from the root *dom*, silence: "but the exile of Edom is 'a burden of silence' for its term has not been disclosed." The Zohar refers to the fact that no term was set for the present exile, unlike previous ones whose duration was known, but Frank could easily have connected it to the mystery of conversion to Christianity. This is a natural source for Frank, who loved the Zohar and rejected most kabbalistic literature. However, it is possible that the passage by Cordovero mentioned earlier added kabbalistic nuances to this mystery; moreover, *Edom* is a symbol of God's highest countenance in the circles associated with the Sabbatean book *Va-avo ha-Yom el ha-Ayin* [I Came Today to the Spring], which was admired by Frank's disciples. See M. A. Perlmuter, *Rabbi Jonathan Eybeschuetz and His Attitude Towards Sabbateanism* [Hebrew] (Jerusalem and Tel-Aviv, 1947), pp. 90–91.

55. More exactly, in the year 5331 (1571), when R. Hayyim Vital was twenty-nine, his soul became "pregnant" with R. Akiba's soul. See Hayyim Vital, *Sefer ha-Hezionot*, Aeskoly ed. (Jerusalem, 1954), p. 135. I believe that this is a crucial detail in the history of Lurianic Kabbala.

56. See note 48. At times, the Kabbala expounds *malkhei Edom* [the kings of Edom] as related to *nimlakh be-da'ato* [consider], given their common Hebrew root (*m-l-kh*). The notion of merging the attributes, found in this midrashic passage, influenced the structure of the kabbalistic *sefirot*. Kabbalists claimed that the *sefira* of *itiferet* [beauty], also called *rahamim* [compassion], is a combination of *hesed* [grace] and *din* [judgment]. However, this notion seems to have been preceded by another, closer to this midrashic passage, claiming that in fact *hesed* combines *din* and *rahamim*. See M. Idel, "Notes on Medieval Jewish-Christian Polemics" [Hebrew], *Jerusalem Studies in Jewish Thought*, 3 (1984): 690–695, and the addendum, ibid., 4 (1985): 219–222.

57. See note 90.

58. Jerusalem Talmud, Taanit 2:1 (65b). See also Genesis Rabba 53:4.

59. A pitchfork [*atar*] is related to the prayers of the righteous through the verse in Genesis 25:21: "And Isaac prayed [*va-yeater*] to the Lord for his wife, because she was barren: and the Lord granted his prayer and Rebekah his wife conceived."

60. These verses were interpreted as if meant for human judges.

61. *Ma'arekhet ha-Elohut* (Mantua, 1558; offset, Jerusalem 1963), 7a–b. According to the exegeses printed on the page, the phrase *the depth of these questions* hints to the mystery of reincarnation.

62. See Saul Lieberman, *Greek in Jewish Palestine: Studies in the Life and Manners of Jewish Palestine in the II–IV Centuries C.E.* (New York, 1942), pp. 185–191.

63. Megilla 15b.

64. *"Otiyyot de-Rabbi Akiva,"* version B, in Abraham Wertheimer, ed., *Batei Midrashot*, Vol. 2 (Jerusalem, 1955), p. 396.

65. *He* refers to the angel (masculine in Hebrew) whereas *she* refers to the attribute (feminine). The comment of the *Masoret ha-Shas*: "It should say 'she said'," provides further support for this version. The parallel version mentioned earlier, in Megilla 15b, also has "he said."

66. See Urbach, *The Sages*, p. 459. See also Ch. 3 in the second edition of my book, *The Sin of Elisha*.

67. *Avot de-Rabbi Natan*, Version A, Ch. 37.

68. Thus in the Munich MSS, and in the printed version: circumcision. According to this formula, the account does not tally. The unity of the body and the circumcised member is explicitly stated in the parallel versions in *Sefer Bahir* 82, 168.

69. Ibid., 172.

70. Thus in the Munich MSS, whereas in the printed version "one" was added.

71. Thus in the Munich MSS, and in the printed version: emissaries.

72. See note 66.

73. As shown by M. Idel, "The Problem of the Sources in the *Bahir*" [Hebrew], in *The Beginnings of Jewish Mysticism in Medieval Europe*, p. 58. See also his *Kabbala*, p. 124.

74. See the article by M. Idel, ibid., pp. 55-72 and his book, ibid., pp. 122–128. See M. Idel, "The World of Angels in Human Form" [Hebrew], in Dan and Hacker, *Studies in Jewish Mysticism, Philosophy and Ethical Literature presented to Isaiah Tishby*, pp. 1–66. See G. G. Stroumsa, "Forms of God: Some Notes on Metatron and Christ," *Harvard Theological Review* 76 (1983): 269–288. On God's attributes as "shapes," see M. Fishbane, "Some Forms of Divine Appearance in Ancient Jewish Thought," in J. Neusner, E. Frerichs, and N. M. Sarna, eds., *From Ancient Israel to Modern Judaism: Essays in Honor of Marvin Fox* (Atlanta, 1989), pp. 261–270.

75. On chairs, see note 90.

76. See Liebes, *The Sin of Elisha*, pp. 34–41, 98–105; p. 38, n. 1, contains references to the extensive literature on this topic.

77. See p. 31.

78. *Shoher Tov* [Midrash on Psalms] 9, 2 and parallel versions.

79. See p. 39. Many views on God's attributes have been quoted in R. Johanan's name; some of these appear in Section II and some will be quoted later.

80. Kabbalists saw this parallel as identifying between "the Kingdom of Heaven" and *Keneset Israel*. See, e.g., *Sefer Otsar ha-Kavod*. However, as I explain, this is not the literal reading.

81. See p. 12.

82. I disagree with the claim of *Otsar ha-Kavod* that the term *batei brai* [outwardly] is a copyist's mistake.

83. *Zauba'a* is storm in Arabic.

84. See Zohar 19b, *Midrash ha-Ne'elam*: "In the ten crowns of the King there are two tears of the Holy One, blessed be He, that is, two attributes of justice, which come from both these tears. . . . And when the Holy One remembers His children, He drops them into the great Sea, which is the Sea of Wisdom, in order to sweeten them." See also Zohar III:132a, *Idra Rabba*. The Zohar also includes beautiful and realistic descriptions that develop the early myth while preserving its integrity, such as Zohar II:9a, *Midrash ha-Ne'elam* or II:196a. On the other hand, in Luria's writings, as usual in his Kabbala, the myth becomes extremely complex and elaborate. See *Sha'ar Ma'amarei Rashbi* (Jerusalem, 1959), 8a.

85. The same story is quoted a few lines earlier in R. Eliezer's name, but in a different version: "As is written (Jeremiah 25:30) 'The Lord shall roar from on high, and utter His voice from His holy habitation; He shall mightily roar because of His habitation.'" The continuation of this verse "He shall give a shout, as they that tread the grapes, against all the inhabitants of the earth," was quoted earlier in the description of the *zeva'ot*.

86. He apparently expounded *panim* [face] as the similar sounding *pamalia* [family or retinue].

87. Meir ben Todros ha-Levi Aboulafia, *Yad Ramah on Sanhedrin* (Warsaw, 1895), 85b. Compare to a similar picture in Berakhot 29b: "Even at the time when Thou art filled with wrath [*ebrah*] against them, like a pregnant [*ubarah*] woman, may all their need not be overlooked by Thee."

88. On this myth in Sabbateanism see Y. Liebes, "New Writings in Sabbatean Kabbala from the Circle of Rabbi Johathan Eybeschuetz" [Hebrew], *Jerusalem Studies in Jewish Thought* 5 (1986): 309–312. I point out the kabbalistic and midrashic sources of this myth and also refer to the literature (see note 44.) Nevertheless, this topic requires further research, and

particularly the Lurianic stage. Sabbateans also related this issue to the breach in the closed shape of the final Hebrew letter *mem*—see ibid., pp. 291–292. The first source on this question is the talmudic passage quoted at the opening of Section IV, where it is claimed that the letter was closed when king Hezekiah was not appointed Messiah.

89. Aaron Yellinek, ed., *Midrash va-Yosha'* (Leipzig, 1853; offset, Jerusalem, 1967), pp. 39–40.

90. See, e.g., *Pesikta de-Rav Kahana*, 23, 3. In Sanhedrin 38b, the chairs—from the verse in Daniel 7:9: "Thrones were placed, and an ancient of days did sit"—are identified as "one for justice and one for mercy," although this exegesis was heatedly contested.

91. Another version reads: "Blasted be the spirit." Maimonides, see the appendix to this essay, writes "the minds."

92. It is called "the yeast in the dough" in a parallel version in Berakhot 17a: "And what prevents us? The yeast in the dough and the subjection to the foreign powers."

93. See the appendix to this essay.

94. See G. Scholem, *Jewish Gnosticism, Merkaba Mysticism and Talmudic Tradition* (New York, 1960), pp. 44–49.

95. See Hagigah 15a and Liebes, *The Sin of Elisha,* pp. 40–45.

96. See M. Idel, "The Land of Israel in Medieval Kabbalah," in L. A. Hoffman, ed., *The Land of Israel: Jewish Perspectives* (Notre Dame, Ind., 1986), pp. 170–187. See also Idel, "The Problem of the Sources in the *Bahir,*" pp. 66–67.

97. Jerusalem Talmud, Berakhot 1:8 (3c), and parallel versions.

98. See p. 34.

99. See G. Scholem, "Shekhina: The Feminine Element in Divinity" in his *On the Mystical Shape of the Godhead* (New York: 1991). On this matter, Scholem seems to have drawn too sharp a distinction between kabbalistic literature and that preceding it. Moshe Idel also expressed this view in a personal communication. See also M. Idel's book, *Kabbala,* pp. 128–136. An attempt to describe the myth of the *Shekhina* as developing in a continous sequence from the Bible to the Kabbala appears in R. Patai, *The Hebrew Goddess* (New York, 1978). On the other hand, Abelson's classic book is concerned precisely with the abstract idea and not with the myth, which he considers as a "personification." See J. Abelson, *Immanence of God in Rabbinical Literature* (London, 1912). In various articles, Eliot Wolfson has expressed views similar to mine on the *Shekhina* and on the antiquity of Jewish myths. I could not make sufficient use of them in the present essay.

100. See Zohar I:155a, and many parallel versions.

101. See *Ma'arekhet ha-Elohut*, 92a; Zohar I:20a.

102. Another example can be found in *Pirke de-Rabbi Eliezer*, end of ch. 34, and the gist of this notion appears already in the Jerusalem Talmud, Berakhot 5:2 (9b); for the earth to be able to deliver those buried in it when the time comes to resurrect the dead, God must first "heal" the earth. The Zohar deals extensively with this matter in I:181b–182a, where the earth is also the *Shekhina*; during redemption, because of the aboundance bestowed on it, the *Shekhina* will grant souls to the dead (at times it seems that the bodies come out from the lower earth and the *Shekhina* is the source of the souls, although at times it seems that the lower earth is an aspect of the *Shekhina*). The passage is a kabbalistic development of a source from the *Midrash ha-Ne'elam*, Zohar I:124a–126b. The exegesis focuses on the story of Abraham's slave (equated in both sources with the angel Metatron) who was sent to find a wife—that is, to revive the body—for Abraham's son—that is, for the soul. Unlike the version of the *Midrash ha-Ne'elam* in the *Zohar* the slave is also the *Shekhina*, and all the rest of the kabbalistic symbolism is interpreted accordingly.

103. See Idel, "The Land of Israel in Medieval Kabbala."

104. Thus in the early Kabbala and in the Zohar, e.g., I:181b. Indeed, in the *Tikkunei Zohar*, Metatron is a lower entity and acts as the servant of the *Shekhina*.

105. *Ma'arekhet ha-Elohut*, 110a–b.

106. See Liebes, *Sections of the Zohar Lexicon*, p. 33, n. 26, and other references there.

107. See M. Idel, "On the Land of Israel in Medieval Jewish Thought" [Hebrew] in M. Hallamish and A. Ravitsky, eds., *The Land of Israel in Medieval Jewish Thought*, (Jerusalem, 1991); also H. Pedayah, " 'Flaw' and 'Correction' in the Concept of the Godhead in the Teachings of Rabbi Isaac the Blind" [Hebrew], in Dan, *The Beginnings of Jewish Mysticism*, pp. 229–233. Both scholars point to the continuity between the midrashic and the kabbalistic idea and expound in this spirit the passage in Ta'anit 5a: "Said R. Johanan: The Holy One, blessed be He, said, 'I will not enter the heavenly Jerusalem until I can enter the earthly Jerusalem.'" Relying on the kabbalistic tradition and on early sources, Idel rejected Urbach's claim that heavenly Jerusalem was of limited importance in rabbinical literature. See E. E. Urbach, "Earthly Jerusalem and Heavenly Jerusalem," in Urbach, *The World of the Sages*, pp. 376–391. I would like to add my own to Idel's remarks as well as comment on Urbach's conclusions. Urbach wrote at the opening of his article (p. 376): "R. Johanan's comments. . .ascribe only minor importance to heavenly Jerusalem. As long as the Holy One, blessed be He, does not enter earthly Jerusalem, the destroyed city, he does not enter heavenly Jerusalem either;

therefore, the building of earthly Jerusalem takes precedence." The conclusion of the whole article, as it appears in the last sentence, is based on this presumption (p. 391): "For the Rabbis, heavenly Jerusalem is nothing but the outcome of the growth and the building of earthly Jerusalem. . ." I believe that R. Johanan's statement is an important and paradoxical innovation; because of His love for the people and his empathy with their grief, God was willing to refrain from entering His beloved city. (The expression *avo' bi-Yerushalaim* [I will enter Jerusalem] may hint to sexual connotations in this context, as in the parallel versions in Gnostic literature and in the exegeses of the early Kabbalists, who replace *avo* [enter] with *ezdavveg* [mate], as shown by Moshe Idel.) *Tanhuma*, a late midrash, does indicate the precedence of earthly Jerusalem: "Because of His great love for earthly Jerusalem, He made another heavenly one" (Exodus 38.) Moreover, from Origen's letters and from other sources, we learn that the idea of the *Shekhina*—also called *Wisdom, Earth*, and *Jerusalem*—was widespread amongst Jews. See "The Kabbalistic Myth as Told by Orpheus," in this volume, p. 176, n. 86.

108. Asi Farber-Ginat, "The Concept of the Merkaba in Thirteenth Century Jewish Esotericism: "Sod Ha-Egoz" and Its Development" [Hebrew], Ph. D. Dissertation, Hebrew University, Jerusalem, 1987, pp. 231–244. See also Idel, *Kabbala*, pp. 191–197. See another view in Dan, *The Early Kabbalistic Circles*, pp. 159–165.

109. See, e.g., *Nahmanides' Commentary on the Torah*, Genesis 38:29; Zohar I:180b–181a; see the references quoted in Mikhal Oron, ed., *Sha'ar ha-Razim* by R. Todros Aboulafia (Jerusalem, 1989), p. 49, n. 19.

110. Sukka 29a: "Our Rabbis taught: When the sun is in eclipse, it is a bad omen for idolaters; when the moon is in eclipse, it is a bad omen for Israel, since Israel reckons by the moon and idolaters by the sun."

111. See, e.g., Zohar III:79b. *Ma'arekhet ha-Elohut*, 106a–109a. See also M. Cordovero, *Pardes Rimonim*, Section 18, called "The Waning of the Moon" and also *Ets Hayyim* in Lurianic Kabbala, Section 36, also called by the same name. See also references quoted in note 109.

112. See, e.g., Megilla 15b.

113. See, e.g., Zohar III:181b.

114. According to Isaiah 46:3: "Hearken to me, O house of Jacob, and all the remnant of the house of Israel, who are borne by me from birth, who are carried from the womb."

115. In another version, the Gentiles crush them—*monim lahem*—and oppress them; however, the other meaning of *monim* is reckon, in which case it would be *monim lah*—reckon by her, rather than *monim lahem*. I believe the version *monim lah* is the correct one.

116. See, e.g., *Ra'aya Meheimana*, Zohar II:187b–188a. Rabbi Hayyim Vital, *Ma'amar Pesi'otav shel Avraham Avinu* (Jerusalem, 1988), p. 5 (bound with other writings in the anthology *Ketavim Hadashim me-Rabbenu Hayyim Vital* [Jerusalem, 1988]).

117. See Berakhot 63a–b; Ketubot 111a; and others. See *Pirke de-Rabbi Eliezer*, Ch. 8; Exodus Rabba, Ch. 15.

118. Thus in several places in Moshe Idel's studies, and in Farber, "The Concept of the Merkaba." On the similarities and differences between these two layers see J. Dan, "A Re-Evaluation of the 'Ashkenazi Kabbala,'" in *The Beginnings of Jewish Mysticism in Medieval Europe*, pp. 129–135.

119. See note 110.

120. Compare Exodus Rabba, 15:6: "Should you enquire why Esther is compared to the moon, the answer is that just as the moon renews itself every thirty days, so did Esther. . ."

121. *Sefer Hasidim* (Bologna, 1538), 119b, n. 1154. (In the Mossad ha-Rav Kook edition [Jerusalem, 1973], pp. 571–572). Indeed, this passage is part of the section originally in the *Sefer Hokhmat ha-Nefesh* by R. Elazar from Worms (see, e.g., in the introduction by I. Marcus, *Sefer Hasidim*, facsimile edition of the MSS [Jerusalem, 1985], p. 10) but I did not find this passage in either the printed or the MSS editions of the *Sefer Hokhmat ha-Nefesh*. Even if the source of this passage is in the writings of R. Elazar, it still belongs to the literature of the German pietist movement.

122. See Rashi and Tosefot, Megilla 22b; Hagiga 18a; Rosh Hashana 23a. See also *Tur and Shulkhan Arukh, Orakh Hayyim*, 417.

123. Quoted in the *Darkhei Moshe*, on the *Tur* (ibid.).

124. See Zohar III:79a–b.

125. See, e.g., Zohar III:187b: "And it seemed thus to Jacob but only as a symbol, since it is written (Genesis 29:9): 'And Rachel came', and this is the shape of another Rachel, as is written: 'A voice was heard in Ramah. . . Rachel weeps for her children.'" See also Liebes, *Sections of the Zohar Lexicon*, pp. 182–183.

126. Note 99 and ff.

127. Baba Batra 99a; Yoma 59a–b. On this question, its significance, the parallel versions and its influence on Kabbala, see Idel, *Kabbala*, p. 165. See Liebes, "New Writings in Sabbatean Kabbalah."

128. See note 106.

129. See more in the next Section.

130. See p. 23.

131. See *Sefer Bahir*, 102, 113, 119. See Joseph Gikatila, *She'arei Ora* (Warsaw, 1883; offset, Jerusalem, 1960), 19a–20a.

132. See Zohar I:182a.

133. See Urbach, *The Sages*, pp. 67–69.

134. See Gikatila, *She'arei Ora*, 48a–52a.

135. See *Otsar ha-Kavod* on Rosh Hashana 31a; *She'arei Ora* (ibid.), 8a–9a. See also Idel, *Kabbala*, pp. 166–170.

136. See B. Zak "The Exile of Israel and the Exile of the *Shekhina* in *Or Yakar* of Rabbi Moses Cordovero," *Jerusalem Studies in Jewish Thought*, 1 (1982): 157–178.

137. See *Sha'ar Ha-Kavvanot* (Jerusalem, 1902), 79a–80c (on Pesah, *drush* a). On these ideas and their development in Sabbateanism, see Liebes, "New Writings in Sabbatean Kabbala," pp. 191–294.

138. In his book against the Galileans, Julian admits that biblical myths may possess deep significance when taken beyond their literal meaning, but neither Jews nor Christians tend to approach myths in this fashion.

139. See G. Scholem, *Major Trends in Jewish Mysticism* (New York, 1961), pp. 7–8.

140. See p. 51.

141. See Genesis Rabba 19:4. See also Ariela Dim, *Zot ha-Pa'am: Eser Nashim mi-Tokh ha-Tanakh* (Jerusalem, 1986), pp. 18–20. After her death, Y. Liebes edited the book and added an introduction.

142. See Liebes, *The Sin of Elisha*, pp. 148–158.

143. See p. 21.

144. See Y. Kaufmann, *The History of Israelite Religion* [Hebrew] (Tel-Aviv, 1960), Vol. I, p. 666; Vol. III, pp. 509–510: "Human sacrifice in Israel...reflects the self-bewilderment of the Israelite religion."

145. See Exodus 13:2; 12–13.

146. See Tur Sinai, *Ha-Lashon veha-Sefer* (Jerusalem, 1952), pp. 122–181.

147. Jeremiah 7:31; 19:5; 32:35.

148. Jeremiah 7:21–23. Similar views are shared by other prophets, as is well known.

149. Quoted in Eusebius, *Praeparatio Evangelica*, I:10, 33; see also I:10, 44; IV:16, 11.

150. Leviticus 27:29; Judges 11:30-40.

151. See Kings II 3:26-27.

152. Maimonides' views, as formulated in *Hilkhot Yesodei ha-Tora* 5, in *Sefer ha-Mitzvot, Mitzvot Ase* 9, in the *Epistle on Martyrdom* and in the *Epistle to Yemen*, provide a good illustration of this ambivalence. This question is much beyond the scope of this work and a hint will suffice in this context. Even though he compared the sufferings of forced conversion to an offering on the altar, Maimonides commanded us not to spare loss of wealth or even exile to avoid martyrdom and does not mention dying for "the sanctification of the Name." See the end of the first chapter in the *Epistle to Yemen*.

153. See Zohar I:66b; I:245a. This matter remains mysterious here, but is clarified in the Hebrew essay by R. Moshe de Leon, *Sod Eser Sefirot Blima*, G. Scholem ed., in *Kovetz Al-Yad* 8 (1976): 381. The whole matter, including the pertinent sources, is discussed extensively in Y. Liebes, " '*Tsaddik Yesod Olam*': A Sabbatean Myth" [Hebrew], *Da'at* 1 (1978): 107-108.

154. See, e.g., Exodus 15:11; Judges 11:24; Samuel I 26:19.

155. According to the prophet Malachi, in his time the whole world worshipped God—Malachi 1:11. Compare Cyrus' statement in Ezra 1:2:. Deutero-Isaiah indeed suggests a slightly different approach—Isaiah 45:4.

156. See Y. Liebes, "*Ha-tikkun ha-kelali* of R. Nahman of Bratslav and Its Sabbatean Links," in this volume, p. 135, and the addendum in *Zion* 46 (1981): p. 354.

157. Phylacteries, from the Greek *philacterion*, talisman for keeping. Compare Genesis 4:15.

158. See Exodus 12: 22-23.

159. Zohar III:121a. See Liebes, "The Messiah of the Zohar," and n. 311.

160. See I. Tishby, *The Wisdom of the Zohar* [Hebrew], Vol. I (Jerusalem, 1957), pp. 285-295. Tishby spoke of the "dualistic trend" and of the "limits of duality." On the other hand, Dorit Cohen Eloro, in a lecture at the Conference on the Study of the Zohar, at the Hebrew University in 1988, claimed that we must speak of the "monistic trend" and of the "limits of unity." See also I. Tishby, *The Doctrine of Evil and the Kelippah in Lurianic Kabbalism* [Hebrew] (Jerusalem, 1963). Tishby also favored dualism in this work, but points out that it is limited by many restrictions and by monistic theories.

161. See *Pirke de-Rabbi Eliezer*, ch. 46, which refers to the scapegoat as a "bribe" to Satan, and thus often in the Zohar, such as I:114b.

162. See Leviticus 9, and Nahmanides commentary on Leviticus 9:7.

163. See Zohar I:64b-65a.

164. Compare the notion of divine catharsis in connection with the death of "the Ten Martyrs," see notes 48 and 49.

165. See Zohar II:32b–35b. See Liebes, "The Messiah of the Zohar."

166. My book *The Sin of Elisha* is grounded on this approach, which I show to be the source of talmudic mysticism and the cause of its limitations. This approach is also helpful in explaining the sins of Elisha ben Avuya and others who entered the *pardes*, as opposed to Rabbi Akiba, the only one capable of attaining the right mixture of love and fear. On this duality in the Zohar and in the *Sefer Bahir*, see Liebes, "The Messiah of the Zohar." I believe this was also the background to the Hayyun controversy, which is connected to the struggle against Sabbateanism, on which see Liebes, "The Ideological Basis of the Hayyun Controversy."

167. This is a translation of the Arabic original. The authograph, which most scholars confirm as authentic, appears in the facsimile edition of Moshe Sasson, *Commentary to the Mishnah by Moshe ben Maimon* (Copenhagen, 1961), part II, p. 304. This edition was printed with a new Hebrew translation by J. Kafeh, *The Mishna with a Commentary by R. Moshe ben Maimon* [original and translation], *Seder Nezikin* (Jerusalem, 1965), p. 216.

168. Amos Goldreich, with whom I consulted, suggested this translation.

169. The translator is apparently Shelomo Ibn Ya'akov. See M. Goshen Gottstein, "The Thirteen Principles of Maimonides as Translated by Alharizi" [Hebrew], in *Likutei Tarbiz V: Studies in Maimonides* (Jerusalem, 1985), p. 309. Alharizi's translation is more accurate: "And we must believe in the Messiah, exalt him and love him," ibid., p. 319. The third translation, which appears at the opening of Itzhak Abrabanel's *Rosh Amana* seems bizarre: "And we must remember redemption [*ge'ula*, which was apparently mistaken for *ha-gedula* greatness] and the love of God." Kafeh translated literally and thus did not decide on this issue: "And to believe in greatness and love."

170. Namely, heresy against the Torah and the Prophets, but in the article in the Commentary on Sanhedrin, he is considered guilty of heresy against God.

171. Aviezer Ravitzky pointed this out to me.

172. Ze'ev Harvey brought this to my attention.

173. See Isaac Shailat, ed., *Letters and Essays of Moses Maimonides* [Hebrew], Vol. I (Jerusalem, 1987), pp. 99–100.

174. Kappah edition, pp. 207–208.

175. It has often been indicated that Maimonides's description of messianic times was influenced by Aristotle's epistle to Alexander the Great. This epistle is preserved in an Arabic translation and, before Maimonides,

R. Moses Ibn Ezra had already commented on its pertinence to messianic times; see S. M. Stern, *Aristotle on the World State* (Columbia, S.C., 1970). From Ibn Ezra's comments, it appears that naturalistic descriptions of messianic times based on this Aristotelian epistle had been known before him. This seems to be evident from the fact that Ibn Ezra included the epistle in the wrong place, immediately after his controversy with those who take miraculous description of messianic times out of context. It appears then, that Ibn Ezra copied the epistle from his opponent, without realizing that it was antithetical to his own intentions. See A. S. Halkin, ed., *Moshe ben Ya'akov ibn Ezra: Kitab al-Muhadara wal-Mudhakara* (Jerusalem, 1975), pp. 268–271.

176. *Politeia* 8, 546a. This has already been noted by J. Kraemer and Warren Harvey.

177. Following my Hebrew translation (Y.L.) of Maimonides's Commentary on the Mishna.

178. See Aviezer Ravitzky, " 'In Man's Measure': Messianic Times for Maimonides" [Hebrew], in Zvi Baras, ed., *Messianism and Eschatology* (Jerusalem, 1984), pp. 191–220.

2. The Kabbalistic Myth as Told by Orpheus

1. The two common forms of the name are Erikapaios or Erikepaios

2. R. Eisler, *Weltenmantel und Himmelszelt* (Munich, 1910), p. 475.

3. G. Scholem, *From Berlin to Jerusalem* [Hebrew] (Tel-Aviv, 1982), pp. 150–153 (with omissions). This passage is translated from the expanded Hebrew version of the autobiography.

4. G. Scholem, *The Kabbala in Provence* [Hebrew], ed. R. Schatz (Jerusalem, 1963, mimeo), p. 52.

5. I. Baer, *Israel Among the Nations* [Hebrew] (Jerusalem, 1969), p. 112.

6. In my view, an erotic note is also apparent in the name of this book, influenced by Moses' description in the Zohar.

7. See his autobiography *From Berlin to Jerusalem*, p. 125.

8. See, e.g., his book *Elements of the Kabbalah and Its Symbolism* [Hebrew] (Jerusalem, 1976), Ch. 8. In the first part of this chapter !pp. 259–274), Scholem concentrated on an attempt to demonstrate the rather problematic claim that the mythical character of the *Shekhina* is a kabbalistic innovation.

9. See the first chapter of ibid., "Mysticism and Religious Authority," pp. 9–35.

10. For a review on the development of this view, prominently represented by Gilles Quispel, see I. P. Culianu, "The Angels of the Nations and the Origins of Gnostic Dualism" in R. van den Broek and M. J. Vermaseren, eds., *Studies in Gnosticism and Hellenistic Religions Presented to Gilles Quispel on the Occasion of His 65th Birthday* (Leiden, 1981), pp. 78–91; E. M. Yamauchi, "Jewish Gnosticism?" in K. Rudolph, ed., *Gnosis und Gnostizismus* (Darmstadt, 1975).

11. See my "The Messiah of the Zohar," in *Studies in the Zohar* (Albany, forthcoming).

12. See B. A. Pearson, "Jewish Elements in Corpus Hermeticum 1 (Poimandres)," van den Broek and Vermaseren, in *Studies* in *Gnosticism and Hellenistic Religons*, pp. 336–348.

13. See Y. Liebes, "Chistian Influences in the Zohar" [Hebrew], *Jerusalem Studies in Jewish Thought* 2 (1983): 43–74.

14. M. Idel, "The Concept of the Torah in *Hekhalot* Literature and Kabbala" [Hebrew], *Jerusalem Studies in Jewish Thought* 1 (1981–82): 23–84.

15. M. Idel "The Evil Thought in the Deity" [Hebrew], *Tarbiz* 49 (1980): 356–364.

16. M. Idel, "The *Sefirot* Above the *Sefirot*" [Hebrew], *Tarbiz* 51 (1982): 239–280.

17. M. Idel, "The Image of Man Above the *Sefirot*" [Hebrew], *Da'at* 4 (1980): 41–55. Recently, Idel has also adopted this course when explaining several issues in the *Sefer Bahir*. See M. Idel, "The Problem of the Sources of the *Bahir*" [Hebrew], in J. Dan, ed., *The Beginnings of Jewish Mysticism in Medieval Europe*, Jerusalem Studies in Jewish Thought 6 (Jerusalem, 1987). See also M. Idel *Kabbala: New Perspectives* (New Haven, Conn., 1988).

18. See my "The Mesiah of the Zohar."

19. "Secret Scroll" [*Megillat Setarim*] was the meaning of the name of the *Sifra di-Ts'niuta* [Book of Concealment], one of the parts of the Zohar (II:176b–179a). Indeed, the author of the Zohar probably wrote this anonymous and enigmatic text as well, though many passages in the Zohar, especially in the *Idrot*, are supposedly an exegesis of what we have "learned" in the *Sifra di-Tsniuta*. However, it is noteworthy that traces of many ancient and remote myths actually do appear in the *Sifra di-Tsni'uta*; see my "Christian Influences in the Zohar," pp. 53–61. The first Zoharic reference to the "death of the kings," discussed at the end of this essay, is also found here (II:176b), together with the famous Gnostic depiction of the uroboros.

20. I am referring to the *Amon mi-No*, the famous demon of Spanish kabbalistic writings from the time of the expulsion. See M. Idel, "The Origin of Alchemy According to Zosimo and a Hebrew Parallel," *REJ* 145 (1986):

117–124. In this case, as in many others, transitions across religions are complex and pendulumlike. This figure obviously originated in Egyptian religion.

21. A prominent example of this are Luria's messianic doctrines, whose hidden roots appear in the Zohar, as I showed in "The Messiah of the Zohar."

22. See W. K. C. Guthrie, *Orpheus and Greek Religion* (London, 1935), pp. 1–5.

23. See O. Kern, *Orphicorum Fragmenta* (Berlin, 1922), Index II, s.v. *Platon.*

24. See C. H. Gordon, *Before the Bible: The Common Background of Greek and Hebrew Civilizations* (London, 1962).

25. See P. Walcott, *Hesiod and the Near East* (Cardiff, 1966). This book fails to pay enough attention to Jewish material.

26. See Guthrie, *Orpheus and Greek Religion*, pp. 255–256.

27. See Eisler, *Weltenmantel und Himmelszelt*; Guthrie, ibid., p. 145, n. 18. See also the entry *Erikapaios* in *Paulys Real-Encyclopadie.*

28. See Guthrie, ibid., p. 98. For the original Greek, see Kern, *Orphicorum Fragmenta*, p. 147.

29. Eisler, *Weltenmantel und Himmelszelt*, had already pointed to this parallel in the Zohar relying, as usual, on the French translation. However, his quotation appears to be a summary of the Zohar's view, and I was unable to find the exact source.

30. See Guthrie, *Orpheus and Greek Religion*, pp. 97–98.

31. Ibid., pp. 257 ff..

32. This document was first published by J. G. Smyly, *Greek Papyri from Gurob* (Dublin, 1921), and is the first document in the collection. The line discussed here is 22. The wording here is indeed *Pikepaige*, but Smyly had already assumed this to be a corrupted form of Erikapaios. This document was republished by Kern, *Orphicorum Fragmenta*, p. 102, who rechecked the manuscript, and I have followed his reading.

33. See M. Sukkah 4:5 and, in the New Testament, Matthew 21:9, 19; Mark 11:9–11; John 12:13.

34. See C. F. Nims and R. C. Steiner, "A Paganized Version of Psalm 20:2–6 from the Aramaic text in Demotic Script," *Journal of the American Oriental Society* 103 (1983). Indeed, in a discussion at the Institute of Jewish Studies at the Hebrew University in Jerusalem, Moshe Weinfeld disagreed with this thesis and assumed that this parallel is in the model of parallels between Ugaritic and biblical literature.

35. See Guthrie, *Orpheus and Greek Religion*, p. 101.

36. Such as the famous Orphic motto: *Heis Zeus, heis Haides, heis Hlios, heis Dionysos, heis Theos enpaniessi.* See Kern, *Orphicorum Fragmenta*, p. 103; Smyly, *Greek Papyri*, pp. 6–7.

37. See O. Weinrich, *Neue Urkunden Zu Sarapis-Religion* (Tubingen, 1919), pp. 24–31.

38. Ibid., pp 18–19. On Jewish awareness and Jewish interpretation of the cult of Serapis—the identification between Serapis and Joseph—see G. Mussies, "The Interpretatio Judaica of Sarapis" in M. J. Vermaseren, ed., *Studies in Hellenistic Religion* (Leiden, 1979), pp. 189–214.

39. See Smyly, *Greek Papyri*, passages 2, 8.

40. See Guthrie, *Orpheus and Greek Religion*, p. 87; Eisler, *Weltenmantel und Himmelszelt*, p. 393, n. 1.

41. See Guthrie, ibid., p. 86; for the original Greek see Kern, *Orphicorum Fragmenta*, p. 130.

42. This responsum is printed, for instance, in the book *Pardes Rimmonim* by Moses Cordovero, Section 11, Ch. I. On this responsum see also Idel, "The *Sefirot* Above the *Sefirot*," p. 247; and "The Image of Man Above the *Sefirot*," p. 67 and references.

43. See, for instance, The New Testament, The Revelation to John 4:7. This, as is well known, is a Judeo-Christian work.

44. In Proclus' commentary to Plato's Timaeus, dc 30. In the original, it appears in Kern, *Orphicorum Fragmenta*, p. 153, passage 79. See also G. Quispel, "The Demiurge in the Apocryphon of John," in R. M. Wilson ed., *Nag Hammadi and Gnosis* (Leiden, 1978), p. 16.

45. Ibid., p. 22.

46. Ibid., pp. 20–33.

47. See A. F. Segal, *Two Powers in Heaven, Early Rabbinic Reports About Christianity and Gnosticism* (Leiden, 1978).

48. Quispel, "The Demiurge in the Apocryphon of John," p. 26.

49. N. H. Tur Sinai, "*El Shadai*," in his book *The Tongue and the Book* [Hebrew], III (Jerusalem, 1977), pp. 114–120. Rather than separate entities, Tur Sinai sees here two names or different facets of the same divinity.

50. See Tur Sinai, "*Merkava Ve-Anan*," in ibid., pp. 62–72.

51. On the Orphic egg and its parallels, see Guthrie, *Orpheus and Greek Religion*, s.v. *Egg, the Orphic*, and specially pp. 92 ff.; Quispel, "The Demiurge in the Apocryphon of John," pp. 10–24.

52. Eusebius, *Preparatio Evangelica*, I:10.

53. Cited by Quispel, "The Demiurge in the Apocryphon of John," p. 13.

54. As summarized in ibid., pp. 13–14.

55. See *Encyclopaedia Biblica* [Hebrew], s.v. *Philon Mi-Geval*; M. D. Cassuto, *From Adam to Noah* [Hebrew] (Jerusalem, 1953), p. 13.

56. See Quispel, "The Demiurge in the Apocryphon of John," pp. 13–14.

57. For interpretations of this obscure combination see Quispel, ibid., p. 14; Guthrie, *Orpheus and Greek Religion*, p. 94.

58. See Guthrie, ibid., p. 80.

59. I. Tishbi, *The Wisdom of the Zohar*, trans. David Goldstein (Oxford, 1989), I:163. A parallel and, in certain respects, more detailed description, appears in Zohar I:16b; III:135b (*Idra Rabba*); *Zohar Haddash* (Mossad Ha-Rav Kook ed.), 121d (this passage does not belong to the *Tikkunei Zohar*, despite its reference to it in the printed versions).

60. The term *engraving* to describe the Creator's first action obviously resembles the beginning of the *Sefer Yetsira*.

61. See *Raza De-Atvan Gelifin*, printed at the end of the book *Har Adonai* and after *Tsaddik Yesod Olam* (Polonea, 1791), 22a: "This is the mystery of 'it penetrated, but did not penetrate' in the Zohar. . .and understand that the chick was born from the inner part of the egg and the chick was carved from the inner part of the egg and the egg split in two." On the books *Raza De-Atvan Gelifin* and *Tsaddik Yesod Olam*, see my article "*Tsaddik Yesod Olam*: A Sabbatean Myth" [Hebrew], *Da'at* 1 (1978): 73–120. On the hatching and its sources see ibid., pp. 101–104. On the author of these two books see my "The Author of the Book '*Tsaddik Yesod Olam*': The Sabbatean Prophet R. Leib Prossnitz" [Hebrew], *Da'at* 2–3 (1978–79): 159–173.

62. See Y. Liebes, *Sections of the Zohar Lexicon* [Hebrew], (Jerusalem, 1982), pp. 136–167, and mainly 145–151 and 161–164.

63. G. Scholem, "Traces of Gabirol in the Kabbala" [Hebrew], in *Measef Sofrei Eretz Israel* (Tel-Aviv, 1940), pp. 167–168; see also note 65.

64. S. Pines, " 'And He Called out to Nothingness and It Was Split': A Note on a Passage in Ibn Gabirol's *Keter Malkhut*" [Hebrew], *Tarbiz* 50 (1981): 339–347. For further details, see the original Hebrew version of the present essay.

65. It seems that, on this issue, other kabbalists relied on Gabirol's philosophical book *Fons Vitae*. See G. Scholem, *The Beginning of Kabbala* [Hebrew] (Jerusalem and Tel Aviv, 1948). Also G. Scholem, *Origins of the Kabbala* (Philadelphia, 1987), pp. 340–343, and G. Scholem, "*Schopfung aus Nichts und Selbstverschankung Gottes*," *Eranos-Jarbuch* 25 (1957): 92–93.

66. The phrase *turned nothingness into being* is worded differently in other versions. One of these wordings—"and it was made with fire and it is"—is printed in I. Gruenwald's edition as part of the text, whereas the others are cited in the footnotes. See I. Gruenwald, "A Preliminary Critical Edition of *Sefer Yetsira," Israel Oriental Studies* (1971): 149. However, it is inconceivable that a version such as "Turned nothingness into being" could be a copier's mistake, the more so because it relies on parallel versions before and after: "Created reality from chaos, turned nothingness into being, and hewed great columns from ungraspable air."

67. Genesis Rabba 2:4. In reply to R. Joshua's question "Whence are the feet?" Ben Zoma answers "From nowhere, Rabbi." S. Lieberman, *Tosefta Ki-fshutah*, Hagiga (New York, 1962), pp. 1292–1294, interpreted this as meaning that Ben Zoma had said: "I am not coming from the *ayin*" and linked this to Gnostic views. If Lieberman was right, then *ayin* appears as the name of a possible provenance. But I believe this interpretation is unacceptable. First, the wording "From nowhere, Rabbi" is not found in the parallel versions that appear in both Talmuds and in the Tosefta, and even differs from several other versions of Genesis Rabba. Second, I do not believe that Ben-Zoma's quest (or even Elisha ben Avuya's quest) had a Gnostic background, as I show at length in my book *The Sin of Elisha: The Four Who Entered Paradise and the Nature of Talmudic Mysticism* [Hebrew] (Jerusalem, 1986). The rabbis did not question their views, and only found fault with the mode of their quest. Ben Zoma was not censored because of his beliefs, but rather because he was so deeply immersed in his thoughts about the cosmos at the moment of Creation that he became oblivious to his status and duties in this world, to the extent of failing to return his teacher's greetings. His statements about the higher and nether waters are not at all parallel to the Gnostic views alluded in Lieberman about the higher and the nether world, the world of light and the world of darkness. The higher waters are not normatively "better" than the nether ones. Nor did Lieberman point to a parallel use of the word *ayin*. Tova Be'eri has recently referred me to the expression *yesh me-ayin* [ex nihilo] in the work of a tenth century poet.

68. Dan, *The Beginnings of Jewish Mysticism in Medieval Europe*, pp. 80–85.

69. For the Greek source, see Kern, *Orphicorum Fragmenta*, p. 134. For the English translation, see J. Van Amersfoort, "Traces of an Alexandrian Orphic Theogony in the Pseudo-Clementines," in van den Broek and Vermaseren, *Studies in Gnosticism and Hellenistic Religions*, pp. 16–17. See also Quispel, "The Demiurge in the Apocryphon of John," p. 19.

70. Compare *Tanhuma, Tazri'a* 3: "Come and see this peacock, with its 365 kinds of colors, and it was created from one drop of whiteness."

71. See Amersfoort, "Traces of an Alexandrian Orphic Theogony," who correctly points out that the claim had already been raised by W. Heintze,

"Der Klemensroman und seine Griechischen Quellen," TU 40, 2 (1914). See also Quispel, "The Demiurge in the Aprocryphon of John."

72. Basilides's work is preserved in Hypolito's *Refutatio*, 7, 21, 5; it is also quoted in Quispel, ibid., p. 20 and in Amersfoort, ibid., p. 25, where the Greek version also appears. Quispel, ibid., mentions further sources for the cosmic egg story.

73. See G. Scholem, *Major Trends in Jewish Mysticism* (New York, 1961), p. 264; and I. Tishby, "Gnostic Doctrines in Sixteenth Century Jewish Mysticism," *JJS* 6 (1955): 146–152.

74. The Nag Hammadi Library (San Francisco, 1977), p, 41. See note 92. In this book, p. 38, there is an interesting parallel to a poem by Gabirol "I Love Thee," concerning the secret tradition the poet had heard about "the whole" aspiring to be like its Creator. I also found a very similar poem in a book by the Arab mystic El-Arabi; see my "Rabbi Solomon Ibn Gabirol's Use of the *Sefer Yetsira* and a Commentary on the Poem 'I Love Thee'," pp. 122–123. The *Evangelium Veritatis* is apparently Valentinus's book—also from Egypt!—and I believe some of its statements reflect Jewish influence. Thus, for instance, I found (p. 45) a homily on the term *teshuva* [repentance], certainly derived from a Hebrew or Aramaic ambiguity. The controversial allegorization of the notion of the Sabbath (p. 44) also attests to links with Jews. For a most detailed bibliography on all that has been published concerning this book up till 1971, see D. M. Scholer, *Nag Hammadi Bibliography* (Leiden, 1971), pp. 119–128.

75. *De Ebrietate*, ch. 32. My friend G. Stroumsa mentioned this passage to me in this context.

76. *De Opificio Mundi*, ch. 23.

77. *Shaar Ha-Hakdamot* (Jerusalem, 1809). Yosef Avivi mentioned this text to me.

78. In his commentary on the Zohar, *Or Ha-Hama* II:51b, see B. Sak, "On R. Abraham Galante's Commentary" [Hebrew], *Misgav Yerushalaim: Jerusalem Studies in Jewish Literature* (Jerusalem, 1987), p. 84.

79. See Y. Ben-Shlomo, *The Mystical Theology of Moses Cordovero* [Hebrew] (Jerusalem, 1965), p. 62. On the formula "withdrew from Himself into Himself," see Sabbetai Sheftel Horowitz, *Shefa Tal* (Hanau, 1912), f.30a, 45b. Sheftel was Cordovero's spiritual disciple and failed to mention Luria even once. *Tsimtsum* always appears in his writings with the addition of the formula "from Himself into Himself," which is common in Cordovero and never found in Lurianic writings. May we conclude that the so-called Lurianic doctrine of *tsimtsum* in fact preceded Luria and might be found in some of Cordovero's writings not in our possession? It is not so hard to assume that this is an ancient doctrine, because inklings of it appear already in the

writings of Nahmanides and his contemporaries (see G. Scholem, *The Kabbala in Gerona* [Hebrew] (Jerusalem, 1964), pp. 286–291). Moreover, the doctrine of *tsimtsum* is not central in Luria's writings, and in some of the Lurianic descriptions of the origins of emanation it does not appear at all. See B. Sak, "R. Moses Cordovero's Doctrine of *Tsimtsum*" [Hebrew], *Tarbiz* 58 (1989): 207–238.

80. On the kingdom of *Ein-Sof* as the place most suitable for building worlds, see my *"Tsaddik Yesod Olam*: A Sabbatean Myth," p. 84, n. 71.

81. As I. Tishby showed in his book *The Doctrine of Evil and the Kelippah in Lurianic Kabbala* [Hebrew] (Jerusalem, 1963), pp. 56–61. Similarly, see R. Israel Saruk in the preface of his commentary to the *Sifra di-Ts'niuta*, printed at the end of his book *Limmudei Atsilut*. The relations between Saruk and Luria's kabbalistic approaches have been extensively considered, and still require further discussion. This kabbalistic view was accepted by and developed in Sabbatean literature, as I pointed out in my "Tsaddik Yesod Olam: A Sabbatean Myth."

82. See *Sha'ar Ha-Hakdamot*, I, *Hakdama* 4 (Jerusalem, 1910), 6b: "Then did the *Ein-Sof* gather itself at its center point, precisely at the middle of its light." Similarly, *Ets Ha-Hayyim*, *Sha'ar* I:2 (Jerusalem, 1910), I:11c. See R. Meir Paparesh's comment there: "Our rabbis said so relatively to us," pointing to the difficulty roused by the mention of a center point in an apparently simple and infinite entity.

83. See Guthrie, *Orpheus and Greek Religion*, pp. 80, 101–102.

84. Ibid., pp. 80–81, 104–106.

85. See, for instance, the description in Proclus' commentary to Plato's Timaeus, Kern, *Orphicorum Fragmenta*, p. 199, and Guthrie's English translation, ibid, p. 81.

86. In my "The Messiah of the Zohar." See also my "How the Zohar Was Written" [Hebrew], in J. Dan, ed., *The Age of the Zohar*, Jerusalem Studies in Jewish Thought 8, (Jerusalem, 1989), pp. 66–68.

87. As did the author of *Va-Avo ha-Yom el ha-Ayin* [I Came Today to the Spring]. See excerpts in M. A. Perlmuter, *Rabbi Jonathan Eybeschuetz and His Attitude Towards Sabbateanism* [Hebrew] (Jerusalem and Tel-Aviv, 1947), pp. 90–91.

88. See Quispel, "The Demiurge in the Apocryphon of John," p. 17 and references; Amersfoort, "Traces of an Alexandrian Orphic Theogony," p. 82. On Jewish and Christian versions of this formula, see my "Christian Influences in the Zohar," pp. 59–60.

89. See Zohar II:122b–123b; III:131b [*Idra Rabba*]; 140a [*Idra Rabba*] 286b–291a [*Idra Zuta*]. This became a main tenet of Lurianic Kabbala.

90. See Guthrie, *Orpheus and Greek Religion*, pp. 82, 97; Amersfoort, "Traces of Alexandrian Orphic Theogony," pp. 18, 21, and the Orphic text he quoted there from Proclus' commentary to Plato's Timaeus, p. 24—the text quoted from Damasceus.

91. In my "The Messiah of the Zohar."

92. See Quispel, "The Demiurge in the Aprocryphon of John," pp. 9–10.

93. Zohar I:22a–b. The passage belongs to the *Tikkunei Zohar*. I discussed this passage in my article "A Messianic Treatise by R. Wolf, the Son of R. Jonathan Eybeschuetz" [Hebrew], *Kiryat Sefer* 57 (1982): 168–170. It is worth noting that the creative God is also called *Marei de-Biniana*, a translation of the Demiurge. Other Gnostic descriptions also precede kabbalistic notions of the *Shekhina*; many of these Gnostics were Jews, and their doctrines could have been handed down to the kabbalists. We thus find that a Gnostic doctrine on the *Shekhina*, called *wisdom, land* and *Jerusalem*, reached Origen via Jews who had hinted at it in a commentary on Genesis 1:2. See J. C. M. van Winden, *"Terra autem stupida quadam erat admiratione*: Reflections on a Remarkable Translation of Genesis 1:2," in van den Broek and Vermaseren, *Studies in Gnosticism and Hellenic Religions*, pp. 458–466. See also the beginning of *Evangelium Veritatis*. Further evidence can be adduced from the Kabbala (Zohar I:39b).

94. See my "The Messiah of the Zohar."

95. Ibid.

96. Y. Dan, "Anafiel, Metatron and the Creator" [Hebrew], *Tarbiz* 52 (1983): 447–457.

97. See M. Idel, "The World of Angels in Human Form" [Hebrew], in J. Dan and J. Hacket, *Studies in Jewish Mysticism, Philosophy and Ethical Literature Presented to Isaiah Tishby on His Seventy-Fifth Birthday* (Jerusalem, 1986). M. Idel directed me to this parallel.

98. See H. Wirshuvsky, *Three Studies in Christian Kabbala* [Hebrew] (Jerusalem, 1975), pp. 39–51.

3. Sabbatean Messianism

1. See Y. Liebes, "The Ultra Orthodox Community and the Dead Sea Sect" [Hebrew], *Jerusalem Studies in Jewish Thought* 1 (1982): 137–152. See pp. 143, 149.

2. See, e.g., S. J. Ish-Horowitz, *Me'ayin U-Le'an* [Hebrew] [From Where to Where] (Berlin, 1913), pp. 259–286.

3. From Shazar's studies, his article on R. Samuel Primo and his editing of *Sipur Ma'ase Sabbetai Zevi* [The Story of Sabbetai Zevi] are worth special attention. Izhak Ben-Zvi studied the Doenmeh sect intensively; Sokolov translated into Hebrew and added comments to Alexander Kraushar's book, *Frank i frankisci polscy* (Warsaw, 1895).

4. G. Scholem, *The Messianic Idea in Judaism and Other Essays* (New York, 1971), p. 1. It must be noted that Scholem did not explicitly discuss Sabbateanism in this article nor did he particularly stress the political aspects in his study of the movement, though he did not object to them.

5. On messianism in the rabbinic period and in Maimonides, see Y. Liebes, "De Natura Dei: On the Development of the Jewish Myth," in this volume pp. 35–42, 61–64.

6. I pointed to new material on this question in the following articles: Y. Liebes, "New Writings in Sabbatean Kabbala from the Circle of Rabbi Johathan Eybeschuetz" [Hebrew], *Jerusalem Studies in Jewish Thought* 5 (1986): 191–348; see p. 192, n. 4, and references. Y. Liebes, "A Messianic Treatise by R. Wolf the Son of R. Jonathan Eybeschuetz" [Hebrew], *Kiryat Sefer* 57 (1982): 148–178 and 368–379; see pp. 175–178 and 377–378. Y. Liebes, "The Author of the Book *Tsaddik Yesod Olam*: The Sabbatean Prophet R. Leib Prossnitz" [Hebrew], *Da'at* 2–3 (1978–79): 159–173: see p. 169. Y. Liebes, "*Ha-tikkun ha-kelali* of R. Nahman of Bratslav and Its Sabbatean Links," in this volume. Y. Liebes, "New Light on the Matter of the Ba'al Shem Tov and Sabbetai Zvi" [Hebrew], *Jerusalem Studies in Jewish Thought* 2 (1983): 564–569.

7. On the distinction between the national and the sectarian stages of the movement as marked by Sabbetai Zevi's conversion, see G. Scholem, "Redemption Through Sin," in Scholem, *The Messianic Idea in Judaism and Other Essays*, pp. 86–94; G. Scholem, *Sabbetai Zevi: The Mystical Messiah* (Princeton, N.J.: 1973), pp. 687–693. I accept this distinction, though I object later to one aspect of the thesis presented in these sources.

8. Ibid., pp. 327–354.

9. For the letter and comments, see ibid., pp. 267–314.

10. Ibid., p. 674.

11. See G. Scholem, "New Documents on R. Nathan of Gaza from the Collections of R. Mahallalel Halleluya in Ancona" [Hebrew], *Harry A. Wolfson Jubilee Volume* (Jerusalem, 1965), 225–241; see p. 237. On the host's insistent requests for consolation, see p. 230. I believe these circumstances explain the relatively large number of references to earthly redemption in these documents.

12. See B. Richler, "From the Collections of the Institute of Microfilmed Hebrew Manuscripts of the Jewish National and University Library in Jerusalem," *Kiryat Sefer* 58 (1983): 194–197.

13. Nathan Shapira, *Tuv Ha-Aretz* (Venice, 1454). As I. Tishby and B. Zak showed, the book is a compilation of excerpts drawn mainly from Cordovero's Kabbala and only partly from Luria. These excerpts had been taken from the book by R. Abraham Azzulay, *Hesed Le-Avraham*, who, in turn, took them from the book *Or Yakar* by Moshe Cordovero.

14. See G. Scholem, "Regarding the Attitude of Jewish Rabbis to Sabbateanism" [Hebrew], *Zion* 13–14 (1948–49): 47–62; see p. 57.

15. See G. Scholem, "Redemption Through Sin," pp. 47–48 (the abrogation of the *Torah De Beri'a* is suggested here only as an hypothesis). See also M. Benayahu, "The 'Holy Brotherhood' of R. Judah Hasid and Their Settlement in Jerusalem" [Hebrew], *S. Z. Shazar Jubilee Volume*, pp. 131–182; see pp. 135–136.

16. See Y. Liebes, "The Messianism of R. Jacob Emden and his Attitude Toward Sabbateanism" [Hebrew], *Tarbiz* 49 (1980): 122–165.

17. See Scholem,"Redemption Through Sin," p. 122 and n. 50. Scholem quoted here most of R. Johathan Eybeschuetz's homily opposing the return to the Holy Land. This homily was preserved only in R. Jacob Emden's writings, and Scholem was therefore slightly doubtful of its attribution to Eybeschuetz. However, many other instances of Emden's quotes from the writings of Eybeschuetz and his circle have since been proven accurate. The style of the homily is also appropriate to Eybeschuetz, and I believe there is no room for doubt regarding this attribution. Moreover, the notion that even in messianic times Jews will not go to the Holy Land appears in other writings by Eybeshuetz, which he himself published.

18. See Scholem, "Redemption Through Sin," pp. 122–123.

19. Ibid., p. 119. See also G. Scholem, *The Dreams of the Sabbatean R. Mordechai Ashkenazi* [Hebrew] (Jerusalem, 1937).

20. On this dispute, see I. R. Molho and A. Amarillo, "Autobiographical Letters of Abraham Cardozo" in *S. Z. Shazar Jubilee Volume*, pp. 183–241. My friend Y. Barnai pointed out that, though not explicitly stated, opposition to R. Jehuda's immigration may also be at the source of this dispute.

21. See G. Scholem, ed., " '*Gey Hizzayon*': A Sabbatean Apocalypse from Yemen" [Hebrew], *Kovetz Al-Yad* (new series) 4 (1946): 103–142.

22. See G. Scholem, ed., "Apocalyptic and Messianic Chapters on R. Mordechai Eisenstadt" [Hebrew], *Sefer Dineburg* (Jerusalem, 1949), pp. 237–262.

23. The best-known excerpt (as was already known to R. Jacob Emden) includes the three songs by Nathan of Gaza (for the first day of Passover, for the seventh day of Passover, and for the festival of Shavuot). These poems were written in the model of Luria's Shabbath songs and, because of their

exoteric character, do not include Nathan's new Kabbala though they do contain hints of Sabbetai Zevi's messianism. Another quote is from Nathan's *tikkunei teshuva*, see I. Tishby, *Paths of Faith and Heresy* [Hebrew] (Ramat Gan, 1964). However, as Tishby pointed out: "Most of the *tikkunei teshuva* are imbued with Luria's ascetic spirit and his theory of *kavanot*, without any special Sabbatean overtones" (p. 37).

24. See G. Scholem, "The Messianic Idea in Kabbalism," in *The Messianic Idea in Judaism and Other Essays*, pp. 37–48. It appears that the notion of historical *tikkun* as a symbol of *tikkun* in higher worlds, common in early Kabbala, is neither appropriate to Lurianic Kabbala nor to the Kabbala of Nathan of Gaza, in which all worlds are part of one continuum.

25. See Scholem, *Sabbatai Zevi: The Mystical Messiah*, pp. 687–693 and Scholem, "Redemption Through Sin," pp. 86–93.

26. On this wording, its meaning, and development, see my "New Writings in Sabbatean Kabbalah from the Circle of Rabbi Johathan Eybeschuetz," pp. 330–331.

27. In *Sod Emunat Adonenu* [The Secret of Our Master's Faith], which Scholem published in *Sabbatai Zevi: The Mystical Messiah*, pp. 316–317.

28. See Y. Liebes, "Sabbetai Zevi's Attitude Towards His Own Conversion" [Hebrew], *Sefunot* (new series) 2 (1983): 267–307.

29. For two of them, see *S. Z. Shazar Jubilee Volume*. One was published by Rivka Shatz and the other by Izhak Ben Zvi (in fact, Yael Nadav).

30. Was published in G. Scholem, *Studies and Texts Concerning the History of Sabbateanism and Its Metamophorses* [Hebrew] (Jerusalem, 1974), pp. 370–421.

31. See G. Atias, G. Scholem, and I. Ben-Zvi, eds., *A Book of Sabbatean Poems and Praises* [Hebrew] (Tel-Aviv, 1948).

32. See G. Scholem, "Commentary on Psalms from the Circle of Sabbetai Zevi in Adrianople," in *Alei Ayin: A Homage to S. Z. Schocken Following his Seventieth Birthday* (Jerusalem, 1948–1952), pp. 157–211; see p. 177.

33. Ibid., p. 198. The Messiah converting to Christianity is referred to as *haben yakir li Ephraim* [my beloved son Ephraim] and is probably considered to be the Messiah Son of Joseph. The writer relied here on *Zohar Ki Teze*, most certainly intending the statement in *Ra'aya Meheimana* found there (Zohar III:276b). According to this statement, it is claimed that because of Jeroboam's sin, Joseph and his progeny, namely, the Messiah Son of Joseph, are doomed to "be profaned by idolatry" (thus in the first printed version whereas in later ones, because of Christian censorship, it was changed to *aku"m*, an acronym standing for star worshippers). Literally, the Zohar does not mean that Joseph and his progeny shall worship idols, but that they will

suffer among strange peoples and the Messiah Son of Joseph will be killed; this meaning is clear from a parallel, contiguous version: "that he and his progeny will not be profaned *among* idol worshippers." This statement from the Zohar is often found in Sabbatean literature, usually in connection with Sabbetai Zevi himself, though he is in fact regarded as the Messiah Son of David. On his conversion, see G. Scholem, "New Sabbatean Documents from the Book *Toei Ruah*" [Hebrew], *Zion* 7 (1942): 172–196; see pp. 183–184, n. 65. (As mentioned, unlike Scholem, I believe the word *progeny* in the literal meaning of the statement in the Zohar hints at the Messiah Son of Joseph.) Abraham Miguel Cardozo, who was born a Christian of Marrano ancestry, apparently tried to place himself into this scheme, slightly changed it for his purposes, and proclaimed that the Messiah Son of Joseph will not become a Christian but will be born a Christian and abandon his religion. See Molho and Amarillo, "Autobiographical Letters of Abraham Cardozo," pp. 237–238. However, it is clear that it is not Cardozo who is intended in the Commentary to Psalms, which specifically alludes to entering Esau's religion rather than leaving it.

34. See, e.g., "A Frankist Commentary to the Hallel" [Hebrew], in G. Scholem, *Studies and Texts Concerning the History of Sabbateanism and Its Metamophorses*; G. Scholem, ed., "A Frankist Letter on the History of Faith" [Hebrew], in *Sefer Dov Sadan* (Tel-Aviv, 1977), pp. 346–360; G. Scholem, "A Sabbatean Will from New York," in *The Messianic Idea in Judaism and Other Essays*; G. Scholem, "A Frankist Document from Prague," in *Salo W. Baron Jubilee Volume*, Vol. II (Jerusalem, 1975), pp. 787–814.

35. Liebes, "A Messianic Treatise by R. Wolf the Son of R. Jonathan Eybeschuetz," pp. 163–166, 174–175.

36. See Scholem, *Sabbetai Zevi: A Mystical Messiah*, pp. 206–207.

37. This work has not been published. For the beginning stages of research on it, see H. Wirshuvsky, "The Sabbatean Theology of Nathan of Gaza" [Hebrew], *Kenesset* 8 (1944): 215–245.

38. See G. Scholem, ed., "Nathan of Gaza's Letter on Sabbetai Zevi and His Conversion," in G. Scholem, *Studies and Texts Concerning the History of Sabbateanism and Its Metamophorses*.

39. See Tishby, *Paths of Faith and Heresy*, pp. 204–226.

40. See Y. Liebes "*Tsaddik Yesod Olam*: A Sabbatean Myth" [Hebrew], *Da'at* 1 (1978): 120–173.

41. See my "The Author of the Book '*Tsaddik Yesod Olam*', The Sabbatean Prophet R. Leib Prossnitz."

42. See Y. Nadav, "A Kabbalistic Treatise of R. Solomon Ayllion," *S. Z. Shazar Jubilee Volume*, pp. 301–347.

43. See my "New Writings in Sabbatean Kabbalah from the Circle of Rabbi Johathan Eybeschuetz."

44. See *"Derush Koddesh Israel Le-Elohav,"* in G. Scholem, "Two New Theological Texts by Abraham Cardozo," *S. Z. Shazar Jubilee Volume*, pp. 243–300; see p. 261.

45. See Molho and Amarillo, "Autobiographical Letters of Abraham Cardozo," p. 202.

46. See, e.g., ibid., pp. 191, 222.

47. See Y. Liebes, "Miguel Abraham Cardozo—Author of the *Raza di-Meheimanuta* Attributed to Sabbetai Zevi and the Error in Attributing the *Iggeret Magen Abraham* to Cardozo" [Hebrew], *Kiryat Sefer* 55 (1980): 603–616.

48. See ibid., p. 605, n. 17.

49. See Molho and Amarillo, "Autobiographical Letters of Abraham Cardozo," p. 229.

50. See Y. Liebes, "The Ideological Basis of the Hayyun Controversy" [Hebrew], *Proceedings of the Eighth World Congress of Jewish Studies*, Division C, (Jerusalem, 1982), pp. 129–134.

51. Metz, 1847. See G. Yosha, "The Philosophical Foundations of Abraham Miguel Cardozo's Theory of Divinity" [Hebrew], M.A. thesis, Hebrew University of Jerusalem, 1985, pp. 200–205. In the book by Lopez, 101a–103b, is an abstract of Cardozo's book *Boker De-Avraham* [Abraham's Morning] called *Derush Be-Inyan Ha-Emuna Ha-Amittit* [Essay on the True Faith]. In my article "Miguel Abraham Cardozo—Author of the *Raza di-Meheimanuta,"* pp. 613–614, I claimed that Cardozo himself wrote this abstract, whereas Yosha convincingly argued that Lopez wrote it.

52. For a discussion and a description of a wonderful example, see Y. Liebes, "A Crypto Judeo-Christian Sect of Sabbatean Origin," *Tarbiz* 57 (1988): 349–384.

53. For instance, R. Israel Hazzan, who remained Jewish, greatly admired those who succeded in converting with Sabbetai Zevi—see notes 32 ff. It is also worth noting the extended contacts of R. Jonathan Eybeschuetz and his son Wolf with the Doenmeh sect and the Frankists, see G. Scholem, "Baruchia—the Sabbatean Heresiarch in Salonika" [Hebrew], *Zion* (1941): 119–147, 181–202, see pp. 199–200. Further evidence can be found in the close links between those Frankists who remained Jewish (mostly in the Prague community) and their apostate brothers. Even Cardozo, despite his virulent attacks against apostates, is very admired in the Doenmeh poems and ranks second only to Sabbetai Zevi, see Atias, Scholem, and Ben-Zvi, eds., *A Book of Sabbatean Poems and Praises*, poem 34, pp. 55–56, and Scholem's notes there. This poem deals with the love and the unity between Sabbetai Zevi and Cardozo. See also poem 47, p. 68, and poem 127, p. 131.

4. Sabbetai Zevi's Religious Faith

1. This article reproduces the text of a lecture, and there is thus no place in it for a detailed analysis of the sources. The material found here is discussed mainly in my articles "Sabbetai Zevi's Attitude Toward His Own Conversion" [Hebrew], *Sefunot* (new series), 2 (1983); "Miguel Abraham Cardozo—Author of the *Raza di-Meheimanuta* Attributed to Sabbetai Zevi and the Error in Attributing the *Iggeret Magen Avraham* to Cardozo" [Hebrew], *Kiryat Sefer* 55 (1980): 603–616; 56 (1981): 373–374, which include bibliographical references and detailed philological analyses.

2. See my "Miguel Abraham Cardozo."

3. These statements are cited in G. Scholem, *Sabbetai Zevi: The Mystical Messiah* (Princeton, 1973), pp. 861, 904.

4. The letter was published by A. Amarillo, "Sabbatean Documents from the Saul Amarillo Collection" [Hebrew], *Sefunot* 5 (1961): 266–268.

5. Ibid.

6. The letter was published by G. Scholem, "A Letter from Hayyim Malakh" [Hebrew] *Zion* 13 (1946): 172.

7. According to the testimony of Israel Hazzan. See Scholem, *Sabbetai Zevi: The Mystical Messiah*, p. 861.

8. In the view of M. Benayahu, "The Sabbatean Movement in Greece" [Hebrew], *Sefunot* 14 (1971–77): 65–66.

9. See Scholem, *Sabbetai Zevi: The Mystical Messiah*, pp. 685–686.

10. I. Tishby published this testimony and discussed its contents in "R. Meir Rofe's Letters of 1675–1680 to R. Abraham Rovigo" [Hebrew], *S. Z. Shazar Jubilee Volume* (Jerusalem, 1959–1960; [*Sefunot* 3–4]), 86–87, n. 69.

11. This is the source for a similar idea often found in the writings of Cardozo, who relies on it for understanding the fate of the Marranos. This notion is indeed found among the Marranos before Sabbateanism.

12. A statement combining Numbers Rabba, 19, and Rashi's commentary to Numbers 19:2.

13. See the letter by Sabbetai Zevi published by Amarillo, "Sabbatean Documents," p. 252.

5. *Ha-Tikkun ha-Kelali* of
R. Nahman of Bratslav and Its Sabbatean Links

English translations are available for several of the classic works of Bratslav Hasidism mentioned in this article. Changes were often made in these translations in the present text.

Hayyei Moharan was published as *Tsaddik: A Portrait of Rabbi Nachman by Rabbi Nathan of Breslov*, trans. Abraham Greenbaum, Breslov Research Institute (Jerusalem and New York, 1987).

Shivhei Ha-Ran and *Sihot Ha-Ran* appeared as *Rabbi Nachman's Wisdom*, by Rabbi Nathan of Nemirov, trans. R. Aryeh Kaplan, Breslov Research Institute (Jerusalem and New York, 1973).

Likkutei Moharan by Rebbe Nachman of Breslov, trans. Moshe Mykoff, Breslov Research Institute (Jerusalem and New York, 1989). Only Vol. I, Lessons 1–16 have been translated.

Likkutei Eitsot appeared as *Advice* by R. Nathan of Breslov, trans. Avraham Greenbaum, Breslov Research Institute (Jerusalem and New York, 1983).

1. These leanings are obvious, and scholars have already pointed them out. The Bratslav phenomenon might help to clarify a thorny and controversial issue: the status of messianism in Hasidism in general. Although Bratslav Hasidism adopts an unusual stand on this question, it is still part and parcel of the Hasidic movement. R. Nahman, the Baal Shem Tov's great-grandson, was not an alien force in the Hasidic movement, and his doctrines can be explained as an outgrowth of general Hasidic teachings. I agree with S. Dubnow's statement: "The young grandson of the Besht, R. Nahman of Bratslav. . .has supposedly heralded a 'new Torah' to the world but, in fact, he simply took known *'tsaddikical'*[!] Hasidic teachings to an extreme, through reductio ad absurdum." See *History of Hasidism* [Hebrew] (Tel-Aviv, 1975), p. 290. The present study, on the nature of Bratslav messianism, might help disclose similar features in other Hasidic groups too.

2. See *Hayyei Moharan*, where R. Nahman is quoted as saying: "There has never been a *hiddush* [novelty] like me in the world" (*Shivhei Moharan*, His Attainments 7). See also the apology of Bratslav Hasidim for this statement in *Hashmatot le-Hayyei Moharan* [Omissions to *Hayyei Moharan*] 1, where it is claimed that R. Nahman purposely made this statement, to evoke controversy! See also note 81. In Bratslav terminology, *hiddush* also means wonder (see *Shivhei Moharan*, His Attainments 17: "Who said I am a wondrous man") as well as the suggestion of new ideas (ibid., 39 and His Opposition 1). These two meanings are related because, according to R. Nahman, there is no greater wonder than the possibility of innovation. New in the sense of wonder appears already in the Talmud, Shabbat 30b, as an exegesis on Ecclesiastes 1:9.

3. See A. Green, *Tormented Master: A Life of Rabbi Nahman of Bratslav,* Alabama University, 1979. This is a good biography of R. Nahman, describing his spiritual development alongside his life history. Green's book appeared too late for intensive use in the present article. The active messianic stage in R. Nahman's life (1805–1806) is described in Chapter 5. See also J. Weiss, *Studies in Bratslav Hasidism* [Hebrew] (Jerusalem, 1974), especially Chapter 12, and M. Piekarz, *Studies in Bratslav Hasidism* [Hebrew] (Jerusalem, 1972), especially Chapter 3.

4. See for instance *Kokhvei Or* [Stars of Light] by Abraham Hazzan (one of Bratslav's most important Hasidim, photostated anew in Jerusalem, 1972) p. 128: "I wrote above that he [R. Nahman] was also called the Son of David and, were it not for the wanton slanders counseled by Samael, redemption would have come in his time." Although in less explicit terms, reflecting the influence of self-censorship, R. Nahman himself confirmed this view in his writings. Due to the "wanton slanders" (that accused R. Nahman of Sabbateanism), the treatment of messianic issues in Bratslav writings became extremely esoteric, see note 7. Later writings disclose a great deal more than earlier ones—though indeed not everything!—and scholars of Bratslav have therefore resorted to a reverse philological method—the later, the more original! This method can also rely upon the meticulous care that Bratslav Hasidim have taken with R. Nahman's original writings. Their admiration for him has reached the point where the greatest possible praise is to convey his words accurately, contrary to the tendency prevalent in other Hasidic schools, where miracle tales are often added to embellish the rabbis' deeds. For Bratslav Hasidim, there is no greater wonder than R. Nahman's historical personality and "too much is too little" (compare also R. Nahman's attitude to miracle-working *tsaddikim* on p. 124). However, I have lately encountered some exceptions to this rule. For instance, a new version of the Bratslav legend in the book *Siah Sarfei Kodesh* (Jerusalem, 1988) seems less authentic than previous ones.

5. See, for instance, his celebrated saying: *"Main faierl vet shoin tluen biz mashiah vet kumen"* [My fire will burn until the Messiah comes] *Hayyei Moharan,* Uman 45.

6. *Hayyei Moharan, Shivhei Moharan,* His Attainments 34. We should also mention in this context his belief that he was part of the Davidic dynasty—*Hayyei Moharan, Shivhei Moharan,* His Spiritual Struggles 67—as well as his messianic hopes for his son. This issue is discussed in the scholarly studies mentioned in note 3.

7. *Hayyei Moharan, Sihot Moharan,* Devotion to God 117: "The main source of hope is in the concept of 'beyond time' attained by the *tsaddikim,* who are the embodiment of the Messiah." It is clarified later that the reference is to R. Nahman himself: "Shortly before his death, I heard from his holy mouth that he was now going along with his teaching on the verse: '. . .this day have I begotten thee'. . .[in Psalms 2:7. This verse is a reference to the

king, God's Messiah] who is 'beyond time,' etc. [The 'teaching' is in *Likkutei Moharan* II:61, where the messianic allusion is more explicit: "The Messiah...will in the end be told by God: 'My son, this day have I begotten thee']....From what he said I understood that he was referring to the tremendous effort that he [R. Nahman himself!] was making to bring many souls closer to God, as yet without success." The issue of "beyond time" and its relevance to R. Nahman as the Redeemer is beyond the scope of this essay. See notes 11 and 38.

See also *Likkutei Moharan* II:32, where he spoke of a messianic aspect present in every human being, and particularly in the *tsaddik*, whose books must be burnt because of it. This clearly hints to the burning of R. Nahman's books, and particularly the messianic ones (see Weiss, *Studies in Bratslav Hasidism*, pp. 189–248; it also seems to be making an ideological case for the esoteric character of messianic hints, see note 4). Incidentally, other Hasidic schools share the notion of a messianic facet latent in every human being. This notion does not preclude the special messianic status of the *tsaddik*, whose soul combines and includes those of all his Hasidim; for sources and clarifications, see I. Tishby, "The Messianic Idea and Messianic Trends in the Growth of Hasidism" [Hebrew], *Zion* 32 (1967): 35.

See also *Sihot ha-Ran* 93, where it is claimed that the great *tsaddikim* (including R. Nahman himself) are as a belt for the Messiah. Green's suggestion in *Tormented Master*, that R. Nahman saw himself as the Messiah Son of Joseph, should also be taken into account. Some of the references quoted by Green would indeed seem to point in this direction, but this understanding does not exhaust R. Nahman's view. Elsewhere, R. Nahman sees himself as standing above both Messiahs, the Messiah Son of David and the Messiah Son of Joseph, see note 92. In this context, we should also consider the Bratslav belief in R. Nahman's future return from death (Ibid., p. 197, and his references to Weiss and Piekarz). It is not yet clear how this return was conceived, whether R. Nahman would return as himself or in some other incarnation.

Even if R. Nahman were not the final redeemer, he was certainly considered the Messiah of his generation. This notion is in line with the Lurianic view that God sends a spark from the Messiah's soul in every generation to bring redemption if the generation is worthy and, if it is not, at least in order to sustain it in Exile. On this notion, see *Sefer Ha-Likkutim* [The Book of Gleanings] from Isaac Luria's writings (Jerusalem, 1913), 81:a,b, on Isaiah 38. See also the book by Nathan Shapira, *Tuv Ha-Arets* (Venice, 1655), p. 38, and the usual printed version of this book (Jerusalem, 1891; photostated anew in Jerusalem, 1972), p. 32. Green (p. 191) claims this view appears in *Emek ha-Melekh* [The Mystical Depths of the King] by Naftali Bachrach (Amsterdam, 1648), and relies for this on D. Tamar, *Sefunot* 7 (1963): 176, who had justifiably cited this source. Tamar also quoted a similar claim in the name of the kabbalist Moshe Prager. Nathan of Gaza, Sabbetai Zevi's prophet, also suggested this view in his *Derush Ha-Tanninim* [Treatise on the Dragons], published by G. Scholem in the collection of writings by Nathan of Gaza called *Be-Ik'vot Mashiah* [In the Messiah's Footsteps] (Jerusalem,

1944), p. 21. This view is also quoted by Hayyim Yosef David Azzulai in *Midbar Kadmut* 40:4. It was on these grounds that R. Yaacov Emden appropriated for himself the messianic spark of his generation, as I showed in my article "The Messianism of R. Jacob Emden and His Attitude Toward Sabbateanism" [Hebrew], *Tarbiz* 49 (1980). See also the next note. This Lurianic notion is a kabbalistic development of the statements cited in Maimonides' name in the *Dispute of the Sages of Tortosa* (from the early fifteenth century), though I could not trace them in Maimonides's work. These statements appear in I. D. Eisenstein, *Otsar Vikuhim* (New York, 1928), p. 109: "And Maimonides wrote that the Messiah was not born on the day of the destruction of the Temple, but that he [in reference to the author of the talmudic statement in the Jerusalem Talmud, Berakhot 2d, 5a, who had claimed that the Messiah was born on the day the Temple was destroyed] had meant to say that, from that day onward, a man is born in every generation worthy of being the Messiah, if Israel will be worthy of redemption." Luria interpreted this notion according to the doctrine of the sparks in every soul, and assigned to the potential Messiahs the task of sustaining the generations unworthy of redemption.

8. See, for instance, *Likkutei Moharan* I:64,5: "Know that through song, the *tsaddik*—who is like Moses—can raise souls from disbelief (!)." See there, extensively. On song, see note 131; see also next two notes and note 92.

Moses' link with the figure of the Messiah is an ancient idea, which appears in rabbinic sayings (for example; "As the first redeemer, so the last redeemer," Numbers Rabba, 11:3). An additional kabbalistic concept is pertinent here (drawn from the later parts of the Zohar—*Ra'aya Meheimana* and *Tikkunei Zohar*) regarding "the *hitpashtut* [egression] of Moses in every generation" and implying that, in every generation, Moses reappears embodied in another person or in the sages of the time. This notion, combined with the concept of the return of the messianic spark in every generation, (see note 7) influenced R. Nahman's messianic consciousness. Other kabbalistic messianic figures, with whom R. Nahman felt particular affinity, had also been considered as incarnations of Moses—Rabbi Simeon b. Yohai in the Zohar, Isaac Luria, R. Moses Hayyim Luzzato, and Sabbetai Zevi (see next note). On the idea of "the *hitpashtut* of Moses in every generation" and its sources, see my *Sections of the Zohar Lexicon* [Hebrew] (Jerusalem, 1977; offset, 1984), pp. 303–304. On the one hand, this notion resembles that of Averroes' active intellect that becomes embodied in the sages of each generation and, on the other, it has an interesting parallel in the perception of Moses in Samarian religion.

9. Piekarz, *Studies in Bratslav Hasidism*, pp. 13–15, has already pointed to the special link between R. Simeon b. Yohai and R. Nahman and to R. Nahman's presumed superiority, and we could mention many other references. On R. Simeon b. Yohai's messianic image in the Zohar and in the Kabbala, see my "The Messiah of the Zohar," in Y. Liebes, *Studies in the Zohar* (Albany, forthcoming). R. Nahman indeed identified with R. Simeon b. Yohai, but also

with other messianic figures, and there is no contradiction in this: He saw himself as the continuation and culmination of a series of redeemers and disclosers of kabbalistic mysteries that had sustained the world, including R. Simeon b. Yohai, Isaac Luria, and R. Israel Baal Shem Tov (*Hayyei Moharan, Shivhei Moharan, His Attainments* 39). See also Green, *Tormented Master*, p. 186; and see also note 8.

10. On R. Nahman's superiority, see the last note; on his advantage over Moses, see p. 126, and over the *Baal Shem Tov*, see p. 140.

11. *Likkutei Moharan* I:60,6. The tales of *shanim kadmoniot* [former years] (Malachi 3:4) are a counterpart to the tales of *bekerev shanim* [in the midst of the years] (Habakuk 3:2), whose concern is to translate the mysteries of the Torah (the Kabbala) into narrative language. Therefore, it is not possible to see the tales of "former years" (included in the *Sippurei Ma'asiyyot*) as a guise for Lurianic Kabbala. Many interpreters of the tales have ignored R. Nahman's explicit statements on this count.

The difference between these two types of tales parallels the difference between *Attika Kaddisha* and *Ze'er Anpin* in the *Idra Rabba* of the Zohar. The Zohar assumes that *Attika Kaddisha*'s doctrine is the one that will be revealed in messianic times whereas, until then, the common Jewish view had been that of the *Ze'er Anpin* (Zohar III:130a). For an extensive discussion see my article, "The Messiah of the Zohar." Hence the messianic attributes that R. Nahman pinned on his tales of "former years." The term *former years* also hints to *Attika*, which means old, as well as to a special facet of R. Nahman, who said about himself "I am the 'Elder of the Elders' " (*Hayyei Moharan, Shivhei Moharan*, His Attainments, 32). The *Elder of the Elders* is also one of the names of *Attika Kaddisha* (Zohar III:128b). The meaning of this title and its relevance to the young R. Nahman (who died at age thirty-nine) is made clearer through R. Nahman's attitude to time, see notes 7 and 38. R. Nahman also resorted to this name to irk his opponent—"the Old Man of Shpola." Obviously, tales of "former years" also mean, quite simply, stories about the past and, in popular parlance, legends.

12. See note 2. See also *Hayyei Moharan, Shivhei Moharan*, His Attainments 24: "I will lead you by a new way, that has never existed before. It is indeed an ancient way and yet, it is completely new."

13. Thus in the Zohar, where the figure of R. Simeon b. Yohai is all-pervasive, and in Lurianic Kabbala, regarding the personality of Isaac Luria and even that of Hayyim Vital. See my article, "The Messiah of the Zohar."

14. R. Nahman was the great-great grandson of the *Baal Shem Tov* and the grandson of R. Nahman of Horodenka.

15. An extremely surprising parable, supplying unique evidence of the *tsaddik*'s profound dependence on his *Hasidim*, appears in *Sihot ha-Ran* 24. The Hasid giving alms to the *tsaddik* is a metaphor for a coachman driving the *tsaddik* to God. The coachman helps God and the *tsaddik* overcome their

predicament, which, paradoxically, is due to their deep mutual longings and only worsens as they draw nearer. See also note 28. R. Nahman's apparently blunt and crude solution to a spiritual problem described with such great subtlety is quite typical. Compare a similar parable in *Hayyei Moharan, Sihot Moharan,* Devotion to God 4.

This situation, caused by irreparable longings whose fulfillment might bring death, calls to mind the famous parable of "The Heart and the Spring," in the tale of the third beggar in *The Seven Beggars,* where a man helps to bring the heart and the spring closer. This parallel sheds clearer light on the identity of the helper—it is the Hasid giving alms to his rabbi, who is honored with the title *der emeser ish hesed* [the truly pious man]. It must be mentioned in this context that R. Nahman refers elsewhere to the spiritual value attached to wealth: He sees man's wealth as part of his soul and as a symbol for it (*Likkutei Moharan* I:25, 29, 68, 69).

This dependence of the *tsaddik* on the Hasid is well illustrated in R. Nahman's exegesis of Psalms 145:17 (The Lord is righteous [*tsaddik*] in all His ways, and gracious [*hasid*] in all His deeds): "When does the *tsaddik* merit to have God in all his ways. . .when the hasid is in all his deeds—when the followers of the *tsaddik,* called Hasidim, take care of all his deeds" (*Hayyei Moharan, Sihot Moharan,* Devotion to God 85).

This argument, meant to justify the Hasidim's financial support of the *tsaddik,* does not appear in any other Hasidic source. The usual claim put forward in Hasidic literature is that, when supporting the *tsaddik,* it is the giving Hasid who benefits rather than the receiving *tsaddik.* R. Nahman too suggested this argument: "When I take money or something else from someone, I am really giving something to him. For my taking is actually giving" (*Sihot Ha-Ran* 150.) See J. Dan, *The Hasidic Tale* [Hebrew] (Jerusalem, 1975), p. 170.

R. Nahman needed his Hasidim not only for financial support, but as an audience for his teachings, which would also accept them and abide by them. This need is often stressed in Bratslav literature, in the course of elucidating the cosmic implications of the Hasidim's acceptance of their leader. This literature also includes some somber descriptions of R. Nahman's fears of loneliness and abandonment, which he experienced over long periods. On this point, see Weiss, *Studies of Bratslav Hasidism,* pp. 42 ff.

16. See, for instance, "The whole world needs me. Obviously you do, you yourselves know how much you need me, but even all the *tsaddikim*. . .and even the nations of the world" (*Hayyei Moharan, Shivhei Moharan,* His Attainments 10) and "I am the only leader in this generation and there is no other like me in the world" (ibid., 18).

17. *Hayyei Moharan, Shivhei Moharan,* Avoidance of Philosophy 13.

18. *Hayyei Moharan, Shivhei Moharan,* His Followers 92.

19. "Scholars are called advice," *Likkutei Moharan* I:41. "Advice" [*Eitsa*] in Bratslav language means leadership or Hasidic custom, hence the name of the Bratslav book of practical behavioral guidance—*Likkutei Eitsot.*

20. See, for instance, *Hayyei Moharan, Shivhei Moharan*, Avoidance of Philosophy 6.

21. See, for instance: "And he spoke to me about ways of serving God, which usually entail great suffering.... He then said: But this does not mean you, since you must alwyas be joyful" (*Hayyei Moharan, Sihot Moharan*, Devotion to God 141).

22. A further instance is the tale of *The Seven Beggars*, which opens with the words: "What do you know of joy out of melancholy, I will tell you how people were happy once." It must be noted that the whole theme of this tale is redemption (see Dan, *The Hasidic Tale*, pp. 144–171. This tale still merits a detailed analysis). As we shall see (p. 139), the end of the tale is related to *ha-tikkun ha-kelali* and the joy accompanying it.

23. *Sihot Ha-Ran* 151–154; *Hayyei Moharan*, Uman 31; *Yemei Moharnat* (Jerusalem, 1977), 35a–37a.

24. R. Nahman had indeed prepared a written outline of this teaching the day before (as he obviously did not write on the Sabbath), which was literally reproduced at the end of the teaching. However, it is precisely from this outline that we learn about R. Nahman's spontaneity—the main part of this teaching, dealing with the *tsaddik*'s simplicity, is missing, whereas many other elements, such as R. Nahman's advantage over Moses, were added in the course of the teaching and will be analyzed later (p. 126). R. Nahman's low spirits when delivering this teaching might explain both the additions and the omissions.

25. See Piekarz, *Studies of Bratslav Hasidism*, pp. 21–55.

26. Compare with the words of the blind beggar in *The Seven Beggars*, who boasted his memory was so long he remembered nothing. The Yiddish original (*Ich gedenk gornisht*) entails a double entendre: I remember nothing, and I remember the "nothing" or the void, which is the name of the supreme kabbalistic *sefira, keter*. On the high virtue of forgetfulness, see note 38.

Incidentally, Sabbetai Zevi also sought relief from his bouts of depression by delving deeply into their meaning, as described by a witness in a letter (A. Amarillo, "Sabbatean Documents from the Saul Amarillo Collection," *Sefunot*, 5 [1961]: 261: "He kept talking about it...hoping that illumination would thereby be returned to him.")

27. Because "whoever is not obligated [*mehuyav*] to fufill a commandment, cannot perform this obligation on behalf of others" (Berakhot 20b). The widespread Hasidic exegesis of this rabbinic dictum relies on a further meaning of *mehuyav*—guilty or sinful—to justify the *tsaddik*'s descent into sin to uplift others.

28. The ten utterances whereby the world was created (according to Avot 5:1) are the highest facet of the ten commandments. The relatively low status

of the commandments is intimated elsewhere in R. Nahman's writings. Thus, for instance, in the parable discussed in note 15 (*Sihot Ha-Ran* 24), the commandments serve to distract the *tsaddik* from his yearnings for God, which threaten to kill him. The relation between the hidden Torah of the "ten utterances" and the one realized in the commandments is, in my view, like the relation between the tales of "former years" and those "in the midst of the years," see notes 11 and 29.

29. These circumstances, of *katnut* and childish pranks, are meticulously described in the account of R. Nahman's journey to the Holy Land. In *Shivhei Ha-Ran*, The Account of R. Nahman's Pilgrimage to the Holy Land 22, we are told that R. Nahman observed the commandments as the patriarchs had done before the giving of the Torah—Jacob fulfilled the commandment of *tefilin* through the sticks he peeled while watching Laban's sheep. Elsewhere, R. Nahman formulated this as follows: "On this journey, I have fulfilled the entire Torah in every aspect" (*Hayyei Moharan* Journey to the Holy Land 14). The way to the Holy Land as taking precedence over the Torah and the commandments is identified here (*Likkutei Moharan* II:78) with *derekh eretz* (literally, the way to the land, but also a term signifying decency and high-principled behavior). According to the rabbis, *derekh eretz* preceded the Torah (Leviticus Rabba 9:3).

30. This interpretation of one passage in this teaching appears in *Yemei Moharnat* (see note 23; see also note 61).

31. *Hayyei Moharan*, Conversations Relating to His Teachings 15.

32. See *Likkutei Moharan* I:7: It is worth noting in this context that, contrary to the land of Israel, the city of Jerusalem has no place at all in R. Nahman's doctrine. He did not even bother to go to Jerusalem during his journey and never even mentions it in his accounts of the journey.

33. See the "Prayer for the Privilege of Reciting a Prayer at the Holy Shrine of Our Rabbi, of Blessed Memory, in Uman." This prayer is printed, for instance, at the end of an edition of *Likkutei Moharan* printed in Jerusalem in 1968 (in the state of Israel!) where it is said: "And the only remnant left to us after the death of our holy rabbi is his holy shrine, marked by the holiness of the land of Israel."

34. Bratslav Hasidim have assembled these teachings in several places, such as *Likkutei Eitsot*, s.v. the land of Israel.

35. Due to self-censorship, the messianic features of this teaching were toned down in the printed version of *Likkutei Moharan*. They are more pronounced in the adaptation of this teaching in the book by R. Nathan of Bratslav, *Likkutei Halakhot* (*Orah Hayyim*, Rules Concerning Meals 4), where this teaching is related to issues concerning *Rosh Ha-Shana*, and justifiably so, as it was indeed delivered on *Rosh Ha-Shana* 5565 (1804) (according to *Hayyei Moharan*, Conversations Relating to His Teachings 59). *Rosh Ha-Shana*

was the most important holiday in Bratslav Hasidism; R. Nahman repeatedly warns his Hasidim lest they fail to come together on this day. The most important teachings in *Likkutei Moharan* were delivered over these *Rosh Ha-Shana* gatherings. Moreover, R. Nahman often related to the high spiritual aspect of *Rosh Ha-Shana* (see *Hayyei Moharan*, His Birthplace, Residence and Travels 24). There are hints to the fact that, in Bratslav Hasidism, the rank of *Rosh Ha-Shana* parallels that of the land of Israel. The holiday of *Rosh Ha-Shana* indeed seems most fitting to denote a stage beyond time, beyond nature, and beyond the intellect. In *Likkutei Halakhot* 20, R. Nathan clarified more explicitly the allusions relating to the victory over the wicked intimated in this teaching. The wicked hinder the way to the land of Israel and will be defeated by being delivered to the Gentile authorities, who will be bribed for this purpose, see p. 143.

36. The complete version of this saying was not printed in the teaching itself and appears in *Hayyei Moharan*, next to the one mentioned in note 31.

37. The source of this saying is in the book *Behinat Olam* by R. Jeda'iah Bedersi (thirteeth–fourteenth century) as follows (chapter 13, verse 33): "The purpose [*takhlit*] of knowing you [God] is that we should not know you." The intention here is to stress human lowliness and the limitations of human knowledge and, in this context, the word purpose implies end or culmination. R. Nahman however, interprets *takhlit* as aim, thereby radically changing the meaning of this saying.

38. "One must study at ease, following the order of the pages, without halting at difficult passages and even without investing too much effort in remembering the contents" (*Sihot Ha-Ran* 76).

In Jewish culture, forgetfulness was considered a grave flaw. R. Nahman was aware of it but still claimed that: "Most people think of forgetting as a defect, but I consider it a great benefit" (*Sihot Ha-Ran* 26). Further on, R. Nahman explained the virtue of forgetfulness by means of a surprising parable (the source of this parable is in Leviticus Rabbah 19:2): "In the books [perhaps alluding to Kohelet Rabbah on Kohelet 1:13] it is said that we were given the power to forget so that the Torah would always be beloved to its learners as on the first time. Because one forgets, even when one goes back to something he has already learned, it is like learning it anew. And there is a parable about one who learns and forgets. Men were hired to fill leaky barrels, and all they poured into the barrels spilled out. The fools said: 'Since everything leaks out, why should we toil and fill the barrels?' But the wise said: 'What do I care? I get paid by the day and my wages are the same even if the barrels leak.' Thus, even if he forgets what he has learned, his reward is not reduced."

This parable is built on the model of many others found in talmudic literature and the New Testament, dealing with wise and industrious slaves as opposed to foolish and lazy ones. However, in all these parables, the wise slave always try to please his masters by the success of his labors while the foolish and lazy one simply complies with the formal requirements of the king's command (see Shabbat 152b–153a). On the other hand, R. Nahman's ideal of a wise slave calls to mind an irresponsible soldier, uninterested in the purpose of his actions and involved in the mechanical performance of his duties. Moreover, it is worth mentioning that, in Greek mythology, filling leaky barrels is considered one of the punishments meted out to the wicked in Hades (this was the punishment of the Danaides) whereas here it appears as the desirable and pleasing deed. In *The Myth of Sisyphus*, Albert Camus turned Sisyphus, condemned to push uphill a stone that always rolls down again, into his human ideal. This might be evidence of the similarities between Camus' philosophy and R. Nahman's thought.

This attitude of R. Nahman toward forgetfulness might be helpful in clarifying his attitude to time. R. Nahman indicates several times that he is very young, just born, and still a very old man (see, for instance, the blind beggar in *The Seven Beggars*, and also notes 7 and 11). I do not think that these point to eternity beyond time but rather to life in a constantly renewed present, in line with his approach to learning and forgetfulness.

Incidentally, Sabbetai Zevi also imagined that "all the things he did in his periods of illumination are like a dream and he has forgotten their cause and their reason," as attested by his prophet Nathan of Gaza (in a letter published in Amarillo, "Sabbatean Documents," p. 264). But, unlike R. Nahman's, Sabbetai Zevi's forgetfulness is described negatively, as one of the torments afflicting the Messiah.

39. The source for this metaphor is Rashi's commentary to Deuteronomy 22:14 (originally in the Sifre).

40. Maimonides (*Guide of the Perplexed* I:37, 54), claims that Moses had aprehended everything a man can grasp, except for seeing His face. R. Nahman seems to rely on this saying when he argues that Moses too was unable to see God's face. I believe the term *face* here is related to R. Nahman's admonition to his generation, as having fallen "from all seventy faces of the Torah," see note 11.

41. According to the New Testament (Epistle to the Hebrews 3:5) Moses was as a slave and Jesus as a son.

42. In the Zohar too (II:70a) the rank of the "son," which is opposed to that of the "slave," is parallel to that of the "*tsaddik*."

43. *Sihot Ha-Ran*, 130. Also *Hayyei Moharan*, New Stories 20. I believe this parable is a development of another one by the Besht, found in the book *Keter Shem Tov* (photostated anew, Jerusalem, 1976), 50c.

44. This phrase refers to his humble station, his few followers, and R. Nahman's constant fears of abandonment by his Hasidim (see his nightmare in *Hayyei Moharan*, New Stories 11 and the interpretation by Weiss, *Studies in Bratslav Hasidism*, pp. 42 ff.). On the *tsaddik* who has no position but his status is higher than those who do, see also *Likkutei Moharan* I:51: "There is one [*tsaddik*] who overtly has no power but, nevertheless, covertly and in

great secret, rules over all his generation, and even over all the *tsaddikim* of his generation. . ." If any doubts remain regarding the fact that this *tsaddik* is R. Nahman himself, this intention is made explicit in *Hayyei Moharan*, Conversations Relating to His Teachings 24.

45. Compare *Likkutei Moharan* I:22: "Know that there are those who reprove their generation, and they are called *raglin* [feet] because they are *limmudei Elohim*, namely, that they ostensibly teach God, and give Him advice." (*Limmudei Elohim* and *raglin* are kabbalistic symbols for the *sefirot* of *nezah* and *hod*.)

46. This is explicit in the teaching as it was delivered; also according to Exodus Rabbah 45:5 and Deuteronomy Rabba 2:2.

47. According to Yoma 75a.

48. The Kabbala claims that Moses' virtue is "knowledge"and that the sexual sin affects the brain, because the source of the seminal drop is in the brain. During the Exodus, Moses amended Adam's sexual flaw (see *Etz Ha-Hayyim* 32:1, *Sha'ar Ha-Kavvanot*, Pesah, 1)

49. Shabbat 87a.

50. As appears from the indices to both *Likkutei Moharan* and *Likkutei Halakhot*, which connect between the teachings in *Likkutei Moharan* and the discussions derived from them in *Likkutei Halakhot*.

51. An example might be found in Weiss, *Studies in Bratslav Hasidism*, p. 155, as well as in R. Nathan's statement earlier.

52. *Hayyei Moharan, Sihot Moharan*, Devotion to God 152: "He said that for him men and women were equal. When he saw a woman he never had even the slightest inkling of an improper thought, and it was exactly the same as if he were looking at a man. He said he feared neither women nor angels. . ."

53. R. Nahman's view is based on an ancient medical outlook often cited in kabbalistic books (*Sefer Bahir*, Margaliot ed., 83 and very often the Zohar, I:247b; see also Nathan of Gaza's statement, p. 144), claiming that the seminal drop has its source in the brain and, while descending, it spreads throughout the limbs. R. Nahman hence concluded that the sexual sin, related to semen, is linked to the intellectual sin, whose source is also in the brain, and includes the sins pertaining to all the limbs. This point is discussed at length in *Likkutei Moharan* I:29 (on the messianic character of this teaching, see Piekarz, *Studies in Bratslav Hasidism*, p. 68, and note 54). See also *Likkutei Moharan* I:19, where it is claimed that the sin of adultery encompasses the sins of the seventy nations of the world. See also *Likkutei Moharan* I:36.

54. In *Likkutei Moharan* I:19 (note 53) it is claimed, regarding the all-encompassing nature of adultery, that the *tikkun* of this particular sin requires

the transgressor to personally go to the *tsaddik* and hear the *tsaddik*'s words from his own mouth; reading them in a book will not suffice (see also *Likkutei Moharan* I:20). The *tikkun* of adultery is brought about by the *tsaddik*'s tongue. A special feature characterizes the personal meeting with the *tsaddik*—the face of the *tsaddik* is like a mirror that reflects the speaker's face, until the Hasid sees himself there and understands the seriousness of his transgression. See also *Hayyei Moharan, Sihot Moharan*, Devotion to God 51, where R. Nahman extols praises on those to whom he had appeared in dreams.

55. See G. Scholem, "The *Tsaddik*," in *Elements of the Kabbala and Its Symbolism* [Hebrew] (Jerusalem, 1959).

56. In "The Messiah of the Zohar," I discuss the connection between R. Simeon b. Yohai, R. Nahman's archetype, and the *sefira* of *yesod*, as well as the sexual-messianic significance of this link. In *Likkutei Moharan* I:29$_6$, R. Nahman explicitly alluded to his link with R. Simeon b. Yohai and precisely in this context. He quoted the Zohar, where it is claimed that only in R. Simeon b. Yohai's generation was it allowed to quote from the Kabbala in public, because its secrets are related to sexual *tikkun*; see note 60. In its cosmic meaning, this *tikkun* was complete only in the times of R. Simeon b. Yohai, who symbolizes the *sefira* of *yesod*. Sabbateans had emphasized the messianic meaning of this *sefira* as embodied in man, and by the time it reached Hasidism, this notion was permeated with Sabbatean influences. I have discussed this question extensively in "*Tsaddik Yesod Olam*: A Sabbatean Myth" [Hebrew], *Da'at* 1 (1978), especially pp. 77–79 and in "The Author of the Book '*Tsaddik Yesod Olam*': The Sabbatean Prophet R. Leib Prossnitz" [Hebrew], *Da'at* 2–3 (1978–79): 169, where I stressed the terminological continuity between the Sabbatean Leibele Prossnitz and Hasidism. It is worth mentioning in this context that, according to the "*Megilla* of Bratslav Hasidism" (note 95), R. Nahman's adversaries accused his disciple (R. Nathan?) of being a great-grandson of R. Leibele Prossnitz.

57. *Likkutei Moharan* II:5$_6$. In this context (5$_7$), the *tsaddik ha-dor* is called *maginnnei erets* [defenders of the land]. I deal at length with this issue in p. 141.

58. See *Likkutei Moharan* I:2, 1–2: "Because the Messiah's main weapon is prayer. . . he receives this weapon through Joseph's virtue, meaning through sexual chastity." Also *Likkutei Moharan* II:32: "Every one, according to his level of holiness and purity, has a messianic aspect [see note 7]. . . .The messianic aspect hinges mainly on abstaining from adultery. . . . Know that 'the breath of our nostrils, the anointed of the Lord' (Lamentations 4:20) becomes a zealous spirit, seeking adultery wherever he might find it." See also the book by a Bratslav Hasid, N. Z. Koenig, *Neve Tsaddikim* (Bene-Berak, 1969), p. 79. Koenig quoted from the esoteric book *Megillat Setarim* (this book has not been printed and is not available to scholars. See Weiss, *Studies in Bratslav Hasidism*, pp. 189–214). According to this quote, R. Nahman wanted to bring the Messiah by doing away with nature (namely, eliminating the sexual instinct) with the help of Joseph's virtue—sexual chastity.

59. See, for instance, *Likkutei Moharan* I:43, which opens "Know that when one hears the talk of a wicked, clever man, one is led to adultery."

60. See note 56. See "The Messiah of the Zohar," where I develop this idea at length.

61. See Appendix I.

62. When describing the sin of the Sabbateans, the Hasidim sometimes linked their doctrinal sin to their actual sexual perversions. See R. Zadok Ha-Cohen on Sabbateanism (as quoted by G. Scholem, "Redemption Through Sin," in G. Scholem, *The Messianic Idea in Israel* [New York, 1971], p. 348, n. 23): "they [the Sabbateans] came to the end that they came to because they engaged in the study of the Kabbala with their hearts full of lust and therefore materialized much [of its spiritual meaning]; and in consequence of the fact that they saw references to copulation, kissing, embracing and so forth [in what they read], they yielded to lascivious passions, may God preserve us from the same, and committed great evil." Scholem also cited the Seer of Lublin, who wrote in a similar vein. Indeed, the Sabbateans reached peaks previously unknown in Judaism, not only in their sexual licentious practices, but also in their daring sexual descriptions of the highest spheres of divinity. See my articles "The Author of the Book '*Tsaddik Yesod Olam*': The Sabbatean Prophet R. Leib Prossnitz," p. 167; and "New Writings in Sabbatean Kabbala from the Circle of R. Jonathan Eybeschuetz," *Jerusalem Studies in Jewish Thought* 5 (1986): 191–398.

63. *Likkutei Moharan* I:207.

64. These were the cosmic circumstances during the Sabbatean-Frankist crisis, as explained later.

65. According to the Kabbala, the *gevurot* represent God's harsh judgment, essentially close to evil.

66. On the danger of sexual sin attached to great "wisdom" see the discussion on Moses, note 48.

67. Thus according to Luria (for instance, *Ets Ha-Hayyim* 5:3: "The *gevurot* of *da'at* [wisdom] were concealed in the mouth through God's mystery. . . . At His will, God exposes these concealed letters in the mystery of voice and speech." The five utterances are the five loci of articulation where sounds originate in the mouth, as mentioned in the *Sefer Yetsira*. The link between *gevurot* and speech is also suggested at the beginning of this teaching by the wording of the verse: "*u-gvuratkha yedabberu*" [they shall talk of thy power—*gvuratkha* (Psalms 145:11)].

68. Lurianic Kabbala teaches that some forms of *tikkun* in the supernal worlds are attained only through the death of those attempting it. See *Sha'ar Ha-Kavvanot (Keri'at Shema and Nefilat Appayyim)* 5. It is claimed in the latter that, at times, *kavvana* is not sufficient and one must literally die, while in *Keri'at Shema*—one must die for the sanctification of the Name.

69. Referring to Jacob Frank, who converted to Christianity with his followers in 1759, only a few months before the Besth's death.

70. It is not clear who R. Nahman is alluding to, but I believe this statement should be considered as important historical evidence of the high scholarly achievements of some of the Frankists.

71. Hinting to their apostasy, as it was then that the Frankists converted to Catholicism.

72. As is well known, the Frankists called themselves contra-talmudists. In their disputes with the rabbis, they consistently villified and denigrated the Oral Law and eventually instigated the burnings of the Talmud.

73. This is apparently a reference to the blood libel in which the Frankists provided the priests with "proofs" from Halakhic literature, showing that Jews are commanded to drink Christian blood during Passover (see p. 141, an issue apparently raised by Arye Leib of Shpola in his accusations against R. Nahman). It is worth noting that even this act is described in very mild terms.

74. I could not find any other source for this. On the holes in the heart, see p. 140.

75. See Zohar I:153b (in a slightly different version).

76. *Likkutei Moharan*, I:12. Sabbetai Zevi too was perceived in this manner. His prophet, Nathan of Gaza, said of him in *Derush Ha-Tanninim*, p. 44: "He is the mystery of the Torah, and the heart of the Torah will only be revealed through him." In a similar vein, Sabbetai Zevi spoke about himself in his letter to his brothers published in *Sefunot* 5 (1961): 267.

77. The reference is to Makkot 22b: "How dull-witted are those other people who stand up [in deference] to the Scroll of the Torah but do not stand up [in deference] to a great scholar because, while in the Torah Scroll forty lashes are prescribed, the Rabbis come and [through their exegesis] reduce them by one." However, although in the talmudic passage the scholar appears as superior to the Torah scroll, R. Nahman assumed they are on a par.

78. In the same teaching mentioned earlier, note 76.

79. Sukka 49b, in a different version.

80. Proverbs 31:26.

81. This issue is beyond the scope of this essay. See Weiss's book, *Studies in Bratslav Hasidism*, especially Chapters 2 and 8. The teaching hinted in note 76, *Likkutei Moharan* I:12, deals with the *tikkun* of a *mitnagged* scholar in this manner. See also note 2.

82. According to Hasidic tradition, the Besht himself was quite close to this view. See *Shivhei Ha-Besht*, Horodetsky ed. (Tel-Aviv, 1947), p. 106: "Once, on the eve of *Yom Kippur*, the Besht saw a powerful threat looming over Israel, that they would lose the Oral Law [hinting at the burning of the Talmud counseled by the Frankists]. . . he was enraged at the *rabbis* and said it is because of them that lies are fabricated"—after the burning of the Talmud, the Besht targeted his fury against the rabbis rather than against the Frankists. His sorrow after the Frankist apostasy is well known—he saw it as the amputation of a limb from the *Shekhinah* (*Shivhei Ha-Besht*, p. 108), unlike rabbis such as Jacob Emden and others, whose feeling was Good riddance! On the Besht's spiritual closeness to the Frankists, see also note 94.

83. See, for instance, *Likkutei Moharan* I:118: "Our sages said [apparently referring to Sanhedrin 98a, and Rashi's commentary there] that the Messiah suffers for the whole of Israel, as it is written 'But he was wounded because of our transgressions'(Isaiah 53:5). The *tsaddik ha-dor* in every generation suffers for the whole of Israel and alleviates their pain, because he is as the Messiah. And it is written in the Zohar [III:280a, *Ra'aya Meheimana*]: 'He is made to suffer for all of us.'" All the elements making up this passage are indeed found in other ancient sources but, in this particular configuration, they appear most frequently in Sabbatean writings. The Sabbateans often used the saying from *Ra'aya Meheimana* in reference to Moses [the Messiah], who suffers for the transgressions of Israel. For instance, see the letter by Nathan of Gaza, published by Scholem, on the conversion of the Messiah (*Studies and Texts*) which includes a long passage on Moses' suffering based on this statement in *Ra'aya Meheimana* (ibid., pp. 241–245). This Sabbatean notion too was clearly influenced by Christianity.

84. In this meaning, the expression *torat hesed* is also found in *Likkutei Moharan* I:283. Weiss, *Studies in Bratslav Hasidism*, also discussed this teaching (pp. 182–183) and clarified that one important dimension of *torat hesed* is that it refers to those who transcend the esoteric. Moreover, Weiss also showed that *torat hesed* describes an aspect of King David that led to his persecution by Saul and unequivocally demonstrated that, in this teaching, King David is R. Nahman and Saul is Arye Leib of Shpola. Once the Sabbatean associations of this concept have been clarified, it might be seen as lending further credence to the hypothesis that R. Arye Leib grounded his persecution of R. Nahman on an accusation of Sabbateanism (see note 95). Weiss also discussed another teaching dealing with the rivalry between Saul and David and showed that it has a bearing on two levels: the dispute between the Old Man of Shpola and R. Nahman as well as the early roots of the strife, namely, the controversy between R. Nahman and his attempted *tikkun* of the Sabbateans (see note 131). Moreover, as Arye Leib had accused R. Nahman of Sabbateanism, so did R. Nahman see his dispute with him as an extension of the Sabbatean controversy.

85. Unlike the meaning of this term in the Talmud, on which R. Nahman relied explicitly. *Torat hesed* in the Talmud is the one studied in order to be

taught to others, without in any way specifying that it originates or is aimed at the wicked or the Gentile nations.

86. See G. Scholem, *Sabbetai Zevi* (Princeton,N.J., 1973), pp. 813, 863–864. See also my "Sabbetai Zevi's Attitude Towards His Own Conversion" [Hebrew], *Sefunot* (new series) 2 (1983).

87. *Likkutei Moharan* I:14.

88. Zohar II:69a (with changes).

89. Proverbs 5:15.

90. R. Nahman seems to be hinting at the Messiah's well-known answer to the Besht's question. Asked about the time of his coming, the Messiah replied with the verse "Your wellsprings shall spread outward." In this answer, the word *outward* in and by itself does not yet have the meaning it assumes in R. Nahman's text. This dialogue between the Besht and the Messiah is part of a letter the Besht sent to his brother-in-law, R. Gershon of Kitov, in the Holy Land. The verse does not appear in all versions of this letter; it is found, for instance, in the version printed in the book *Keter Shem Tov*. This parallel seems to emphasize the messianic meaning that R. Nahman had attributed to the *tikkun* of Sabbateanism.

91. In *Likkutei Moharan* I:16 though, this version is censored and the idea is not clearly conveyed. It is explicit in a more original version of this teaching found in *Parpera'ot la-Hokhma* by R. Nahman of Cheryn, which appears in Weiss, *Studies in Bratslav Hasidism*, p. 53, though this version too was censored (as Weiss himself indicated, pp. 189–190) and ends with: "and he said more than was printed."

92. I am referring to the theory by Abraham Miguel Cardozo developed in the text edited by Scholem, *Studies and Texts*, pp. 288–296. Cardozo spoke there of two defiled Messiahs: Messiah ben David is Mohammed and Messiah ben Joseph is Jesus Christ—his father, or his mother's husband, was named Joseph. R. Abraham Abulafia (thirteenth century) had already identified Jesus with the Messiah Son of Joseph. See M. Idel, "Abraham Abulafia: Works and Doctrine," (Ph. D. Dissertation, Hebrew University, 1976). Parallel to these two impure Messiahs, two holy ones emerged, who were charged with the *tikkun* of the two latter ones and their nations. They are the Messiah Son of David—Sabbetai Zevi, who converted to Islam to amend Mohammed—and the Messiah Son of Joseph—Abraham Miguel Cardozo himself, born as a Christian to a Marrano family, who will amend Jesus and the Christians. This theory also appears in the writings of Israel Hazzan, (cited in note 145), p. 198.

The structural similarities between this approach and the one found in *Likkutei Moharan* II:16 are obvious. The main difference is that, for R. Nahman, the two defiled Messiahs are precisely the same two Sabbatean Messiahs who, for Cardozo, are the holy ones. However, in the role of the defiled Messiah Son of Joseph, R. Nahman obviously cast Jacob Frank, who had converted to Christianity, rather than Cardozo, who had been born as a Christian. As for the two holy Messiahs, they were sure to emerge in the future from among Bratslav Hasidim whereas the *tsaddik*, R. Nahman, would include both.

The notion of the *tsaddik* as the reincarnation of Moses and comprising the two Messiahs is well developed in Cardozo's writings, which perhaps inspired R. Nahman. See Cardozo's statements, edited by G. Scholem, *Sefunot* 3–4 (1959–1960), for instance, p. 265. This idea is also pervasive in the writings of Rabbi Moses Hayyim Luzzato, who apparently took it from Cardozo. This is the view suggested by I. Tishby in "Kabbalistic Writings in Oxford Ms. 2593—A Collection of Hidden Words by R. Moses Hayyim Luzzato" [Hebrew], *Kiryat Sefer* (1978): 171, n. 30. Tishby also pointed out the source of this notion in the *Ra'aya Meheimana* and in *Tikkunei Zohar*. In this context, it is worth mentioning the comments by R. Nathan Shapira in his book *Megale Amukkot* 252: "It thus appears that Moses is compounded of two Messiahs—the Messiah Son of David and the Messiah Son of Joseph." See also Appendix II to this chapter.

93. See note 27.

94. According to *Shivhei Ha-Besht*, p. 125: "R. Joel (of Nemirov) told me that Sabbetai Zevi came to the Besht seeking *tikkun*. And R. Joel said that *tikkun* means linking soul to soul and spirit to spirit [thus according to Lurianic Kabbala, obviously in line with the suggestion of affinity and resemblance] He [the Besht] slowly began drawing closer to him, because he [Sabbetai Zevi] was a very evil man. Once, while the Besht was sleeping, Sabbetai Zevi came [apparently in his dream] and tempted him, God forbid, and cast him forcefully until he fell into the deepest abbys [in other words, into the Sabbatean-Frankist heresy leading to Christianity]. The Besht peeked and saw that he had landed with him, may his name be blotted out, on a board. The Besht told us that he [Sabbetai Zevi] had a holy spark, and Samael had trapped him in his net, may God save us, and the Besht heard that his fall was due to pride and anger."

On this passage see also my "New Light on the Matter of the Ba'al Shem Tov and Sabbetai Zevi" [Hebrew], *Jerusalem Studies in Jewish Thought* 2 (1983): 564–569. These claims about Sabbetai Zevi's eminence and his fall because of pride and anger closely resemble R. Nahman's attitude toward the Sabbateans in the preceding passage. I shall show in my discussion that the *tikkun* of Sabbateanism also means the *tikkun* of sadness and anger and their transformation into ecstatic joy (see p. 139 and note 95). The temptation of Christianity may also have parallels in the life of R. Nahman who, in his youth, "was very confused" by the crucifix (*Hayyei Moharan*, His Birthplace, Residence and Travels 7).

95. Previous Bratslav scholars such as Weiss and Piekarz had also suggested this, but the available evidence was limited and flimsy, as Bratslav

literature had consistently deflected these accusations. Suspicions of Sabbateanism are explicitly advanced in *Megillat Hasidei Bratslav*, published by M. N. Litinsky, *Korot Podolia ve-Kadmoniot ha-Yehudim Sham* (Odessa, 1895), pp. 62–63, and reprinted by Weiss, *Studies in Bratslav Hasidism*, pp. 28–29. But Weiss himself unequivocally demonstrated that this was an apochryphal document, (pp. 29–32) and only some of its factual elements were accurate.

Piekarz, *Studies in Bratslav Hasidism*, pp. 71–76, relied on another derogatory expression used by Arye Leib of Shpola (*maginnei erets*) to assume that it entailed an accusation of Sabbateanism against R. Nahman, though he adduced only shaky support in favor of this brilliant hypothesis, which will be expanded and substantiated later (p. 141). Piekarz also hinted (p. 211) that an accusation of Sabbateanism lurked behind the later attacks against Bratslav Hasidim, launched after R. Nahman's death.

I shall attempt to prove that the accusation of Sabbateanism was a crucial element in the controversy against R. Nahman. Thus, I shall show that some traced R. Nahman's *ha-tikkun ha-kelali* to a Sabbatean source (p. 145) whereas others found Sabbatean grounds for his journey to Kamenets (see Appendix I to this chapter). For a further hint to this background to the controversy, see note 84; see also R. Nahman's statement on p. 133, from which it appears that his adversaries tended to accuse him of Sabbateanism whenever possible.

Furthemore, as Weiss had already pointed out in "The Beginnings of Hasidism" [Hebrew], *Zion* 16 (1951): 89–91, n. 14, R. Nahman himself claimed that he had been accused by his adversaries of borrowing his doctrines from his grandfather, R. Nahman of Horodenka (*Sihot Ha-Ran* 211). R. Nahman of Horodenka was one of the ascetic pietists who had preceded the Besht and, after being drawn into the Besht's circle, turned away from ascetic practices (see *Shivhei Ha-Besht*, p. 82.) However, it is very likely that, before drawing closer to the Besht, R. Nahman had been a Sabbatean, as were many other pre-Beshtian ascetic pietists like him, and the claim that R. Nahman of Bratslav had followed in his grandfather's footsteps may rely on this insinuation. Further support might be found in *Megillat Hasidei Bratslav—* if Weiss was right and its factual core is indeed authentic. One of the assertions of the *Megilla* is that Bratslav Hasidim were accused of Sabbateanism on the grounds that their way of worship was sad, unlike the joyful devotion of other Hasidim; compare this to the Besht's claim, in note 94, that Sabbetai Zevi's fall was due to his anger. We are also told in *Shivhei Ha-Besht* that R. Nahman of Hodorenka's strongest ascetic feature was his habit of immersing in a cold ritual bath, an activity that R. Nahman of Bratslav also considered very important, see notes 117 and 118. The charges of joyless devotion might appear strange, as it is well known that there is no higher principle than joy in Bratslav Hasidism. But in R. Nahman's terms, his is "a joy out of melancholy" (p. 139), which brings about the *tikkun* of Sabbateanism (namely, melancholy) and turns it into joy. This connection with R. Nahman of Horodenka is a further illustration of a practice well entrenched in Bratslav literature, where all accusations of Sabbateanism are consistently blurred. Rather than of Sabbateanism, R. Nahman seems to be accused of lack of originality and plagiarism from a "legitimate" source. For a further instance, see p. 145. On the esoteric approach of Bratslav literature to messianic questions in general and Sabbatean issues in particular, see notes 4 and 7.

96. On the controversy over R. Jonathan Eybeschuetz's Sabbatean leanings, which was finally resolved by proving him a Sabbatean, see my " 'Tsaddik Yesod Olam': A Sabbatean Myth."

97. Hayei Moharan, Sihot Moharan, Devotion to God 19.

98. Altona, 1752 (photostated in Jerusalem, 1971, with the addition of several pages).

99. Avdo Meshiho appears there on p. 17, but in a different transposition—meviho instead of meshiho.

100. See the letter by Nathan of Gaza (cited in note 83), p. 268: "Until Noah came, who is as the Sabbath...that is the year when Amirah [an acronym for adonenu malkenyu yarum hodo, by which Sabbetai Zevi was usually referred to in Sabbatean literature, resembling the Arabic title emeer] was born, that is as the Sabbath [hinting to the name Sabbetai] that will bring menuha [or peace, hinting at the name Noah, according to Rashi's commentary to Genesis 5:29] to all worlds."

Noah as a symbol for Sabbetai Zevi appears several times in the hymns of the converted Sabbateans from Salonica. See M. Atias, G. Scholem, and I. Ben-Zvi, A Book of Sabbatean Poems and Praises [Hebrew] (Tel-Aviv, 1948). For instance, all of hymn 129 (pp. 132–33) describes Noah's endeavors as a symbol of Sabbetai Zevi, and begins with the words: "The spark of the king Amirah, may his glory be exalted, Noah was a just man." Similarly, in hymn 226 (pp. 201–212). As Scholem pointed out (in n. 1 to this hymn), the source of the notion that Noah alludes to the Messiah is in Tikkunei Zohar, in the passage printed in Sefer Zohar Haddash 113c, Mossad Ha-Rav Kook ed.: "Then the Messiah shall come, who is like Noah, of whom it was said 'this one shall comfort us'(Genesis 5:29)." Christian sources—from Matthew 24:37 onward— which see Noah as a prototype of their Messiah, might have had an influence on the Sabbateans, as well as on the Tikkunei Zohar itself. As such, the typological method of interpretation is derived from Christian sources, see A. Funkenstein, "Nahmnanides' Typological Reading of History" [Hebrew], Zion 45 (1980): 35–59.

101. See Appendix II.

102. Sihot Ha-Ran 102. This comment might shed light on R. Nahman's view that, in order to destroy heretic books, his own books would have to be burned (Likkutei Moharan II:32). A profound analysis of this quite puzzling notion appears in Weiss, Studies in Bratslav Hasidism, pp. 244–248.

103. See the *Derush Ha-Tanninim* by Nathan of Gaza in *Be-Ik'vot Mashiah*, p. 21. "Even when *Amirah* was born, only one spark issued from this root [the root of the Messiah's soul], from the *kelippa* [the realm of evil]; through his labors, he took out the whole source, and even [I reconstructed this version from the note there—Y. L.] after that, God put him through ardous ordeals. Several times, after standing high above, he would fall into the depth of the abyss, and snakes [forces of evil in Nathan's Kabbala] would tempt him by showing mighty signs and asking: Where is your God?! Human reason would be unable to stand this but he clung to his belief. . ." Sabbetai Zevi's victory over the temptation of the "snakes" or the "dragons" is his victory over the dragons themselves, which is the subject of this work (*Treatise on the Dragons*), and will bring cosmic redemption. The temptation of the snakes is not only in the theoretical and theological realms but is also sexual, as might be learned from *"Ha-Mar'e shel Avraham He-Hasid,"* printed in the same anthology, p. 61: "The bastards attached themselves to him [Sabbetai Zevi] and they beat him, and he would not listen, and these are the sons of *Na'ama* [queen of devils] *nig'ei benei adam."* According to the Zohar, as the editor pointed out, *"nig'ei benei adam"* are devils born from improper seminal emissions (III:76b and ff.). According to the *Ra'aya Meheimana* (Zohar II:114b), these are also the torments suffered by Moses.

104. On the essence and the role of faith in Sabbatean doctrine see Scholem, *Sabbetai Zevi*, pp. 210–211 and 282–284. A source is also quoted (pp. 866–867) emphasizing that a faithful ignoramus is superior to the scholars who deny Sabbetai Zevi.

The idea that people will inevitably ask questions about the *tsaddik*, as they will about God, because neither can be apprehended through the mind (*Likkutei Moharan* II:52), originates in the Sabbatean work *Iggeret Magen Avraham*, pp. 138–139: "It is totally impossible for any creature to explain and reconcile that which is unintelligible to the masses. . . because whoever says that he has understood his concerns and his actions [of Sabbetai Zevi] is close to being the Messiah, as in the utterance about God [in R. Joseph Albo's *Sefer Ha-Ikkarim* II:30] 'If I knew Him, I would be He.'" See Weiss, *Studies in Bratslav Hasidism*, pp. 152–154, who had rightfully claimed that there is no precedent for this notion anywhere in Hasidic literature, though Weiss fails to mention its Sabbatean origins. See also the parallels quoted by Piekarz, *Studies in Bratslav Hasidism*, pp. 112–113, though Piekarz did not point to this analogy between the *tsaddik* and God. Piekarz's quote from R. Israel of Riszin, who claimed that the *tsaddik* is as "laws which have no reason," is also originally Sabbatean. Nathan of Gaza often described Sabbetai Zevi in this fashion; see G. Scholem, "R. Eliahu Hacohen Itamari and Sabbateanism" [Hebrew], *Alexander Marx Jubilee Volume* (New York, 1950), pp. 459–460. See also my "Sabbetai Zevi's Attitude Towards His Own Conversion," p. 303.

105. In J. Frank, *The Words of the Master* 574.

106. Thus, for instance, R. Nahman said to his followers (who printed it!) when they reproached him for keeping company with *maskilim*: "How dare you approach me? For me you are just like lint on someone's clothes, that when he blows on it, it floats away" (*Hayyei Moharan*, Uman 24; see Yiddish original there). Frank's arrogance toward his followers pervades *The Words of the Master*; see also Scholem, *Studies and Texts*, p. 119.

107. Thus R. Nahman in *Likkutei Moharan* II:78. See my detailed discussion p. 000. Thus also Jacob Frank, see Scholem, ibid. We also find that Sabbetai Zevi began one of his letters with the words: "The complete fool said." See Scholem, *Sabbetai Zevi*, p. 138.

108. *Ha-tikkun ha-kelali* and the circumstances of its discovery as told by R. Nahman, are extensively described in *Sihot ha-Ran* 141. The theoretical background is provided in *Likkutei Moharan* I:205 and II:92 (the first ending of the book). The *tikkun* was first discussed in 1805, but only in 1809 was it disclosed which ten psalms were to be included in it (*Hayyei Moharan*, Conversations Related to His Teachings 49). For a different view regarding this date, see the book *Neve Tsaddikim*, pp. 66–67. For the ten chapters see note 121.

109. See *Likkutei Moharan* I:29.

110. See Zohar I:219b. Elsewhere in the Zohar (II:62a), after introducing the idea that repentance cannot repair this sin, reservations are conveyed: "unless he repents very much"; namely, unless his penitence is severe. However, this seems to be a later addition, attempting to attenuate the gravity of this offense and, indeed, these words are missing in the *Or Yakar* version (the Zohar with the commentary by R. Moses Cordovero, vol. 4, [Jerusalem, 1967], p. 27). We have also found elsewhere (Zohar II:3b) that fervent penintence helps to repair this sin, though this too might be a later addition. R. Nahman's attitude to these Zoharic statements is extremely interesting. See *Sihot Ha-Ran* 71.

111. Zohar II:3b: " 'Sun and a shield' (Psalms 84:12) this is the holy convenant...as a shield protects man, so does the holy covenant. Whoever keeps this covenant, no harm shall befall him." In Zohar III:214a: "As is written of Pinhas: 'Behold, I give to him my covenant of peace' (Numbers 25:12)—he shall have peace from the angel of death, who shall neither rule over him nor judge him, because he upholds the supreme covenant." Moshe Idel indicated that a similar notion appears in the commentary on the ten *sefirot* by Joseph Gikatila, Vatican Ms. 456 18a: "*Yesod* [the *sefira* of *yesod*]...is *tikkun ha-kol* [the *tikkun* of all]...a true shield, the shield of David [as in the blessing of the *haftara*]. As it is said, 'But thou, O Lord, art a shield for me' (Psalms 3:4)." *Tikkun ha-kol* resembles *ha-tikkun ha-kelali* and a similar expression, *Tikkuna de-kholla*, is found in the Zohar II:219a.

112. A tendency to show more leniency toward the sin of improper seminal emission was one of the innovations of Hasidism, but not all Hasidic

schools agreed on this issue. See R. Schatz, *Quietistic Elements in Eighteenth Century Hasidic Thought* [Hebrew] (Jerusalem, 1968), p. 48.

113. See the end of this essay.

114. See *Neve Tsaddikim*, pp. 67–71, which numbers fifty-four editions until 1967; many more have been printed since. Some of these editions include long doctrinal explanations of *ha-tikkun ha-kelali* as well as several Bratslav prayers composed for this purpose, to be recited in addition to the psalms.

115. See *Studies in Bratslav Hasidism*, p. 191.

116. See the pamphlet by R. Abraham Hazzan, *Yemei Ha-Tela'ot* (Jerusalem, 1933), p. 193 (as quoted by Weiss): "He [R. Nahman] spoke to them and said: When going to war, they wear an armour called *panzer* etc. etc. . . . And he said that the story of this armour would remain secret and should only be revealed to the selected few, but that the *tikkun* through the ten psalms should be revealed to all." "The story of the *panzer*" is apparently known to Bratslav Hasidim, as a Bratslav Hasid informed Weiss. There is also evidence of a manuscript containing this story (in *Neve Tsaddikim*, p. 194). However, it remains esoteric—it has not been printed, and no outsider has had access to it.

The pamphlet *Yemei Ha-Tela'ot* itself, although it has been printed and photostated three times, is also considered esoteric by Bratslav Hasidim, because it includes the "ommissions" from *Hayyei Moharan* that had been censored from the printed versions due to their esoteric character. It also describes the hardships suffered by Bratslav Hasidim as well as their disputes. Bratslav Hasidim were undecided as to whether to print this pamphlet—see Weiss, ibid., p. 36—and it is no longer available for sale. I was told by a Bratslav Hasid that they regretted having printed it, as the times were not suitable. The copy in the Jewish National and University Library in Jerusalem has been lost (or perhaps stolen?) and I have used the various editions available in the Jerusalem Shocken Library.

117. *Sihot ha-Ran* 141: "He said that the first *tikkun* is the ritual bath, that one must immerse in the ritual bath. *Dos ersht is mikveh* [the repetition of this order in the original Yiddish attests to its importance, the more so since in Yiddish a double meaning is entailed and the ritual bath takes precedence both in time and importance]. Another time he said: You must be very careful to immerse in a ritual bath on the same day that you become unclean [through an improper seminal emission]. . . it is most important to immerse on the very same day." See also the end of note 95.

118. *Likkutei Moharan* II:123, where a medical explanation is offered for the benefits of the ritual bath (opening sweat pores). However, it is clear to me that this is not the true reason for submitting to the rigors of a cold ritual bath, and this is simply an attempt to defeat doctors at their own game.

119. On his attitude to doctors during his last days in Uman see *Hayyei Moharan*, Uman 38. On his attitude to doctors and to medicine in general,

see *Sihot Ha-Ran* 50. I have not found such incriminating accusations against doctors even in Moliere's *Le Malade Imaginaire*. About his own use of doctors, his Hasidim typically claimed that he did so "for reasons and mysteries known to him" (*Sihot Ha-Ran* 50).

120. See *Likkutei Moharan* I:29, where *ha-tikkun ha-kelali* is also connected to the giving of charity. The redemption entailed by *ha-tikkun ha-kelali* is what enables the revelation of the Torah's mysteries.

121. The ten varieties of song are hinted in the titles of the psalms, according to Pesahim 117a: "The Book of Psalms uttered ten synonims of praise, viz.: *nitsuah* [victory], *niggun* [melody], *maskil*, *mizmor* [psalm], *shir* [song], *ashre* [happy], *tehilla* [praise], *tefilla* [prayer], *hodaya* [thanksgiving], *halleluja*." This issue has been discussed at length in the Zohar, see an example in the next note. According to R. Nahman, these ten psalms hint at the ten varieties of song and reciting them constitutes *ha-tikkun ha-kelali*: 16, 32, 41, 42, 59. 77. 90, 105, 137, 150. It is not easy to trace the correspondences between these psalms and the ten varieties of song in the preceding talmudic passage. See the explicit interpretation suggested by R. Nahman of Cheryin in *Parpera'ot la-Hokhma* on *Likkutei Moharan* II:92. It seems that some of the psalms, such as 137:1, were chosen mainly because R. Nahman saw them as hinting at a victory over impurity.

122. *Tikkun* 69, 105a, in the Mossad Ha-Rav Kook edition.

123. The exegesis of this pasage in *Sihot ha-Ran* 273 suggests that the princess is not the *Shekhina* but the soul, though it also hints at another, more esoteric dimension: "Know well how far things go." In Nathan of Bratslav's book *Likkutei Halakhot, Even Ha-Ezer, Hilkhot Periyya U-Rviyya* 2:10, the soul is endowed with wider significance and identified with the *Shekhina*: "Hence, the main *tikkun* of the princess—the *Shekhina* that comprises all the souls of Israel—is through the ten varieties of song, the height of all joy."

124. Scholars have already pointed to this: Weiss, *Studies in Bratslav Hasidism*, p. 152 and Dan, *The Hasidic Tale*, p. 161, relying on the exegesis of R. Nahman of Cheryn.

125. See his book *Likkutei Halakhot, Orakh Hayyim, Hilkhot Birkat Ha-Peirot* 4, especially the end. The whole of this *halakha* deals with the land of Israel and its conquest.

126. *Likkutei Halakhot*, as in note 123.

127. *Likkutei Moharan* I:205.

128. Thus at the conclusion of the events surrounding the teaching concerning the simplicity of the *tsaddik* (*Likkutei Moharan* I:78), which I discussed extensively. See note 23 for the pertinent sources. R. Nahman's deep despair was transformed into great joy through the memory of his journey

to the land of Israel and the Hasidim marched out singing and dancing. R. Nahman then claimed, relying on a double entendre in Yiddish, that song depends on the ability to spurn sexual passion. Piekarz quoted this passage, *Studies of Bratslav Hasidism*, p. 45; however, although he interpreted the play on words correctly, Piekarz failed to grasp the further implications, which have now become clear: The shift from sadness to joy implies the overcoming of the evil instinct or *ha-tikkun ha-kelali*, which is the way to the land of Israel and toward complete redemption.

The connection between the pulses and hand clapping appears, for example, in *Likkutei Moharan* I:10$_6$—Dancing and hand clapping nullify harsh justice, heresy, and apostasy and enhance faith in the *tsaddik*. See also *Hayyei Moharan*, His Birthplace, Residence and Travels 12: "I heard him say that we conquered Bratslav with hand clapping and dancing." A note from the editor there explains that hand clapping helps to draw in the air of the land of Israel and helped to cancel the notorious *"Punkten"* edicts.

129. Lilith is alluded in the word *me'orot* [lights] in Genesis 1:14, on the fourth day of Creation. However, because of the spelling, the word was interpreted as *me'era* [curse] (see, for instance, Zohar III:234a) and identified with diphteria that, according to the rabbis (in the Jerusalem Talmud, Ta'anit 4e, 68b) is the disease of the fourth day, when the lights were created (Zohar II:267b).

130. This might be related to the sin of improper seminal emission, as Maimonides wrote in *Hilkhot Deot* 4:19: "Semen constitutes the strenght of the body, its life and the light of the eyes." R. Nahman mentioned in several places the clouds covering the eyes of the *tsaddik*, symbolizing thoughts of heresy and apostasy, particularly the Sabbatean one. See Weiss, *Studies in Bratslav Hasidism*, pp. 52–53.

131. Ibid., pp. 58–60; see note 84. Piekarz added a note clarifying the author's intention. See also *Likkutei Moharan* I:64$_5$, alluding to the melodies of atheistic wisdom that are repaired through the song of the *tsaddik*, who represents faith. These melodies are compared to church music, hinting at the well-known Hasidic practice of adopting Gentile tunes.

132. *Hayyei Moharan*, Conversations Relating to His Teachings 41: "He spoke to us about the issue of *magginei erets*, as the Old Man had called us, etc., and this is also mentioned in that teaching (*Likkutei Moharan* II:5) and see there par. 7."

133. In *Studies in Bratslav Hasidism*, pp. 71–76, he collected all the sources on the various meanings of this derogatory term as used by Aryeh Leib.

134. Arye Leib made his statement in the summer of 1806 (see Piekarz, ibid.). This teaching is from September 1805 (*Hayyei Moharan*, Conversations Relating to His Teachings 59).

135. *Likkutei Moharan*, I:20f and ff.. I discussed another aspect of this teaching in p. 120.

136. I. Tishbi studied these *tikkunim* in "The Repentance *tikkun* of Nathan of Gaza" [Hebrew] in *Paths of Faith and Heresy* [Hebrew] (Ramat-Gan, 1964), pp. 30–51.

137. See the opening of *Derush Ha-Tanninim* by Nathan of Gaza, p. 16: "Therefore, the *tikkun* [from Lurianic Kabbala] of weeping over the exile of the *Shekhina* as we used to do is not to be adopted, and instead [we should adopt] the *tikkun* ordained by *Amirah* [Sabbetai Zevi], as is known to you." And Scholem noted there: "Such a *tikkun* has not reached us." However, it does not seem far-fetched to assume that Nathan of Gaza used Sabbetai Zevi's *tikkun* when ordaining his own *tikkun kelali*. Moreover, by "the *tikkun* ordained by *Amira*," Nathan could have been referring to the new prayer aimed at replacing the Lurianic devotions that he had specified in his letter to Rafael Joseph Gilabi in Cairo (published by Scholem, see the end of Appendix II). Indeed, the context in both the *Derush Ha-Tanninim* and in the letter is similar: The rise of the *Shekhina* in messianic times, as it rises on the eve of the Sabbath. It is possible that the *Derush Ha-Tanninim* was also sent to the same Rafael Joseph in Cairo (see Scholem's introduction, p. 12). In that case, the phrase *as is known to you*, could refer to the letter. This hypothesis would require us to assume a change in the terminological use of the word *tikkun* and claim that, rather than the repair of sins, it implies the repair and unification of the supernal worlds.

138. Quoted by I. Tishbi, "The Repentance *tikkun* of Nathan of Gaza," p. 32, and originally in the manuscript at the Jewish National and University Library in Jerusalem, 8° 159, p. 112a. The name *tikkun-kelali* does not appear in the other manuscripts of the *tikkun* of repentance (see note 144) though they do include the text.

139. See a similar version in note 111. I indeed encountered once the term *ha-tikkun ha-kelali* in reference to the *tikkun* instituted by Luria, but in a quote from Nathan of Gaza! Nathan described his childhood (in his mentioned letter, Scholem, *Studies and Texts* p. 236) as follows: "I studied Torah in purity until the age of twenty and I did *ha-tikkun ha-kelali* that R. Isaac Luria, of blessed memory, had recommended for unremitting sinners though, praise God, I had never intended any offense, but my soul may have been sullied, God forbid, from a previous incarnation." G. Scholem wrote (in the introduction to *Derush Ha-Tanninim*, p. 19) that Nathan of Gaza intended here the *tikkun* appearing in the book *Kanfei Yona* by Menahem Azaria of Fano, Part III, 59. Indeed, I have no doubts that this was Nathan's intention, because it says there (as in the excerpt by Nathan quoted earlier) that this *tikkun* was meant for "whoever has willingly sinned and transgressed." However, the wording *ha-tikkun ha-kelali* does not appear in *Kanfei Yona*. It thus seems to me that Nathan calls the Lurianic *tikkun* (found in *Kanfei Yona*) *ha-tikkun ha-kelali*, under the influence of the name he had previously given to his own *tikkun*. Lately I realized that *ha-tikkun ha-kelali* occurs frequently in the writings of Rabbi M. H. Luzzatte, who is the direct source of R. Nahman.

140. See notes 53 ff.

141. Jerusalem manuscript (see note 138), p. 120b.

142. It is this holy name that is flawed because of man's sins, as Nathan had previously explained at length.

143. On p. 121a.

144. Unlike the ritual instituted by R. Nahman, the *Tikkun Kelali* of Nathan included, in addition to psalms, readings from Isaiah, Jeremiah, and Ezekiel and even the passage "a woman of valor" from Proverbs. Nathan does not speak of ten psalms but of thirty, though the number ten appears in the following context: Ten correspond to the World of Action [*Olam Ha-Asiyya*], ten to the World of Formation [*Olam Ha-Yetsira*], and ten include these two realms when raised to the World of Creation [*Olam Ha-Beri'a*]. Neither did Nathan determine which psalms were to be recited; he only set a number and left the choice open (incidentally, R. Nahman determined the psalms exactly four years after giving a general instruction to recite ten psalms in *ha-tikkun ha-kelali*, see note 108). The thirty psalms are mentioned in all the manuscripts of the repentance *tikkun* by Nathan of Gaza: the Jerusalem Ms. (note 138, p. 112a); the Halberstam Ms. 40 (this is the London Ms., Montefiore 471, N. 5371 in the Institute of Microfilmed Hebrew Manuscripts at the Jewish National and University Library in Jerusalem), p. 41a; the Corneille Ms. (see *Ha-Shahar* 3 [1872]: 627).

Having recourse to the psalms for the purpose of *tikkun* could be seen as a Sabbatean innovation (contrary to the magical uses found in books on "the use of psalms"). There is evidence showing that Sabbetai Zevi and his followers used to "recite psalms and consider them more important than the reading of *mishnayot*" (see A. Freiman, ed., *On Sabbetai Zevi* [Hebrew] [Berlin, 1913], p. 93). The stress on the contrast between reciting psalms and reading *mishnayot* is worth noting; it points to an innovation vis-à-vis Lurianic Kabbala, which had related to the reading of *mishnayot* as the most important form of *tikkun*, as the same Hebrew letters appear in *mishna* and in *neshama* [soul] (see in *Sefer Ha-Shelah* by R. Yeshayahu Horowitz, 181b); it is on these grounds that many associations of *mishnaiot* readers emerged in eighteenth century Eastern Europe (see I. Halpern "Associations for the Study of the Torah and for Good Deeds and the Spread of the Hasidic Movement" [Hebrew], *Zion* 22 [1953]: 209. On the importance of psalms in Sabbateanism see the exegesis of psalms mentioned in the next note.

145. In R. Israel Hazzan's commentary on psalms printed in the appendexes to G. Scholem, "The Commentary on Psalms from the Circle of Sabbetai Zevi in Adrianople," in *Alei Ayin: Zalman Schocken Jubilee Volume* (Jerusalem, 1948–1952), pp. 157–211. The next quote is taken from this source, p. 201.

146. Psalms 51:4. R. Israel Hazzan discussed it in detail. In all the psalms, King David, who is traditionally considered their author, appears as an archetype of Sabbetai Zevi, and Hazzan consistently found that the psalms hint to matters related to Sabbetai Zevi.

147. Hazzan, in *Alei Ayin*, p. 203.

148. The name *Ha-Tikkun Ha-Kelali*, in the sense of repairing the world at the time of redemption, appears in R. Moshe Hayim Luzzato's *Da'at Tevunot* (reprinted in an anthology of his works called *Yalkut Yedi'at Ha-Emet*, 2, [Tel-Aviv, 1966], p. 37), in a passage suffused with Sabbatean ideas: "Nevertheless, in the goodness of His laws, He returned to look at these creatures to attain their complete and total *tikkun* [*ha-tikkun ha-kelali ve-ha-gamur*] which will surely come." I discussed the Sabbatean character of these statements in my article "*Tsaddik Yesod Olam*," p. 94.

149. From "A Collection of Letters on the Sabbatean Movement" [Hebrew], *Kovets Al-Yad* 13 (1941): 211.

150. See Scholem, *Sabbetai Zevi*, p. 458, note 304. Scholem had suggested that "the armour of repentance" in Nathan of Gaza's statement might allude to the *tallit katan* that Nathan of Gaza had strongly insisted must be worn by all the believers, as we know from other sources. It is worth remembering that, in Jewish thought, wearing a fringed garment is often seen as protection from sexual temptation. For instance, in Menahot 44a, it is told that a young man was saved at the last minute from sinning with a harlot by the fringes of his garment striking his face. It was thus appropriate for R. Nahman to connect between *ha-tikkun ha-kelali* (sexual chastity) and the wearing of a fringed garment. I have not found an explicit mention of this connection (though perhaps there is one in the unavailable *panzer* story, see note 116) but there are allusions in *Likkutei Moharan* 1:8, particularly in the last section. R. Nahman claimed there that the four corners of the fringes correspond to King David's songs (namely, the psalms, which are the contents of *ha-tikkun ha-kelali*) and, through the songs and the fringes, we overcome the treachery of the wicked, who prolong our exile.

151. According to Yevamot 97a. Apparently, in an attempt to benefit R. Nahman's soul. See p. 136.

152. *Sihot ha-Ran* 141. The Hasidim thus rely on R. Nahman himself (see note 119) though slightly changing the meaning of his words. R. Nahman had meant that the innovation is in the very possibility of repairing this sin rather than in ordaining the *tikkun*, about which R. Nahman himself had said that others had preceded him, and he had merely succeded in accomplishing their task.

Bibliography

Altmann, Alexander.*Faces of Judaism* [Hebrew], ed. A. Shapira. Tel-Aviv, 1983.

Baer, Yitshak F. *Israel Among the Nations* [Hebrew]. Jerusalem, 1955.

Carlebach, Elisheva. *The Pursuit of Heresy.* New York, 1990.

Dan, Joseph. *The Esoteric Theology of Ashkenazi Hasidism* [Hebrew]. Jerusalem, 1969.

_____. *Studies in Ashkenazi-Hasidic Literature* [Hebrew]. Giv'atyim and Ramat-Gan, 1975.

Elior, Rachel. "Between *Yesh* and *Ayin*: The Doctrine of the Zaddik in the Writings of Jacob Isaac, the Seer of Lublin." In *S. Abramski Jubilee Volume.* pp. 393–455. London, 1988.

_____. "Mysticism, Magic and Angelology: The Angelology of *Hekhalot* Literature" [Hebrew]. In *Sara Heller Wilensky Jubilee Volume.* Forthcoming.

Farber-Ginat, Asi. "The Concept of the Merkabah in Thirteenth Century Jewish Esoterism" [Hebrew], Ph.D. Dissertation, Hebrew University, Jerusalem, 1986.

Gottlieb, Efraim. *Studies in the Kabbala Literature* [Hebrew]. Tel-Aviv, 1976.

Green, Arthur. *Tormented Master: A Life of Rabbi Nahman of Bratslav.* Tuscaloosa, Ala., 1979.

_____. "The Zaddiq as Axis Mundi in Later Judaism." *JAAR* 45 (1977): 327–347.

Halperin, David. *The Faces of the Chariot.* Tubingen, 1988.

Idel, Moshe. "The Concept of the Torah in *Heikhalot* Literature and Its Metamorphoses in Kabbala" [Hebrew]. *Jerusalem Studies in Jewish Thought* 1 (1981–82): 23–84.

_____. "The Evil Thought in the Deity" [Hebrew]. *Tarbiz* 49 (1980): 356–364.

_____. *Golem*. Albany, N.Y., 1990.

_____. "The Image of Man Above the *Sefirot*" [Hebrew]. *Da'at* 4 (1980): 41–55.

_____. *Kabbalah: New Perspectives*. New Haven, Conn., 1988.

_____. "The Magical and Neoplatonical Interpretation of Kabbalah in the Renaissance." In B. D. Cooperman, ed., *Jewish Thought in the Sixteenth Century*, pp. 186–242. Cambridge, Mass., 1983.

_____. "The *Sefirot* Above the *Sefirot*" [Hebrew]. *Tarbiz* 51 (1982): 239–280.

_____. "The World of Angels in Human Form" [Hebrew]. In J. Dan and J. Hacker, eds., *Studies in Jewish Mysticism, Philosophy and Ethical Literature Presented to Isaiah Tishby on His Seventy-Fifth Birthday*, pp. 1–66. Jerusalem Studies in Jewish Thought, 3, Jerusalem, 1966.

Liebes, Yehuda. "The Angels of the Shofar and Yeshua Sar ha-Panim" [Hebrew]. In J. Dan, ed., *Early Jewish Mysticism*, pp. 171–195. Jerusalem Studies in Jewish Thought 6, Jerusalem, 1987.

_____. "The Author of the Book *Tsaddik Yesod Olam*: The Sabbatean Prophet R. Leib Prossnitz" [Hebrew]. *Da'at* 2–3 (1978–1979): 159–173.

_____. "*Tsaddik Yesod Olam*: A Sabbatean Myth" [Hebrew]. *Da'at* 1 (1978): 73–120.

_____. "Golem: a Criticism on the Book by Moshe Idel." *Kiryat Sefer*. Forthcoming.

_____. "The Ideological Element in the Hayyun Controversy" [Hebrew]. *Proceedings of the Eighth World Congress of Jewish Studies*, pp. 129–134. Division C. Jerusalem, 1982.

_____. "Jonah as the Messiah ben Joseph" [Hebrew]. In J. Dan and J. Hacker, eds., *Studies in Jewish Mysticism, Philosophy and Ethical Literature Presented to Isaiah Tishby on His Seventy-Fifth Birthday*, pp. 269–311. Jerusalem Studies in Jewish Thought 3, Jerusalem, 1986.

_____. "The Messianism of R. Jacob Emden and His Attitude Toward Sabbateanism" [Hebrew]. *Tarbiz* 49 (1983): 122–165.

_____. "Miguel Abraham Cardozo—Author of the *Raza di-Meheimanuta* Attributed to Sabbetai Zevi, and the Error in Attributing the *Iggeret Magen Avraham* to Cardozo" [Hebrew]. *Kiryat Sefer* 55 (1980): 603–616, 56 (1981): 373.

_____. "Mysticism and Reality: Towards a Portrait of the Martyr and Kabbalist R. Samson Ostropoler." In I. Twerski, ed., *Jewish Thought in the Seventeenth Century*,. pp. 221–255. Cambridge Mass., 1987.

_____. "The Myth of the *Tikkun* of the Godhead: The Zohar and Jonathan Ratosh" [Hebrew]. Forthcoming.

_____. "Myth versus Symbol in the Zohar and Lurianic Kabbala" [Hebrew]. *Eshel Be'er Sheva,* forthcoming.

_____. "New Light on the Matter of the Ba'al Shem Tov and Sabbetai Zevi" [Hebrew]. *Jerusalem Studies in Jewish Thought* 2 (1983): 564–569.

_____. "New Trends in Kabbala Research" [Hebrew]. *Pe'amim,* forthcoming.

_____. "New Writings in Sabbatean Kabbala from the Circle of R. Jonathan Eybeschuetz" [Hebrew]. *Jerusalem Studies in Jewish Thought* 5 (1986): 191–348.

_____. "A Crypto Judeo-Christian Sect of Sabbatean Origin" [Hebrew]. *Tarbiz* 57 (1988): 349–384.

_____. "Rabbi Solomon Ibn Gabirol's Use of the *Sefer Yetsira* and a Commentary on the Poem 'I Love Thee' " [Hebrew]. In J. Dan, ed., *The Beginning of Jewish Mysticism in Medieval Europe,* pp. 73–123. Jerusalem Studies in Jewish Thought 6, Jerusalem, 1987.

_____. "Sabbetai Zevi's Attitude Towards His Own Conversion" [Hebrew]. *Sefunot* 2, no. 17 (1983): 267–307.

_____. "Shlomo Pines and Kabbala Research." In M. Idel, W. Z. Harvey, and E. Schweid, eds., *Shlomo Pines Jubilee Volume,* Part 2, pp. 16–22. Jerusalem Studies in Jewish Thought 9, Jerusalem, 1990.

_____. *The Sin of Elisha: The Four who Entered Paradise and the Nature of Talmudic Mysticism* [Hebrew]. Jerusalem, 1990.

_____. *Studies in the Zohar.* Albany, N.Y., forthcoming.

_____. " 'Two Young Roes': The Secret Sermon of Luria Before His Death" [Hebrew]. In R. Elior and Y. Liebes, eds., *Lurianic Kabbala.* Jerusalem Studies in Jewish Thought, Jerusalem. Forthcoming.

_____. "Who Makes the Horn of Jesus Flourish." *Immanuel* 21 (1987): 55–67.

_____. "A Messianic Treatise by R. Wolf the Son of R. Jonathan Eybeschuetz" [Hebrew]. *Kiryat Sefer* 57 (1982): 148–178, 368–379.

Meroz, Ronit. "Redemption in the Lurianic Teaching." Ph.D. Dissertation, Hebrew University in Jerusalem, 1988.

Pedayah, Haviva. " 'Flaw' and 'Correction' in the Concept of the Godhead in the Teachings of Rabbi Isaac the Blind" [Hebrew]. In J. Dan, ed., *The Beginning of Jewish Mysticism in Medieval Europe,* pp. 157–285. Jerusalem Studies in Jewish Thought, 5, Jerusalem.

Piekarz, Mendel. *Studies in Braslav Hasidism* [Hebrew]. Jerusalem, 1972.

Rapoport-Albert, Ada. "Self Depreciation and Disavowal of Knowledge in Nahman of Braslav" [Hebrew]. In S. Stein and R. Loewe, eds., *Studies in Jewish Religious and Intellectual History Presented to Alexander Altmann.* pp. 7–33. Tuscaloosa, Ala., 1979.

Schatz-Uffenheimer, Rivka. *Quietistic Elements in Eighteenth Century Hasidic Thought* [Hebrew]. Jerusalem, 1968.

Scholem, Gershom. *Jewish Gnosticism, Merkabah Mysticism and Talmudic Tradition.* New York, 1960.

_____. *Kabbalah.* Jerusalem, 1974.

_____. *Major Trends in Jewish Mysticism,* New York 1961.

_____. *The Messianic Idea in Judaism.* New York, 1971.

_____. *On the Kabbalah and its Symbolism.* New York, 1965.

_____. *On the Mystical Shape of the Godhead.* New York, 1991.

_____. *Origins of the Kabbalah.* Philadelphia, 1987.

_____. *Sabbatai Zevi—The Mystical Messiah.* Princeton, N.J., 1973.

_____. *Studies and Texts Concerning the History of Sabbateanism and Its Metamorphoses* [Hebrew]. Jerusalem, 1974.

_____. *Researches in Sabbateanism* [Hebrew]. Tel-Aviv, 1991.

Stroumsa, Gedaliahu G. "Form(s) of God: Some Notes on Metatron and Christ." *HTR* 76 (1983): 269–288.

Tishby, Isaiah. *Paths of Faith and Heresy* [Hebrew]. Ramat-Gan, 1984.

_____. *Studies in Kabbala and Its Branches* [Hebrew]. Vol 1. Jerusalem, 1982.

_____. *The Wisdom of the Zohar,* 3 volumes. Oxford, 1989.

Urbach, Ephraim E. *The Sages—Their Concepts and Beliefs.* Jerusalem, 1975.

_____. *The World of the Sages: Collected Studies.* Jerusalem, 1988.

Weiss, Joseph. *Studies in Braslav Hasidism* [Hebrew]. Jerusalem, 1974.

_____. *Studies in Eastern European Jewish Mysticism.* Oxford, 1985

Wolfson, Elliot R. "Female Imaging of the Torah: From Literary Metaphor to Religious Symbol." In J. Neusner, E. Frerichs, and N. M. Sarna, eds., *From Ancient Israel to Modern Judaism: Essays in Honor of Marvin Fox,* pp. 271–307. Atlanta, 1989.

_____. "The Image of Jacob Engraved on the Throne" [Hebrew]. In M. Oron and A. Goldreich, eds., *Efraim Gottlieb Memorial Volume.* Forthcoming.

Zak, Berakha. " *'Ha-Kelippa Tsorekh Ha-Kedushah'* " [Hebrew]. In J. Dan and J. Hacker, eds., *Studies in Jewish Mysticism Philosophy and Ethical Literature Presented to Isaiah Tishby on His Seventy-Fifth Birthday,* pp. 191–206. Jerusalem Studies in Jewish Thought, 3, Jerusalem, 1986.

Sources

Following are the original Hebrew sources of the essays published in this book:

1. *"De Natura Dei*: On the Development of the Jewish Myth." In M. Oron and A. Goldreich, eds., *Efraim Gottlieb Memorial Volume.* Forthcoming.

2. "The Kabbalistic Myth as Told by Orpheus." In M. Idel, W. Z. Harvey, and E. Schweid, eds., *Shlomo Pines Jubilee Volume*, Part 1, pp. 425–459. Jerusalem Studies in Jewish Thought, 8, Jerusalem, 1989.

3. "Sabbatean Messianism." *Pe'amim* 40 (1989): 4–20.

4. "Sabbetai Zevi's Religious Faith." In Z. Baras, ed., *Messianism and Eschatology*, pp. 293–300. Jerusalem, 1983.

5. *"Ha-tikkun ha-kelali* of R. Nahman of Bratslav and Its Sabbatean Links." *Zion* 45 (1980): 201–245.

Index

219

Index of Rabbinic Sources and Zohar